P9-CCF-509

Economic Independence and Zambian Copper

edited by
Mark Bostock
Charles Harvey

The Praeger Special Studies program—utilizing the most modern and efficient book production techniques and a selective worldwide distribution network—makes available to the academic, government, and business communities significant, timely research in U.S. and international economic, social, and political development.

Economic Independence and Zambian Copper

A Case Study of Foreign Investment

PRAEGER SPECIAL STUDIES IN INTERNATIONAL ECONOMICS AND DEVELOPMENT

**Praeger Publishers**   New York   Washington   London

PRAEGER PUBLISHERS
111 Fourth Avenue, New York, N.Y. 10003, U.S.A.
5, Cromwell Place, London S.W.7, England

Published in the United States of America in 1972
by Praeger Publishers, Inc.

© 1972 by Praeger Publishers, Inc.

Library of Congress Catalog Card Number: 77-163926

Printed in the United States of America

In 1969, Zambia was the largest producer of copper among developing countries and the third largest producer in the world after the United States and the U.S.S.R., producing 12.2 percent of total world production.

On August 11, 1969, President Kenneth Kaunda announced in a speech at Matero Hall, Lusaka, that he was inviting the mining companies to offer 51 percent of their shares to the Zambian Government. This book seeks to set this event, and the other changes that accompanied it, in the context of the whole history of Zambia's attempts to control its own economy, from the first arrival of foreigners in search of wealth. We also analyze the present and future effects of the takeover on the economy.

In preparing the book, we have tried to integrate the various chapters by working together as much as possible. Although none of the contributors were in Lusaka throughout the writing of the book, all except John Niehuss had many opportunities for discussion of most of its parts and certainly of those parts most closely related to their own chapters. Final responsibility for each chapter remains with contributors, and for the book as a whole with the editors. The views of all the contributors are their own and in no way commit their employers.

An earlier paper, "The Mining Industry in Zambia." was written by the editors and David Murray and distributed privately by Maxwell Stamp (Africa) Limited in December 1969. As Dr. Murray now lives in London, he could not be involved in this book, but we owe him a continuing debt for his contribution to that paper.

We also wish to thank Tom Warke of the University of Zambia for careful and detailed comments on Chapter 7; various people, who probably prefer to remain anonymous, for having been pestered about different points for their opinions; Frankie Bostock for first suggesting that we write a book on the takeover; Celia Harvey for remaining deeply skeptical throughout; Ann Thomson and Judy Spörer for rapid, accurate and good-humored typing of the manuscript; and Judy Slinn for reading the manuscript with great care.

LIST OF TABLES

xiii

TABLES IN THE APPENDIX

LIST OF CHARTS

CHARTS IN THE APPENDIX

LIST OF MAPS

LIST OF ABBREVIATIONS

Amax	American Metal Climax
CIPEC	Intergovernmental Council of Copper Exporting Countries
DCF .	Discounted cash flow
ENI	Ente Nazionale Idrocasbusi
IMF	International Monetary Fund
Indeco	Industrial Development Corporation (of Zambia)
K	Kwacha
LME	London Metal Exchange
Mindeco Ltd.	Government holding company
NCCM	Nchanga Consolidated Copper Mines
NPV	Net present value
RCM	Roan Consolidated Mines
RST	Roan (formerly Rhodesian) Selection Trust
UNIP	United National Independence Party
Zamanglo	Zambia Anglo-American
ZCI	Zambia Copper Investments
Zimco	Zambia Industrial and Mining Corporation

UNITS

Currency

During its colonial period, Zambia used pounds, shillings, and pence, which were always equal to British currency. These units were retained after independence, and Zambia did not devalue when the British pound was devalued in 1967. In January 1968, Zambia decimalized its currency on the basis of 10 Zambian shillings = 1 Kwacha = 100 ngwee. The Zambian Kwacha was thus equal, from its inception to the time of writing this book, to U.S.$1.40, 1 South African Rand, U.K. £0.5833, at the IMF parity rates of exchange. Zambian currency (pounds or Kwacha) has had the same parity with the U.S. dollar since 1949.

It has proved impossible to use one currency unit consistently throughout the book. In general, chapters about the modern Zambian economy use Kwacha, with sterling or dollar equivalents quoted as well where appropriate. Pre-1968 Zambian statistics have been converted to Kwacha for comparability (£1 Zambia = 2 Kwacha). For the period before World War II, we have, in general, used pounds sterling (£1 = 20/-).

The price of copper is now commonly quoted in Zambia in both pounds sterling and Kwacha per metric ton: K750 per metric ton is equal to £437.50 per metric ton, which in turn is equal to 47.64 U.S. cents per lb. Throughout the book, pounds (£) refers to British pounds sterling.

Weights

Copper production and ore reserves were in the past quoted in "long tons" (2240 lbs.) and "short tons" (2000 lbs.) respectively. The world is gradually moving to using the metric ton, which is approximately 2204 lbs. The modern statistics are quoted here in metric tons, but where tax formulas, notably those for calculating royalty and export tax, were based on long tons, the formulas have not been converted.

CHRONOLOGY

1886   Discovery of Witwatersrand gold field in South Africa.

1889   British South Africa Company incorporated by Royal Charter.

1890   Lewanika, Litunga of Barotseland, grants first concession to British South Africa Company agents.

1895   Beginning of prospecting north of the Zambezi River.

1899-1900   British South Africa Company rule over Northern Rhodesia established by British Orders-in-Council.

1900   Granting of "Lewanika concession"—principal concession on which British South Africa Company's claims to ownership of mineral rights in Zambia was based.

1902   Roan Antelope and Bwana Mkubwa claims pegged.

1904   Opening of Sasare gold mine in Petauke district.

1906   Railroad reaches Broken Hill (now Kabwe).

1909   Railroad link to the Copperbelt and Katanga Province in the Congo completed.

1912   Mining Proclamation—first mining legislation in Northern Rhodesia.

1915   First lead produced at Broken Hill Mine.

1922   British South Africa Company begins to issue exclusive prospecting licences.

1924   British South Africa Company hands over administration of Northern Rhodesia to British Colonial Office.

1928   Formation of Rhodesian Anglo-American and Rhodesian Selection Trust.

1931   Roan Antelope and Nkana Mines begin production.

1932   Agreed cut in production of 25 percent at Nkana and Roan Antelope; Nchanga and Mufulira closed down production could start.

1933   Mufulira reopens and begins production.

1936   Nchanga reopens and begins production.

1938   British Secretary of State for the Colonies refers mineral rights question to the British Government Law Officers, who find in favor of British South Africa Company's rights.

1940-45   Copper sold at an agreed price to British Ministry of Supply.

1950   Agreement by Northern Rhodesian Government, British South Africa Company, and British Government that the British South Africa Company enjoy royalties until 1986 subject to payment of 20 percent of royalties to Northern Rhodesian Government.

1953   Formation of the Federation of Rhodesia and Nyasaland.

1955   Chibuluma begins production.

1957   Bancroft begins production (closed 1958, reopened 1959).

1962   New constitution enables African parties to win narrow majority in Legislative Council.

1963   Dissolution of the Federation of Rhodesia and Nyasaland.

October 1964   Independence of Zambia, with Kenneth Kaunda as President. Mineral rights bought from the British South Africa Company.

1965   Chambishi begins production. Unilateral Declaration of Independence in Southern Rhodesia.

1966   Formation of Intergovernmental Council of Copper Exporting Countries (CIPEC). Abandonment of producer price by copper companies.

April	1968	"Mulungushi" speech announced: (1) that no credit would be granted to any non-Zambian or non-Zambian company (defined as any company less than 100 percent Zambian-owned) without the permission of the Bank of Zambia; (2) that all non-Zambians would be refused retail trading licences from the following January, except in the main town centers; and (3) that 27 companies would be invited to sell 51 percent of their shares to the Government, at book value, to be paid for out of future profits.
December	1968	General election: UNIP (President Kaunda's party) returned with a reduced majority.
June	1969	National referendum enables a two-thirds majority in Parliament to make any changes in the constitution (UNIP had such a majority).
August	1969	"Matero" speech announced: (1) that the copper mines would be taken over on a 51 percent basis and new mineral taxation system would be introduced and (2) that the definition of a Zambian company would be immediately relaxed to include any company more than 50 percent Zambian-owned.
December	1969	Heads of Agreement signed.
January	1970	The new Mines and Minerals Act comes into force.
September	1970	Disaster at Mufulira kills 89 miners; loss of production estimated at 200,000 metric tons during 1970-72.
November	1970	Speech in Mulungushi Hall announced: (1) that banks and building societies would be taken over on a 51 percent basis and (2) that all insurance business would be handled by the State Insurance Company within 18 months.

Economic Independence and
Zambian Copper

LOCALITY MAP OF ZAMBIA

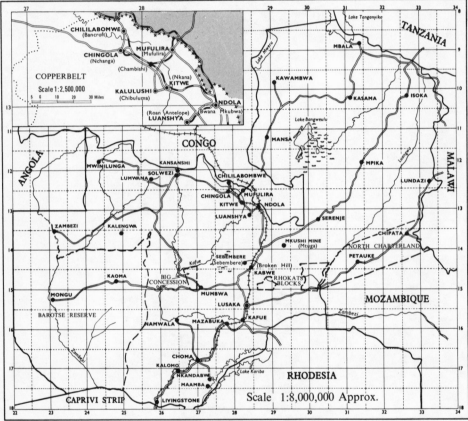

Compiled and Drawn by the Geological Survey Department, The Republic of Zambia, 1971

1

ECONOMIC
INDEPENDENCE

Charles Harvey

INTRODUCTION

The question of economic independence, or nationalism to use a slightly more emotive term, has many ramifications and is not confined to African or even to underdeveloped countries. Such rich industrialized countries as France and Canada have been concerned about the limitations on their independence created by large-scale American investment, and Great Britain is frequently worried by the loss of freedom that arises out of running a reserve currency with inadequate backing.

Nevertheless, the problem is probably most acute in Africa, in the states that have recently become politically independent; certainly, the ideas in this chapter have been formed in Zambia, and in particular by the experience of dealing with the big copper mining companies, whose partial takeover is the main subject of this book.

Zambia is an extreme example of economic dependence. Its colonization from the south, the period of Federal domination by Southern Rhodesia, and British colonial policies left the country, with approximately 100 university graduates and 1,000 secondary school graduates at independence in October 1964.[1] Naturally, a disproportionate number of the graduates were absorbed into government as senior politicians and civil servants, leaving the senior ranks of the private sector much as they had always been—overwhelmingly in the hands of expatriates. At the same time, virtually the whole of

3

TABLE 1.1

Copper Production in Members of Intergovernmental
Council of Copper Exporting Countries, 1965
(percentages)

	GDP	GNP	Exports	Revenue	Employment
Zambia	40	34*	93	68	15
Congo (Kinshasa)	18*	23*	51	45*	2*
Chile	4	3*	65	14	3
Peru	2	1.5*	18	12	1

*Estimated

Source: A. M. J. de Swardt and A. R. Drysdall, "Mining and
Prospecting in Zambia, with Particular Reference to the Work of the
Geological Survey Department" (unpublished, paper read at 50th Anni-
versary Conference of the Geological Survey of Uganda, Entebbe,
July, 1969). (Proceeding in press.)

manufacturing industry, mining, and the financial sector and a large
part of other service sectors (including retailing) were owned by
foreigners. From the Zambian viewpoint, it added insult to injury
that most businesses were owned and controlled from Salisbury or
South Africa. The suspected or actual abuse of these situations has
been a separate reason for some takeovers.

Another and quite different aspect of Zambia's economic dependence is the extraordinary dominance of copper in the economy.
Although many underdeveloped countries depend heavily on a few
primary product exports, Zambia is an extreme case (see Table 1.1).
The resultant problems, in particular that of instability, are dealt
with in some detail in Chapter 4. The point to note here is that,
although takeover, restriction of trading licences to citizens, investment in education, and other measures open to government can be
used to tackle the areas of economic dependence mentioned earlier,
dependence on copper and inability to influence its price are problems about which Zambia alone can do virtually nothing in the short

term. Reduction of dependence on imports and development of alternative exports are essentially very long-term policies and are fraught
with their own difficulties.

Before discussing in detail the problems that arise from large-
scale foreign investment in a country such as Zambia, a few general
points are worth noting. The first concerns the association between
socialism and the search for economic independence. In Uganda, for
example, the 1970 nationalizations were announced as a move to the
left, and the Tanzanian policy of self-reliance has been part of an
explicitly socialist policy. In Zambia too, although President Kenneth
Kaunda's philosophy of Zambian Humanism (not to be confused with
other brands of humanism, although the use of the term is rather mis-
leading) specifically rejects the doctrines of socialism, there have
been socialist policy elements. But in Zambia the choice of public
ownership has been pragmatic rather than ideological: the government has simply used the most easily available means to achieve its
aims (see Chapter 5). Thus, private enterprise has been encouraged
in such fields as retailing, construction, and agriculture, where Zambian individuals and institutions were available to replace foreigners.
The companies that have been taken over continue to be run on largely
capitalist principles, partly because the Government does not have
the personnel to run them in any other way but also because the commitment to a socialist philosophy is not by any means as definite as
the commitment to Zambianization of the economy.

A second point is that many attempts to decrease economic
dependence, especially in countries with a colonial history, have been
as much political as economic. As this book is concerned primarily
with the economic aspects of independence, we have not tried to
analyze in detail the political motives of the takeovers.

POINTS OF CONFLICT

There are points of conflict between private business and the
government in any country, and governments use a whole range of
controls to try to resolve them. Where locally owned companies are
involved, most of the controls have the effect of reducing profits and
thus discouraging investment. However, a situation in which the
decision is simply whether or not to invest is different from one in
which there is a third alternative: to invest somewhere else. In other
words, foreign investors can often go elsewhere and are rather more
sensitive than domestic investors to interference with the profitability
of their investments.[2] Even in a society concerned with avoiding

great inequalities of wealth, high profits can be tolerated if the profits accrue to local institutions and individuals, and especially if they are reinvested. But high profits remitted abroad, although like locally-owned profits contributing to investment incentives, are a direct loss to society. Even reinvestment creates further problems (see below). There are also clashes of interest in other areas, arising out of the shorter time horizons of foreign companies and the greater likelihood of differences in political outlook between foreign companies and host governments.

Some of the points of conflict specific to foreign companies are:

1. Discrimination against local people in employment, promotion, and training opportunities.

2. The outflow of profits, on the ground that they are excessive in absolute terms, in relation to total profits, in relation to present investment size (that is, the past inflow of capital including reinvested profits), or in relation to present inflow of capital.

3. Insufficient reinvestment of profits, which is essentially the same issue as that of outflow of profits, although some inconsistency of criticism often arises here since host countries also object to the building up of foreign-owned assets out of locally-earned profits.

4. Decisions of multinational companies that conflict with local interests, for example on sources of imports, forward and backward linkages; more specifically, the interests of the foreign part of a multinational company—which is typically much larger than its local part in any one host country—are often different from the interests of either the local company operations or the host government.

5. Suspicion that companies can manipulate costs and sales prices in order to shift profits around the world, thereby avoiding local taxes and exchange control regulations.

6. Suspicion that the economic power of foreign companies gives them undue political power.

7. Discrimination against local people in supplying a product, for example, loans supplied by foreign-owned banks and building societies.

LOCALIZATION

Localization of employment and promotion and provision of training can be pursued by various forms of government pressure, as they are in Zambia through Zambianization committees for each sector of the economy. It is also possible to subsidize training programs if necessary. However, it is important here to distinguish between large and small companies. In a large company, it is frequently in the economic interests of management to use local people because they cost less than expatriates. Furthermore, the large company is in a better position to invest in training (and in such welfare services as health, education, and community development, which reduce the migrant element in local labor). First, a large company is more likely to have the financial resources; second, it is more likely to be a monopoly buyer of the specialized skills needed in its own operations. A retailer who trains a shop manager at some expense risks losing him to another retailer or to a business venture of his own. A copper mine that trains a shift boss can afford to pay him much more than he would get anywhere else except in another copper mine, and the few mining employers (essentially two in Zambia) can either agree not to poach each other's men or can afford to assume that they will gain as much as they lose.

A further distinction must be drawn between the large multinational company, where decisions are taken by an executive whose job is not immediately threatened and who can eventually look forward to security of employment through jobs elsewhere in the company or group, and the much smaller expatriate business, where the management's jobs are immediately threatened and where the management may not have alternative job opportunities, especially if they have resided in the country for a long time.

Before independence in Zambia, one would have had to take into account noneconomic prejudices, specifically the power of the white trade unions. In fact, the copper mine management often wanted to go further and faster with local promotion and training than they were able because of white trade union power.[3] Political independence greatly reduced this power; this change, and the placing of noncitizens on expatriate contract terms, must have removed a great deal of the real driving force behind the determination of expatriates to protect their jobs, since they can no longer think in terms of permanent residence in Zambia. This is not to say that all becomes plain sailing after political independence. There may still be a big difference between the directives of the head office and what actually happens on the factory floor, in the workshop, or down the mine. Many expatriates still would like to keep their jobs, and the shortage of even expatriate skilled labor must mean that many have little enough time to get their jobs done, let alone train others to do them as well. In fact, an important part of the problem is that it is the very men whose jobs are most immediately threatened whose cooperation is most needed in the on-the-job training to make localization effective.

Taking ownership or partial ownership in a situation where the same management is retained may or may not increase the possibilities for speeding up localization. Clearly, it depends on how much already was being done; how much short-term loss of efficiency is tolerable; and the quality of local residents put in at board level, the time they can afford to spend learning the business, and the mutual understanding they manage to develop with the remaining foreign management. The ultimate constraint, as in almost all matters concerning economic independence, is local manpower. If local people are available to perform skilled jobs, if able government officials are available to oversee the process of localization, above all if there are men on the government side who are sufficiently knowledgeable about an industry and sufficiently confident of their knowledge to counter the expert arguments of expatriate management, then localization can proceed quickly and smoothly. The whole point, of course, is that such people usually are not available. It is difficult to argue against men who have been hired specifically because they know a lot about a business, and it is easy for disaffected people to sabotage a newly promoted local resident, either by shifting effective decision-making away from him or by making him appear inefficient and thus fulfilling doom-laden prophecies made before the promotion. In mining, there is the vitally important added complication of the safety of thousands of men working underground. Safety is a factor in most industries (although not in commerce), but it is a central feature of mining and it would be a brave and probably foolish government official who tried too hard to hasten localization against expert advice in such conditions.

In commerce, the deep-end method works better, but only if those thrown in have unrealized potential and do in fact start swimming. However, there is an alternative result and a disastrous and lasting drop in efficiency can occur if too much is attempted too soon and if there simply are not enough local residents with enough education and experience to seize the opportunity. Of course, choosing the point in time at which this is no longer true is a large part of the skill needed in dealing with foreign companies; it is not clear that nationalization per se necessarily makes much difference. At worst, it means putting a few overworked permanent secretaries and ministers onto the board where they will have a nominal majority but no time to study the background for their decisions and possibly dispute the advice of minority foreign management. It also means that the threat of nationalization, useful before the event in imposing the government's will, has been removed. At best, nationalization may produce a genuinely better understanding of each side's point of view and thus a more constructive working relationship. Without more local skills and experience, nationalization cannot mean much more in larger companies.

Takeover can be used as an occasion for a formal deal on localization. But, in order to convince a company to agree to a timetable, government would have to guarantee an adequate supply of secondary school leavers and technical college and university graduates to make it possible to meet that timetable. Many companies in Zambia, one suspects, would be only too willing to agree to a Zambianization timetable in return for such a guarantee. In short, time and the education program will do much more than any other government policy to solve this problem. The Chilean copper industry has faced many of Zambia's problems in dealing with large foreign companies, yet in the 1960's it employed only a tiny handful of expatriates. Although this fact in itself proves nothing, it does at least suggest that the real problems lie elsewhere and that, at least in large companies, economic forces will do much of the localization committee's work.

PROFITS

Part of the problem faced by the underdeveloped world in playing host to foreign private investment is illustrated by the following quotation:

During the period 1950-1968 foreign assets of United States-based corporations rose from $12,000 million to $65,000 million. In that same period net outflow of U.S. direct investment fell short of income by over $15,000 million. In other words, overseas assets rose by $53,000 million, while there was a net flow of money to the U.S. of $15,000 million. With reference to British private investment in the developing countries, for example, the following figures are equally pertinent: in 1967, British private investment in the developing countries was £60 million whereas Britain's earnings from past investments amounted to £140 million in the same year.[4]

The quotation ignores the possibility—which is the justification for all capital inflows except grants into poor countries—that investment may increase production sufficiently in host countries to make such payments possible and still leave the host countries better off. A further justification has been the hope that new inflows of foreign investment capital would always grow faster than repayments in the form of repatriated profits. This hope clearly has not been fulfilled, and it is disturbing that one of the net results of foreign investment has turned out to be a large net flow of money to the rich countries.

The above quotation also points up very neatly the dilemma that faces the host country that recognizes the problem and seeks a package of policy measures to ease the strain on its balance of payments without losing the benefits of foreign investment.

Taxation increases reduce both the outflow of profits and the build-up of foreign-owned assets out of locally-earned profits. At the same time, they reduce the profitability of investment and thus risk reducing inflows of new capital by more than the reduction in profit outflow. In addition, tax increases may be in direct conflict with policies of tax concessions to attract foreign investment.

Exchange control restrictions on the repatriation of profits also may reduce capital inflow, since foreign companies must put a lower subjective value on funds forcibly retained in the host country. Such exchange control restrictions also create the fear of worse to come, and are certain to increase foreign ownership of assets in so far as profits are forcibly retained and will be utilized within the country.

The final possibility is some form of local purchase of assets, presumably although not necessarily by government. If compensation is paid, it will mean an increased outflow of funds in the short term to pay for a reduced outflow in the long term. In order to minimize the risk of cutting off future flows of foreign investment, compensation must at least be reasonable, but this exacerbates the short-term balance of payments problem and still runs the risk of not achieving its objective. The growing insistence on partnership in new investment between foreign investors and local interests, public or private, reduces the size of these problems but does not provide a solution to the problem of existing investments. Furthermore, many countries do not have the local financial resources to participate in all new investments.

Countries with adequate supplies of money can afford to deal more radically with foreign investment, being less dependent on future capital inflows. But virtually no underdeveloped country is self-sufficient in technical and managerial manpower or in technology, and in general there is even less likelihood of local development of new techniques in the future because only a very small proportion of all research and development expenditure takes place in the underdeveloped world. Thus, takeover without compensation, which is certain to reduce the inflow of new foreign investment, is a dangerous policy even for countries that do not need the finance.

One of the key questions is whether new technology can be purchased on the open market in the form of new machines, the men to run them, and the men to adapt them to local conditions, without offering equity participation, and, if this can be done, whether hired management will have the same incentives to maximize efficiency without an equity holding. Certainly, hired management has some advantages. For example, it may be possible to write into management contracts some specific localization objectives which, if the contract has a stated time limit, may not conflict with the personal ambitions of management itself. It may be possible to divorce hired management more successfully from the objectives of the multinational company when it is also divorced from ownership—but this approach may at the same time cut the developing country off from new technology.

Of course, restricting the outflow of profits is not the only way to expand production without nationalization. Other more direct ways include the following:

1. Conventional tax incentives, which usually have the disadvantage of a capital-intensive bias. However, they need not have a capital-intensive basis: for example, it is possible to have tax reductions for expansion of employment, even unconventional ones as in Chile where a declining average tax rate was offered for production expansion. All these methods reduce government revenue and probably increase profit flows abroad.

2. Putting up of part of the cost by government (this technique also was used by Chile) or using government influence or guarantees to raise funds—assuming that the government's credit is better than that of a multinational company, which is far from always being the case.

3. The threat, for example, of increased tax rates or tightened exchange control or nationalization if expansion does not take place.

4. The guaranteeing of a market by such measures as price guarantee and protection although the bigger the industry and the more export-oriented it is, the less able government is to do this, at least without huge risk.

5. Numerous other benefits, such as promises of wage control and provision of services.

One should add that the need to provide investment incentive rests on the view that private and public investment criteria differ. They do, in any country. Foreign investment in underdeveloped countries is a special case because of supposed political instability and because of the perfectly genuine fears of host countries that some form of exploitation is embodied in investment by foreign companies, many of whom have incomes much larger than the countries in which they invest. Both factors increase the risk of noneconomic loss by the investor; in fact, the very nature of foreign investment creates this risk since xenophobia, or more politely the desire for economic independence, seems certain to arise from foreign investment situations, especially when they involve unequal partners. The foreign investor thus uses a high subjective discount rate on future profits; yet a host government, which undoubtedly believes in its own future and even more in that of its people, is bound to discount more generously future benefits supposedly reduced by governmental instability.

In short, some government action may be needed to bridge the gap between investors' fears and host countries' needs.

Thus, paradoxically, one form of investment incentive may turn out to be local partnership with foreign investors, even when this approach is imposed forcibly. Partnership reduces the threat of expropriation and gives the foreign investor a chance to formally establish its rights and duties vis-à-vis the host government, while the government makes a public and explicit commitment to the continued success of the investment.

Although taxation and the need for production and wage employment gives government an interest in any investment, equity participation involves government more directly and gives it a glimpse of the private investor's viewpoint. At the same time, by the very fact of government participation it is more difficult to make accusations of economic colonialism, excessive repatriation of profits, or excessive build-up of foreign-owned assets out of locally-earned profits.

As already mentioned, poor countries may not be able to afford this particular form of investment incentive, but the growing need to cope with investors' fears may force some form of participation on even the poorest countries. Furthermore, the disincentive to savings that arises from being able to rely in the short term on inflows of foreign investment could be reduced without throwing the full burden of saving onto a low-income country.

LINKAGES AND INTRA-COMPANY DEALS

In addition to the question of profit retention and reinvestment, the multinational nature of foreign investors creates further problems that do not normally occur when investment is by local interests. Thus, companies that are vertically integrated across national frontiers have an interest in buying and selling from one another. Where a local assembly plant in an underdeveloped country was set up precisely in order to increase exports of parts from the country of origin, the company will normally be slow to encourage local manufacture of parts unless pushed to do so by its host government. Similarly, both Chile and Congo (Kinshasa), for example, continued to export copper in less than fully refined form long after their mining industries were sufficiently large to support local refining, because of the existence of refining capacity in the United States and Belgium.*

Horizontally integrated companies create different problems: plants set up to supply a home market may be prevented from expanding into export markets because of the danger of conflicting with exports from plants under the same ownership in other countries. The case of Ford in Great Britain, which is allowed to export to the United States in competition with American Ford, is an exception.

There are many well-known ways of encouraging backward and forward linkages, including import duties, quotas and bans, and export taxes on unprocessed products. But it may be that the key problem is early identification of the linkages that are possible; once this is done, government has various weapons in a bargaining situation with a foreign company. Partnership may help to provide better information

---

*A recent approach to this problem is illustrated by the deal between Congo (Kinshasa) and Japanese copper mining interests, by which copper concentrates can be exported from the Congo for a limited period only.

about potential linkages, but the important thing is to realize that "natural" forces are unlikely to be in the host country's interest where companies have foreign connections, and therefore a positive government program is required.

If export markets are divided in a way that is against the national interest, the first step, as before, is identification of the problem. Effective action again depends on government's bargaining strength, with the ultimate possibility of severing the overseas connection. However, as always, this action is only possible if a country can manage without foreign management, technology, capital, and inputs.

Manipulation of accounts to avoid local taxes and exchange control regulations can be policed when products are traded internationally outside the umbrella of intra-company trading. It is more difficult to police intra-company purchases from head offices, especially purchases of such items as administrative and research services. Ultimately, high taxes and severe exchange control rules may be self-defeating if the cost and difficulty of policing them is too great.

In this area, as in the "undue" political interference of foreign companies, a host country is limited in the independence it may achieve by the quantity and quality of available manpower and by its ability to do without aid, the supply of which often has been tied to the treatment of foreign investors.

One final point is that the commitment of foreign company management to the parent company can be exaggerated. Senior company men may have lived in the host country for long periods and may have considerable local loyalty. Thus, willingness to cooperate with host governments should not invariably be interpreted as a sinister plot to increase the scope for hostile actions by foreign companies. In addition to the areas of common economic interest that clearly exist, there may also be areas of common interest in a different sense, interest in the survival, prosperity, and development of the country.

DISCRIMINATION IN THE SUPPLY OF
PRODUCTS LOCALLY

The most sensitive sector in which product supply has been discriminatory is loans. Some discrimination has been based on objective criteria that, through no fault of the local people, made them unsuitable customers. But some of the discrimination can be traced to linguistic and cultural differences between lenders and local borrowers and to a lack of urgency among foreign bank managers in the search for new lending criteria and new types of security that would enable them to discriminate between local residents who will and will not be able to repay.

This situation doubtless contributed to large proportions of African bank deposits, for example, being invested in London financial markets[5] and to the desire of African governments to secure further control of financial sectors. However, the development of local capital markets and the training of more local bank managers seems likely to accomplish more than participation by government in expatriate banks. Indeed, the detailed interference by government in the granting of loans opens too many avenues to corruption, inefficiency, and the making of losses. If a government wants to make noncommercial loans, it is probably better done through a government agency or by overt subsidies to commercial institutions.

In other sectors where supply was discriminatory before political independence—such as health, education, electricity, and agricultural extension services—the government now is usually the supplier and thus is in a position to remove discrimination as and when it can and, more importantly, to increase total supply.

TAKEOVER AND BARGAINING STRENGTH

We have examined some of the alternatives to equity participation by government in the search for economic independence and pointed out the limitations to achieving any advance by takeover. But this ignores the point that takeover is often a political necessity; it can become intolerable that major industries or sectors of great sensitivity, such as banking, should be run and owned entirely by foreigners, however many controls the government has at its disposal. It also can be argued that government participation, even though it may be only a small step toward economic independence, is a necessary one as a basis for further steps forward and thus is probably inevitable. In some cases where takeover has been expected for some time, it is as well to get it done and provide a more settled and permanent atmosphere.

How much ownership the government should take and how much it should pay in a takeover situation are largely dependent on the government's bargaining strength. What is more, as is by now clear, how much control the government is actually able to exercise after the takeover also depends on its bargaining strength. Ownership of

100 percent may achieve little or nothing if the government has no real power. The previous owners may actually maintain or even increase their (remittable) profits from company operations through management contracts and favorable sales contracts for both inputs and final products. On the other hand, less than 50 percent ownership may give all the control needed if the government's strength is sufficient to get what it wants in negotiation and to see that it continues to get what it wants after takeover.

The bargaining position of government depends on: (1) its ability to replace the present management should it be withdrawn, either with local residents or with alternative foreign management; (2) its need for future foreign investment because it needs the money; (3) its need for future private foreign investors because it needs their expertise, their techniques, and access to future supplies of technology; (4) the importance of the product to the management/owners or their political masters—for example, key raw materials where alternative sources are in other hands; (5) the proportion of profits the government is already successfully taxing or retaining through exchange control; (6) the ability of government negotiating teams and the experience of government in general in such bargaining situations; (7) the "shock" effect of a takeover announcement—in a situation in which everyone is expecting some form of takeover, the actual announcement is less likely to alienate those with whom government must deal; (8) the size of the local company, both absolutely and in relation to its parent group; and (9) the size of the home market, where a foreign company is selling locally.

ZAMBIA'S BARGAINING STRENGTH

Zambia's bargaining position in negotiating with the copper companies was an interesting mixture of strength and weakness. It was absolutely essential to keep the management and most of the expatriate employees in the industry, both because of their specialized local knowledge and because of the world-wide shortage of men skilled in this field. Turnover of expatriates, and especially the replacement of long-term employees by newcomers on short contracts, already was causing enough problems without risking further departures. Nevertheless, the sheer size of the industry—which is large even in relation to world copper production and to the large mining groups with which the Zambian companies are associated— gave some strength to the government position, since there could be no real question of quick reemployment of the entire expatriate labor force in other countries.

The question of future flows of capital and technology is inseparable from the need to keep the management. Success in keeping the
management probably means continued access to foreign technical
know-how, and a deal satisfactory to the management should by definition be satisfactory to the shareholders they represent and thus
indirectly to the capitalist world. In Zambia's case, this meant that
it was essential to pay "adequate" compensation. One should add that
the flow of technology is not all in one direction since some important
techniques have been developed in Zambia, but this does not make the
country independent of developments elsewhere.

The size of the Zambian copper industry is again important
when discussing its strategic importance. During World War II, for
example, "pressure was brought by the British Government to avoid
a strike at any cost."[6] In fact, it has been said that British policy
in Zambia has always been roughly described by "keep the country
quiet, keep the copper coming out." But Britain buys less than one-
quarter of Zambian copper and must have much less influence on the
companies now than in 1940. Therefore, it is unlikely that Britain's
strategic need to maintain copper supplies added much to Zambia's
bargaining strength; Zambia's need for copper sales is normally much
greater than the need of any of its customers for Zambian copper.
Furthermore, at the time of the takeover, world supply was expected
to increase very rapidly, probably more rapidly than demand in the
short term.[7]

Because the Zambian Government already was taking such a
high proportion of copper profits in taxation and retaining part of the
remainder under exchange control regulations, there was little question of the government seeking to use the takeover as an occasion for
trying to increase its share of the profits. In fact, the tax system
was so badly structured and the exchange control rules were creating
so many problems that they urgently needed changing. Almost any
change was bound to be favorable to the companies, but Government's
bargaining strength was increased by being able to make the changes
as part of the takeover deal, since it always pays to enter a negotiating situation with something to give away, even if it is something
that must be given away in any case.

The haste with which Government decided on the takeover is
neatly illustrated by its having asked the companies to submit their
suggestions for the takeover. This meant that negotiations began in
a framework conducive to company objectives. The companies must
have been sufficiently well prepared, as takeover had been a clear

possibility for some time. For example, in December 1968, several senior copper company men came to a discussion of a paper given at the Zambian Economics Club on a hypothetical takeover scheme and discussed the details rather than challenging the premise.[8] Overseas shareholders were undoubtedly less well prepared, but satisfying their representatives proved sufficient, since the shareholders accepted in due course the settlement made on their behalf.

It is difficult to overemphasize the difference that the great size of the mining industry made to Zambia's negotiating position, in contrast to, for example, Tanzania's negotiating position in regard to expatriate banks. The big international banks could afford to withdraw all their expatriate staff from Tanzania and reabsorb them elsewhere with no problem, and the prospect of expropriation or low compensation as a result may have been worth the risk if the gesture had a salutory effect in other countries. No such gamble was possible with the mines in Zambia, and so for once a small country may have been able to avoid some of the consequences of its size.

COMPENSATION

Compensation can range from nothing to book value, share value, and discounted future profits. None of these, except the first, is really objectively determinable. How much to pay depends fundamentally on whom the country is trying to satisfy. Thinking in terms of future supplies of foreign investment and technology, it is possible to satisfy:

(1) the existing shareholders, plus (2), plus (3);

(2) their compatriots, plus (3);

(3) other capitalist countries' investors;

(4) socialist countries.

The scale should really be two-dimensional, with the second dimension being time. Thus, a payment that succeeds in not scaring off capitalist investors in time should generally satisfy investors from countries where previous shareholders live. The other oddity of the scale is that, the more a country rejects capitalist criteria for compensation, the more likely it is that the socialist countries will be pleased and thus willing to supply technical expertise; this is obviously not an immutable rule, but one can think of examples that support it, such as the Tanzam railroad being built by the Chinese, the Aswan high dam, and the experience of Cuba.

It is possible that some socialist technology is less capital-intensive and thus more suitable to underdeveloped countries, but it has other drawbacks. The transfer of technological skills is made more difficult by language problems, and few countries wish to confine themselves to only one-half of the developed world. It is probable that the time dimension works even in this case in that capitalist investments will eventually return to countries that have expropriated capitalist assets. Despite all the fine speeches by chairmen at annual general meetings, businessmen are always interested if the terms are right.

As to the ethics of deliberately paying less than a "fair price," no such thing as a "fair price" exists. An underdeveloped country should pay as much and no more than will buy what it wants, whether it be management goodwill or investor goodwill. Those individual shareholders who bought shares long ago will have done very well, and those who bought them recently knew the risks they were running. The figures already quoted on international flows of investment money and the damage done in social and racial terms by foreign investors demonstrate easily enough that the ethical arguments are not all one way. A fair price is simply what the two parties can agree to, and so it reflects their bargaining strength and what they want from the deal.

SHOULD ANY COUNTRY ENCOURAGE FOREIGN INVESTMENT?

There is evidence that capital imports are inversely correlated with domestic savings and growth of per capita income. The evidence based on cross-section analysis tells us little about what would happen in an individual country if capital imports increased, nor does it clarify the direction of causation since countries with low rates of growth and low savings ratios may attract more capital according to some criteria of needs. Nevertheless, the figures are highly suggestive and indicate the need to look further at the whole question.[9]

Kaj Areskoug has shown a more direct effect by finding a statistically significant allocation of foreign capital to current consumption in some individual countries. He argues convincingly that this is to be expected since presumably underdeveloped countries wish to optimize consumption over time, and there is no reason to suppose present consumption has zero weight.[10]

From a priori argument, it is clear that the availability of foreign capital must reduce the incentive to save, especially when the main source of savings is public and tax increases are politically difficult. Furthermore, countries that are almost wholly dependent (or wholly dependent like Malawi, which has a negative domestic savings rate) on imported capital for growth have no incentive to develop industries to supply the currently imported needs of development projects, since most if not all aid is tied. Yet industries to supply capital goods are one of the keys to industrial growth. This argument is merely an extension, albeit an important one, of the well-known arguments that capital imports are capital-intensive and so reduce employment growth and are also import-intensive and so reduce output of existing import-competitive industries.

It would be foolish to condemn all imports of capital on the basis of these arguments. What is needed is a greater awareness among underdeveloped countries of the dangers so that they can reject the worst deals and extract much better terms in the future. The full bargaining strength of underdeveloped countries has not been used because of inexperience and ignorance; the grossly suboptimal results are due to these factors as much as to the inherent weakness of an underdeveloped country's economic position. To put it another way, capital flows are going to continue in most countries, so it is better to concentrate on making the best of them than to waste time condemning them all. It would be equally nonsensical to argue for the expulsion of all existing foreign investors from underdeveloped countries. There is clearly a large area of common interest; one is merely concerned to see that current arrangements fall within that area, and if possible nearer to the host country's needs than hitherto.

CONCLUSION

Ownership is only one way of controlling foreign companies. A 51 percent ownership is the cheapest way (assuming some compensation is paid) of acquiring nominal control while retaining some of the benefits of private enterprise, especially incentives to maximize profits and to continue to bring in new techniques. There is no shock effect if partnership is used from the start, but even takeovers may remove uncertainty and, by putting what is already a profit-sharing partnership (through the tax system) on a more sensible basis, they may create a more fruitful atmosphere for development.

The real degree of control that takeover gives to the government depends on the economic and political strength of the two sides, and especially on the experience and knowledge available to the government.

Experience and knowledge will accrue more rapidly through partner-ship, but they are basically products of time, the education system, and real on-the-job training at all levels. Ownership, 51 percent or any other figure, cannot alter the real domestic resources available to government, which determine what government can achieve. How-ever, ownership can alter the deployment of resources, which can produce a significant shift in the balance of economic power and con-trol; ownership may also be the only available way of achieving such a shift short of revolution.

Finally, buying ownership is a way of using domestic savings that, for reasons of absorptive capacity (lack of complementary in-ternal resources to match with imported goods and skills in develop-ment projects), cannot be spent in other ways. Thus, governments lucky enough to have foreign surpluses (and an adequate reserve position) can invest such surpluses in future profits in their domestic industries instead of in U.K. Treasury Bills.

NOTES

1. T. Coombe, "The Origins of Secondary Education in Zambia," African Social Research, I, 3 (June, 1967), p. 173.

2. That foreign investors have been successful in seeking high profits is supported by the figures quoted by P. Baran and M. Sweezy showing that investment abroad by U.S. companies is more than twice as profitable as investment in the United States. See P. Baran and M. Sweezy, "Notes on the Theory of Imperialism," in Problems of Economic Dynamics and Planning: Essays in Honour of Michael Kalecki (Warsaw: Polish Scientific Publishers, 1964).

3. R. E. Baldwin, Economic Development and Export Growth: A Study of Northern Rhodesia, 1920-1960 (Berkeley: University of California Press, 1966), pp. 100-5.

4. "Economic Development and Co-operation Among Non-Aligned Countries," Draft Document No. 23, Third Summit Conference of Non-Aligned Nations, Lusaka, September 1970 (NAC/CONF.3/CM/23), paragraph 19. The figures on U.S. investment were taken from R. D. Woolf, "The Economics of Imperialism," American Economic Review, Papers and Proceedings, May 1970, who in his turn derived them from various issues of Survey of Current Business. The British figures are taken from an article by M. Barrat-Brown in The Spokes-man, May 1970.

5. For East Africa, see W. T. Newlyn, Money in an African Context (Nairobi: OUP, 1967), Chapter 4; for post-independence developments in Zambia, see chapter on money and banking in C. M. Elliott, ed., Constraints on the Economic Development of Zambia (Nairobi; Oxford University Press, 1971).

6. Baldwin, op. cit., p. 101.

7. For a recent summary of the position, see The Economist, November 10-17, 1970.

8. The paper was "A Future for Zambia's Copper Industry?" by M. L. O. Faber, and J. G. Potter in Towards Economic Independence (Cambridge: Cambridge University Press, 1971). Also, there was at least one offer made to Government by the companies soon after independence (October 1964) for a less than majority shareholding in their Zambian operations. We thank Philip S. Coonley, Institute for African Studies, University of Zambia, for reminding us of this.

9. See K. Griffin, Underdevelopment in Spanish America (London; Allen and Unwin, 1970), Chapter 3.

10. Kaj Areskoug, External Public Borrowing: Its Role in Economic Development (New York; Praeger Publishers, 1970).

2

THE LEGACY
OF THE BRITISH
SOUTH AFRICA COMPANY:
THE HISTORICAL
BACKGROUND

Peter Slinn

" Cecil Rhodes has not lived in perpetuity " remarked President
Kenneth Kaunda during his speech announcing the Zambian mining
reforms. President Kaunda also might have noted that the British
South Africa Company, which Rhodes founded, no longer existed except
in name; in 1965, as a result of a merger, it became a wholly-owned
subsidiary of Chartered Consolidated Ltd. However, the role of the
"Chartered Company" (so called because it was incorporated by
Royal Charter in 1889) in the development of the copper industry
prior to independence is a key to understanding the situation that
existed in 1969. The structure of the industry and the legal framework within which it operated can be seen much more readily as a
legacy from the Chartered Company than as a legacy from the Colonial
Office administration.

The Chartered Company's influence had a twofold basis. First,
as a result of its part in the acquisition of what is now Zambia for
the British Empire in the 1890's, the Chartered Company laid claim
to, and was allowed to exercise until independence, the mineral rights
over almost the entire territory. Second, the Chartered Company was
itself directly responsible for the administration of what was then
known as Northern Rhodesia until that region's administration was
handed over to the Colonial Office in 1924. Under these circumstances,
the Chartered Company was able to procure the passing of mining
legislation with the effect that the Chartered Company, deemed to be
owner of the mineral rights, was in a position to dictate by whom and
on what terms and conditions any mineral prospecting or mining was
to be carried out.

The circumstances in which the Chartered Company was alleged to have acquired the mineral rights subsequently led to a dispute that became the cause célèbre of Zambian colonial history (this matter is discussed in detail later in this chapter).[1] The company's Royal Charter empowered it, subject to British Government approval, to "acquire by any concession, agreement, grant or treaty all or any rights, interests, authorities, jurisdictions and powers of any kind or nature whatsoever" within a rather vaguely defined area of south central Africa.

Although Rhodes and his associates were primarily concerned at first with what is now Southern Rhodesia, they did not neglect to send agents north of the Zambezi to make "treaties" with local African rulers and thus to forestall foreign rivals pressing into the area from north, east, and west. In June 1890, one of these agents, Frank Lochner, obtained the first of a series of concessions from Lewanika, the Lozi ruler who dominated the upper Zambezi area.[2] This agreement was "to be considered in the light of a treaty" between the Lozi (or Barotse) people and the Government of Queen Victoria, although it was on the Chartered Company's behalf that Lochner agreed to protect Lewanika and pay him a subsidy. In return, Lewanika granted to the Chartered Company sweeping commercial concessions including "the sole absolute and exclusive and perpetual right and power. . . . over the whole of the territory of the Barotse nation, or any future extension thereof including all subject and dependent territories. . . . to search for, dig, win and keep diamonds, gold, coal, oil and all other precious stones, minerals or substances." Meanwhile, two more of Rhodes' agents, Alfred Sharpe and Joseph Thomson, were dispatched on separate treaty-making expeditions to what are now northeastern Zambia and Katanga Province of Congo (Kinshasa). They failed to obtain any concession from Msidi, the principal chief in Katanga, but they did acquire a miscellaneous collection of agreements allegedly assented to by various chiefs or purported chiefs scattered over northeastern Zambia east of the Kafue. The wording of these documents varies, but generally the chief or individual concerned was promised "British protection" and some small material consideration in return for a grant to the Chartered Company of mineral rights and other commercial concessions. The Chartered Company's original claim to ownership of all Zambian mineral rights was based on the documents obtained by Thomson and Sharpe and the concession signed by Lewanika in its renegotiated form—the "Lewanika concession" of October 17, 1900.

The British Government was induced to give formal approval to the Lewanika concession and the Thomson/Sharpe "treaties." In 1893, H. H. Johnston, the British Commissioner and Consul-General for the

territories under British influence to the north of the Zambezi,
issued "certificates of claim" recognizing inter alia the Chartered
Company's claim to minerals in all of Zambia east of the Kafue and
in what became known as the Katanga Pedicle across the Congo border.
However, Johnston's certificates were of dubious validity and there
were wide areas of Northern Rhodesia where the Chartered Company's
treaty-gathering agents never penetrated.

        Fortunately for the Chartered Company, it was well placed to
establish its claims on a more sound legal basis under the adminis-
trative arrangements made by British Orders-in-Council for the new
protectorates of "Barotziland—North Western Rhodesia" and "North
Eastern Rhodesia" in 1899 and 1900 respectively. These Orders-in-
Council regularized the rather confused situation in which the Chartered
Company's officers had been establishing themselves in Northern
Rhodesia under the distant authority of Consul-General Johnston.
By these orders, both territories were placed effectively under the
administrative and financial control of the Chartered Company, although in North Western Rhodesia formal jurisdiction and legislative
power were vested in the British High Commissioner for South Africa,
who appointed the Chartered Company's Administrator. In North
Eastern Rhodesia, the Chartered Company's Administrator was empowered to make "regulations," but these were subject to the approval
of the Commissioner for the British Central African Protectorate.
Thus was established the system of "Company rule," which, with
various changes of form rather than substance, survived until 1924.*
It is not proposed in this brief historical survey to analyze in detail
the period of the Chartered Company's administration but merely to
point to certain features of significance for the future development of
the territory in general and the mining industry in particular.

        The British Government's attitude toward the Chartered Com-
pany's administration was ambivalent. The permanent officials, who

---

        *The principal formal changes were: (1) the 1905 transfer of
the boundary between North Western and North Eastern Rhodesia
from the Kafue River eastward to the narrow "neck" of Northern
Rhodesia (this transfer played an important part in later controversy
about the validity of the Chartered Company's mineral rights) and
(2) the amalgamation by Northern Rhodesia Order-in-Council 1911
of the two territories under one Chartered Company Administrator,
with legislative power vested in the High Commissioner for South
Africa advised by the Administrator.

remembered the Jameson Raid and the violence in which Southern
Rhodesia had become submerged in the 1890's under Chartered Company rule, were anxious to keep a close watch on the company's activities north of the Zambezi. However, the British Government did not
appoint an official to superintend the company's administration in
Northern Rhodesia on the spot and therefore the Colonial Office was
forced to rely on the company for information about the territory.
As a result, Downing Street's only effective power was to veto or
modify proposals submitted to it by the Chartered Company administration, without the benefit of independent advice as to the circumstances.

Moreover, the Colonial Office was very conscious of the financial
burden borne by the Chartered Company in respect of the administrative
deficit in Northern Rhodesia, and this appears to have inhibited officials
from any vigorous challenge of the methods used by the company to
strengthen its commercial claims. Thus, when the Chartered Company submitted for approval the Lewanika concession of 1909, under
which the chief made over to the company all the land in North Western
Rhodesia outside his tribal reserve in return for a westward extension
of that reserve, an official commented, "I see no reason for attempting
to make the Company pay anything for what they are getting having
regard to the fact that North-West Rhodesia is at present costing
their shareholders over £30,000 per annum."[3] Thus, the Chartered
Company was able to use its period of administrative control to con-
solidate its commercial rights—in particular its mineral rights—the
fruits of which it was to enjoy in full measure after its administrative
responsibilities had ended.

The Chartered Company's own policy toward Northern Rhodesia
and its economic development was determined on the one hand by a
desire to exploit the commercial potentialities of the territory to the
full* and on the other by an acute shortage of development finance.
Northern Rhodesia remained a financial liability to the end; the administrative deficit for the year ending March 31, 1921, was £96,500.
The territory showed no sign of attracting a large influx of European
farmers to snap up the "empty" acres to which the Chartered Company

---

*As Henry Wilson Fox, then the Chartered Company's London
Manager, observed candidly in a memorandum for the Board in 1910,
"the problem of Northern Rhodesia is not a colonization problem. It
is the problem of how best to develop a great estate on scientific lines
so that it may be made to yield the maximum profit to its owner."

had laid claim and thereby to form the basis of a substantial European tax-paying community. The European population in 1921 was a mere 3,500. The chief prop of the administrative revenue remained a "hut-tax" of a few shillings per year collected, sometimes with difficulty, from the African population. The African population also was a major economic asset as a labor reserve to relieve the acute shortage of "native labor" south of the Zambezi. This, however, did not console the shareholders who lamented the burden of the Northern Rhodesia deficit on the Chartered Company's funds, a burden that weighed heavily on the company throughout the period 1900-24 when a critical shortage of funds precluded payment of a single dividend. Following the early euphoria, which caused the company's £1 shares to touch over £8 at the end of 1894, the shares often fell below par. The Chartered Company seems to have enjoyed little support in the City and was forced to keep itself going by periodic increases in ordinary share capital. Thus, the company did not have large sums available to invest in the development of Northern Rhodesia, even if it had wished to do so.

Under the circumstances, the Chartered Company's only real hope of substantial profits from its Northern Rhodesian "estate" appeared to lie in the exploitation of the territory's mineral resources. Evidence of such resources already had come to light in the early 1900's, notably in the form of ancient copper workings. However, as we have seen, the funds were not available to invest in prospecting and mining operations. The Chartered Company therefore sought to rely on the small prospector to make discoveries of sufficient promise to attract the outside capital needed for development.[4] The company's own share of the fruits of that development would be assured since all prospectors first had to make terms with the company as owner of all mineral rights.

The Chartered Company was quick to take steps to ensure that its claims to the mineral rights would not be challenged. Thus, in North Eastern Rhodesia, the Land and Deeds Registry Regulations made by the Chartered Company's Administrator in 1900 vested all unalienated land in the territory in the Company and reserved all mining rights from any grant of land made. In North Western Rhodesia, the concession secured by the Chartered Company from Paramount Chief Lewanika in 1909 certainly was intended by the company to strengthen its title to land and minerals throughout the territory, although the concession's effect has been much disputed. Previously, in 1905, the company had persuaded the British Government to transfer a large slice of North Eastern Rhodesia to North Western Rhodesia. Ostensibly the reason for this request was administrative convenience,

but the company's real object was to strengthen its claim to minerals
in the transferred area.[5]

With the growth of prospecting and mining activity, the Chartered
Company became especially anxious to secure the promulgation of a
mining law, and in 1906 it submitted to the Colonial Office a draft
mining proclamation designed to be applied throughout Northern
Rhodesia. In the meantime, the company issued mineral grants on an
ad hoc basis, reserving for itself a large interest (between 35 percent
and 50 percent) in any claims pegged. Such grants were to be subject
to the Northern Rhodesian mining law if and when promulgated; in
the interim, the mining law of Southern Rhodesia was deemed to
apply.[6] It is significant that the Chartered Company did not consider
the Southern Rhodesian legislation (the Mines and Minerals Ordinance
of 1895) to be a very satisfactory precedent. This legislation created
statutory mining rights and entirely determined the benefits and the
obligations of the holders. The Chartered Company found itself
severely restricted in its freedom of action in dealing with what it
regarded as its commercial assets. Therefore, as H. M. Williams
points out:

> When the Company came to framing the mining legislation
> in Northern Rhodesia . . . care was taken to ensure that
> the terms and conditions on which mining rights could be
> acquired were recorded in a prospecting licence which
> was a matter of contract between the Company and the
> prospector and was not dependent on the statute. . . .
> Care also was taken to ensure that the Company could
> make a special grant of mining rights on its own terms
> and conditions notwithstanding that they might be incon-
> sistent with the other provisions of the legislation relating
> to mining locations.[7]

However, various points in the company's original draft did not
prove readily acceptable to the Colonial Office and a prolonged
correspondence ensued. The principal point at issue was the appor-
tionment of mining revenue between administrative and commercial
accounts. The Chartered Company asserted that, since its mining
rights were held by virtue of its concessions without reference to its
administrative obligations, it had complete discretion as regards the
employment of mining receipts and, moreover, that there was nothing
to prevent any future administration from taxing the mineral assets
by legislation. However, under Colonial Office pressure, the Chartered
Company reluctantly agreed to treat certain mining licence fees as
administrative revenue.[8]

The Mining Proclamation was issued and came into force throughout Northern Rhodesia on July 1, 1912; it was destined to remain on
the statute book until 1958. Under its provisions, the objectives
catalogued by H. M. Williams in the passage quoted above were
achieved. The Mining Proclamation was to constitute a major obstacle
to any attempt to challenge the British South Africa Company's entrenched influence over mining policy and development. The preamble
stated "the right of searching and mining for and disposing of all
minerals and mineral oils in Northern Rhodesia . . . is vested in the
British South Africa Company." Even if this preamble is not deemed
to have had the effect by itself of conferring statutory title on the
Chartered Company, the provisions of the law were based on a clear
assumption that the company held legal title to all mineral rights.
The Chartered Company had acquired a degree of control over mining
operations that was to arouse strong criticism in the future as a
major copper mining industry became established, but in 1912 there
was no indication of the scale on which this industry ultimately would
develop.

In the early years, the only important financial figures to take
a close interest in Northern Rhodesia's minerals were Robert Williams
and Edmund Davis. The latter was an associate of Cecil Rhodes and
much later was to become a Director of the Chartered Company and
Deputy Chairman of Rhodesian Anglo-American. His major initial
venture involved not copper but the lead and zinc deposits discovered
in 1902 at Broken Hill (now Kabwe). The existence of the Broken Hill
mine provided the impetus for the Chartered Company's one major
departure during its years of administration from its policy of keeping
its own financial commitment in Northern Rhodesia to the absolute
minimum.* The railroad from Bulawayo and the south reached Kalomo
in 1904. On the basis of assurances from Davis in respect of the
traffic that would be generated by the Broken Hill mine, the Chartered
Company agreed to guarantee debentures issued by the Mashonaland
Railway Company to finance the northward extension of the line, which
reached Broken Hill in 1906. However, in May 1907 consignment of
ore from the mine was suspended, and the Kalomo/Broken Hill extension lost £6,500 in its first year of operation. Members of the
Chartered Company Board were appalled to find that, since Davis and

---

*For example, as far as risking its own funds was concerned,
the Chartered Company often requested a mining concern to give up
a substantial share in the enterprise in return for the grant of a
concession.

his syndicate had themselves incurred no financial responsibility for
the line, the Chartered Company was left with the liability for what
one director called "the disastrous fiasco at Broken Hill." In 1908,
the Chartered Company was in such difficulty in respect of its liability
for railway debentures that it was forced to ask the British Government
for financial support. However, the Chartered Company was informed
that, since it claimed exclusive entitlement to its commercial assets
as distinct from the public revenues of the territories that it administered, the Government had no interest in protecting those assets by
active financial assistance.

The problem of railroad finance eventually was resolved by the
further extension of the line to the Congo border in 1909, a development financed by Robert Williams to carry traffic from the already
flourishing copper mines of Katanga. This rail line also passed
through what was later to become the Copperbelt, and therefore was
available to carry the traffic of the mines there. However, the earlier
Broken Hill episode illustrates the paucity and uncertainty of the
finance available for the development of Northern Rhodesia during
the greater part of the period of Chartered Company rule, when the
company notably failed in its objective of solving the problem "of
how best to develop its great estate on scientific lines."[9]

The beginning of the 1920's ushered in the dramatic years of
Zambia's short colonial history, during which a neglected labor
reserve was to become one of the world's leading copper producers.
The initial impetus for this "industrial revolution" was provided by
the British South Africa Company's belated decision to encourage
mineral exploration on more "scientific lines." According to Sir
Theodore Gregory, the company's "forward" policy was inspired by
Edmund Davis, who gave the following account to the shareholders
in 1926: "It was early in 1923—or it may have been late in 1922—
that I suggested to the members of this Board that they should place
the development, or at any rate the prospecting, of Northern Rhodesia
in the hands of syndicates with ample capital, properly managed, and
with the necessary technical staff at their disposal."[10] The successful
implementation of this policy paved the way for rapid and remarkable
development of the industry that Zambia eventually was to inherit at
independence. The principal factors involved in this achievement are
briefly summarized below.

The British South Africa Company had been careful to ensure
that the territory's mining law, although minutely regulating the
activities of small prospectors, did not restrict its power as owner
of the mineral rights to make, over large areas, "special grants" of

prospecting and mining rights to which many of the provisions of the mining law did not apply. Therefore, between 1922 and 1926, the company issued six grants of exclusive prospecting rights for a period of years over a total area of 148,300 square miles. This vast area, which included the whole of the present Copperbelt, was closed to holders of ordinary prospecting licences. As Sir Henry Birchenough, the Chartered Company's President, explained to shareholders in 1928, "Exclusive rights . . . are an indispensable condition of large scale company prospecting"[11] since powerful companies needed time and security in which to operate if they were to embark on expensive prospecting programs.

The grantee of an exclusive prospecting licence had to undertake to expend a minimum annual sum on prospecting activities and to make over to the Chartered Company some financial interest in the venture (e.g., an allotment of shares). The grantee was entitled not only to peg as many mining locations as he required but also to receive a "Special Grant" of mining rights over a much larger area if this was justified. The provisions of the 1912 Mining Proclamation only applied insofar as they were not inconsistent with any of the provisions of such a Special Grant. Furthermore, the Special Grant of mining rights usually was made for an indefinite period. As grants of this type formed the documents of title on which the great mines of the Copperbelt were developed and on which those mines were still held at the time of independence, their importance cannot be overestimated. Originally issued by the British South Africa Company, these grants were destined to survive for some years the transfer of that company's rights to the Zambian Government.

The Chartered Company's willingness to encourage large-scale prospecting and mining development with such grants would have been of little avail, in view of the company's own unwillingness or inability to put up with the necessary cash, if the "syndicates with ample capital" mentioned by Edmund Davis had not been willing to risk their money in Northern Rhodesia. However, the interest shown by two of the most influential figures in world mining finance at that time, Alfred Chester Beatty and Ernest Oppenheimer, proved of decisive importance in making the necessary development funds available. Each man played a major part in financing the "concession companies" that carried out the first great prospecting campaign. There is not space here to analyze the complicated interplay of financial groupings during the development years of the Copperbelt,[12] and it is sufficient to note that by 1928 the important mining properties had been effectively divided between Oppenheimer's Rhodesian Anglo-American group and Chester Beatty's Rhodesian Selection Trust (RST) group,

including their respective subsidiaries.* Both parent companies
were incorporated in England. The new scale of operations is indicated by the fixing of the original capital of Rhodesian Anglo-American at £2.5 million, an amount that "very speedily proved inadequate."[13] The Chartered Company had minority holdings, acquired
under the terms of the relevant concessions, in some of the RST
group's mines, but it had far stronger links with the Rhodesian Anglo-
American group. By 1930, Rhodesian Anglo-American had become
the largest individual shareholder in the Chartered Company, which
in turn had a sizable stake in Rhodesian Anglo-American. Henry
Birchenough, Drummond Chaplin, Edmund Davis, Dougal Malcolm,
and Ernest Oppenheimer all sat on the boards of both companies.

The new prospecting operations revealed that large sulfide orebodies existed in the Copperbelt area below the surface outcrops of
oxide ores (see Chapter 3).** This discovery encouraged the financiers
to make further funds available, and by June 1930 Edmund Davis was
able to inform Rhodesian Anglo-American shareholders that drilling
estimates indicated the existence in the company's areas of a total
of 585 million metric tons of 4.5-percent ore.[14] Production from the
Roan Antelope and Nkana mines began in 1931 and at Mufilira in 1933.
Initial growth was severely restricted by the effects of the great
depression, but the future status of Northern Rhodesia as a major
producer of the world's copper was assured.

While these developments of such enormous importance to the
future of the Zambian economy were taking place, an event of considerable political significance occurred. On April 1, 1924, the
British South Africa Company ceased to be the administering authority
for the territory and was replaced by a "Crown Colony" type of government on the traditional Colonial Office pattern (Northern Rhodesia

---

*However, it should be remembered that important direct fi-
nancial links existed between the Anglo-American and RST groups.
For example, the Anglo-American group retained a substantial
minority in RST's Mufilira mine, which was originally acquired as
a result of the Bwana Mkubwa Copper Mining Company's retention
of a one-third holding in the concession in which the future Mufilira
mine was situated (see Chapter 3).

**Sulfide ores must be subjected to a more complex process than
oxides in order to convert the pure copper. However, by the 1920's
the technical difficulties of this "flotation process" had been overcome.

retained the constitutional status of a protectorate). Thus the Chartered Company lost its useful privilege of being in many respects politically independent. Henceforth it was to be confronted with a "Northern Rhodesian Government" with which the company's commercial interests, previously open only to the scrutiny of distant Whitehall, might come into conflict. Thus the problem of governmental control of the mining industry first appeared in the years after 1924 as the Northern Rhodesian Government sought to establish some means of influencing mining policy and acquiring a larger share of mining profits. However, at this stage the Government was not involved in any significant clash with the copper producers, from whose activities the major part of the Government's income tax revenues were derived, either directly or indirectly. There was no thought of fundamentally interfering with the operation of the mines or with the producers' profits, although important questions concerning industrial unrest and African advancement involved a rather reluctant Government in the mining industry's problems. However, both the local Government and the Colonial Office found themselves in frequent conflict with the British South Africa Company, which continued to play a key role in questions of mining policy and finance by virtue of its retention of the mineral rights throughout almost all of Northern Rhodesia under the terms of the agreement by which it gave up the administration of that territory. (There were areas where the Chartered Company had alienated its mineral rights; the largest of these was the North Charterland Concession on Zambia's eastern border. Also, the Chartered Company's rights in the "Barotse Reserve" were restricted.)

Clause 3(g) of the September 1923 agreement between the British Government and the Chartered Company (known as the Devonshire Agreement after the then Colonial Secretary) provided that: "the Company shall retain and the Crown shall recognise the Company as the owners of the mineral rights acquired by the Company in virtue of the concessions obtained from Lewanika in North-Western Rhodesia and concessions in North-Eastern Rhodesia covered by the . . . certificates of claim issued by Sir H. H. Johnston." Although the Chartered Company already was embarked on its efforts to encourage large-scale prospecting—the Rhodesian Congo Border Concession was granted in February 1923—all the evidence suggests that the parties to the agreement could not at that time have had any appreciation of the potential value of the rights, which were regarded as one of the lesser bargaining counters in an across the board financial settlement.

Later, much was to be made of the failure of the 1923

Conservative Government to carry out the recommendation of the
Buxton Committee (which was appointed by Winston Churchill, the
Coalition Colonial Secretary) that the question of the Chartered Company's claims to land and minerals within Northern Rhodesia be
referred to the Privy Council; this failure to act was thought to be
the result of the Chartered Company's influence over Conservative
ministers.[15] However, the available evidence suggests that the Government's decision was motivated only by a desire to reach a quick
settlement without recourse to expensive and cumbersome litigation
(the Privy Council had taken four years to reach a decision on similar
questions relating to Southern Rhodesia).

The first Governor of Northern Rhodesia, Sir Herbert Stanley,
assumed office on April 1, 1924. At first, the change was more
apparent than real. The Chartered Company's administrative staff
remained at their posts and the acting Administrator, Richard Goode,
became "Chief Secretary" of the new Government. There were no
funds forthcoming from the British Government for development
purposes, and the only prospect—and that a distant and uncertain one—
lay in the local mining industry. However, as we have seen, under
the existing legislation, which was not affected by the change of
government, the effective control of any such development rested
with the Chartered Company. Commenting in 1926 on unofficial
pressures on Government to encourage prospecting, Stanley observed:

> The conditions in Northern Rhodesia with regard to min-
> erals differ from those obtaining in other East African
> Territories. The revision of the local mining law . . .
> involves numerous difficulties. . . . The encouragement
> or discouragement of prospecting depends at present
> upon the policy of the British South Africa Company
> rather than upon the policy of the Government.[16]

A long struggle then ensued to replace the obsolete mining law
of 1912; this goal was not to be achieved until the 1969 Mines and
Minerals Act removed the last vestiges of the system established
under the Chartered Company's regime. Ostensibly, legislation
was the one field where the local Government had a fairly free hand,
and as early as October 1924 Stanley suggested that in light of the
change of administration the mining law would require amendment.
He also suggested that the Chartered Company be consulted about
any proposed changes. The Colonial Office in reply requested that a
draft ordinance be prepared in consultation with the Chartered Company.[17] After some delay, Governor Maxwell, who succeeded Stanley
in 1927, forwarded the draft to the Colonial Office. The Colonial

Office and the Legal Committee of the Imperial Institute (which were
brought in as advisers) both felt that the draft was not entirely satisfactory, but the British South Africa Company uncompromisingly
rejected Maxwell's proposals, arguing that no substantive changes
whatsoever were necessary in the existing mining law.

In the negotiations that began in 1930, the Chartered Company's
objective was to delay any changes for as long as possible, as was
the case in its later struggle to retain possession of the mineral
rights. The argument in favor of changes was that by 1930 the 1912
Mining Proclamation had become "wholly unsatisfactory, in places
unintelligible and largely unworkable." It was pointed out that, although
the Chartered Company had retained its mineral rights under the 1923
agreement, with certain insignificant exceptions it had given up its
claims to unalienated surface land, which had passed generally to
the Crown. Therefore, it was inappropriate that the Chartered Company rather than the Crown should exercise statutory powers to deal
with the surface in the interests of mining. Similarly, it was no
longer appropriate for the Chartered Company to have unfettered
control over the issue of prospecting licences and mining grants.
Furthermore, the Government needed wide residual powers to ensure
that the copper industry was operated in the interests of the community as a whole. The Copper Restriction Agreement of 1932 had
provided an alarming precedent for a sharp cutback in production as
a result of an agreement between international mining interests. It
was therefore proposed to empower the Government to forbid the
suspension and enforce the commencement of mining operations and,
in extreme circumstances, to confiscate unworked mining locations.

Proposals such as those described above were strongly opposed
by the Chartered Company, which was particularly incensed by the
proposed restriction of its power to make Special Grants of exclusive
prospecting and mining rights; in a communication to the Colonial
Office, the Chartered Company stated:

> It is in a great measure owing to grants of this character
> that the recent great developments of the copper mining
> industry in Northern Rhodesia have taken place. . . .
> [The Company] ought to be free to dispose of its mineral
> rights to its assignees in any way that it thinks best to
> the advantage of its shareholders whose interests must
> necessarily be bound up with the maximum and most
> profitable development possible of the mineral resources
> of Northern Rhodesia.[18]

Leslie Pollak, the Managing Director of Rhodesian Anglo-American Ltd., with which the Chartered Company had very close financial
links, informed Governor Maxwell that the proposed changes "would
create so grave a feeling of uncertainty as to diminish if not completely destroy the zeal and enterprise with which at huge cost to
the operating companies but to the great advantage of the country the
mineral resources are being prospected and developed."[19] Apart
from this intervention, however, the copper producing companies
appear to have played no direct part in these negotiations.

Eventually, a compromise between the Chartered Company and
the Colonial Office was hammered out at a series of meetings in 1933
and 1934. The Colonial Office abandoned "anything on the lines of
compelling working or forcing prospecting," but remained firm on
certain points such as Government control over surface leases and
the general need for entirely new legislation, which the Chartered
Company continued to resist.

The Chartered Company's delaying tactics proved successful,
at least in the short term. By the time agreement had been reached
on the provisions of the draft ordinance, the whole question of reform
of the mining law was put in suspense when the new Governor, Sir
Hubert Young, raised fundamental points concerning the validity of
the Chartered Company's mineral claims, to which the proposed new
law would have given unassailable statutory authority. The painfully
negotiated bill was put aside; considered so urgently necessary in
1927, it was not passed until 1958.

The 1930-35 negotiations suggest that the problems faced by the
independent Zambian Government with regard to the mining industry
had been identified to some extent by the pre-war colonial Government,
although the political climate at that time made inevitable a rather
different outcome than that of 1969. In the 1930's, the Chartered
Company's claim to be "as free as possible to deal with their mineral
estate" clashed with a growing feeling among civil servants in the
Colonial Office and the Northern Rhodesian Government that, in view
of the administration's general responsibility for the welfare of the
territory as a whole, it was incumbent upon the Government to ensure
that mining was carried out along the best possible lines, regardless
of ownership.

The shelving of the proposed mining ordinance occurred in the
immediate pre-war years as a fierce controversy developed concerning the validity of the Chartered Company's title to the mineral
rights, which were recognized as an asset of considerable actual and

enormous potential value. Under the terms of the grants of mining
rights made by the Chartered Company to the copper producers, the
latter were bound to pay to the company a percentage royalty on the
gross value of every ton of copper produced. The actual percentage
was calculated on a complicated sliding scale formula based on the
current London Metal Exchange quotation. The most significant
feature of this arrangement, which was to survive until 1969, was that
the royalty was payable so long as a mine produced copper; the profitability of the mine was irrelevant. For this reason, in the 1950's
the copper producers themselves, particularly those in the RST group,
came to press for changes in the royalty system. However, in the
1930's it was not the method of computation of the royalties that was
challenged but the legal entitlement of the Chartered Company to
collect them. Insofar as this title was based on the Lewanika concessions, it had been challenged as early as 1921 when Lewanika's
successor Yeta petitioned the British High Commissioner in South
Africa for the cancellation of the concession. Settler opponents of
the Chartered Company also bitterly opposed the company's retention
of commercial rights under the Devonshire Agreement of 1923.
However, the Chartered Company's total mining revenue derived from
Northern Rhodesia in the year ending September 30, 1925, was a paltry
£12,781.

By 1938, the situation was changing rapidly. The Pim/Milligan
Commission appointed in 1937 to investigate the financial and economic
position of Northern Rhodesia found that money was urgently needed
for expansion of the central social services; this money would be
available if the government received a larger proportion of the proceeds of "the country's only really important industry, the mining
industry."[20] The Pim/Milligan Commission drew attention to the
fact that the Northern Rhodesian Government's income tax receipts
from the copper producers were reduced not only by the operation of
double taxation relief-since the companies concerned then had their
headquarters in London, the tax receipts were shared between the
United Kingdom exchequer and the local government—but also because
the royalty paid to the British South Africa Company counted as a
production cost allowed against tax liability.

The Pim/Milligan Commission also noted that the 1923 Devonshire Agreement had proved "a remarkably good bargain" for the
Chartered Company, whose mining revenue for the year ending
September 30, 1937, reached £310,955, of which £274,149 represented
copper royalties. Therefore, it was not surprising that the European
elected members in the Northern Rhodesia Legislative Council, whose
ranks Roy Welensky had just joined, were quick to challenge the basis

of that bargain by putting down a motion in December 1938 requesting
that the question of the validity of the Chartered Company's title to
mineral rights be referred to the Judicial Committee of the Privy
Council. The Legislative Council was informed that the British Government had recently given "prolonged and careful consideration" to
this question, and would shortly be in a position to communicate its
conclusions on the matter.[21] This was the first public intimation of
the lengthy and detailed examination of the question that had been
proceeding in both the Colonial Office and the Lusaka Secretariat,
culminating in a reference to the Law Officers in July 1938.[22]

Sir Hubert Young, Governor of Northern Rhodesia, originally
raised the question of the validity of the Chartered Company's title
to mineral rights with the Colonial Office in 1935. He was very sensitive to settler opinion and was afraid that the new mining ordinance—
which conferred a statutory title on the Chartered Company—would
provoke opposition in the Legislative Council. Young also had doubts
about the terms of a proposed settlement between Lozi Paramount
Chief Yeta and the Chartered Company with regard to a longstanding
dispute about the application of the original concessions to the "Barotse
Reserve"; Young thought the terms of the compromise reached,
might be deemed to strengthen the Chartered Company's general title.
Young's initial queries encountered a strong feeling in the Colonial
Office that it was no longer practicable to alter the mineral rights
position and that efforts should be concentrated on getting through the
new mining law. However, Young rapidly became convinced that it
could not be right for a private company to retain in perpetuity "the
entire mineral rights over a territory half as large again as France,
and if they have in fact no legal claim to them, I as Governor of the
territory feel that I should be failing in my duty if I acquiesced in
the existing position."[23]

Young initiated in Lusaka a monumental research exercise and
came to a conclusion that Clause 3 (g) of the 1923 Devonshire Agreement left open the question of the actual territorial extent of the rights
granted under the various concessions. He went on to argue that the
Lewanika concessions could not have conferred legal title to mineral
rights in any part of the Copperbelt area on the Chartered Company
because this area was at all times outside Lewanika's jurisdiction.
Young even alleged that the Chartered Company had systematically
misled the Colonial Office as to the true position and that the British
Government was now entitled to reinterpret the 1923 agreement.

Although Young did not attempt to challenge the Chartered Company's title to the rights on the east bank of the Kafue insofar as their

validity was based on the Thomson/Sharpe treaties and Johnston's
certificates of claim, his attack on the west bank rights was serious
enough since it affected royalties from Nkana and Nchanga. However,
official opinion in the Colonial Office, particularly among the lawyers,
was unimpressed by Young's arguments and only after persistent
pressure was he able to persuade Secretary of State William Ormsby-
Gore to agree in April 1938 that the matter should be referred to the
Law Officers. The latter proved as unimpressed by Young's arguments
as the Colonial Office; their opinion, delivered in October 1938,
found against Young on all major points. In their view, even if Lewanika's jurisdiction was assumed never to have extended over any
part of the Copperbelt, the Crown and the Chartered Company had
agreed to treat it as so doing in 1900 and subsequent agreements and
legislation had been based on the company's possession of the rights.
The Law Officers rejected allegations of fraud against the Chartered
Company and considered that on grounds of good faith the Crown was
precluded from challenging the company's title. Armed with this
opinion, the Colonial Office sought to silence the Chartered Company's
public and private critics in Northern Rhodesia by the publication in
March 1939 in the official gazettes of the Northern Rhodesian Government of a dispatch to Governor Young from Malcolm MacDonald
(who had succeeded Ormsby-Gore as Secretary of State) explaining
that the Chartered Company's mineral rights were valid and could
not be challenged. However, this was not the end of the story, although
the issue did not receive significant public attention again until after
World War II.

On the eve of World War II. the major problems concerning
the development of the Northern Rhodesian mining industry for the
remainder of the colonial period were already identifiable. The industry was at last recovering from the slump, and a period of remarkable prosperity lay ahead. However, the local government, although
overwhelmingly dependent for its revenue on that single industry,
exercised little effective control over it. While compiling his report
in 1937, Sir Alan Pim found that "Government has no real policy on
any of the big issues and though they have money for the moment,
prospects are uncertain . . . altogether it [Northern Rhodesia] is a
depressing place."[24] The subsequent failure to carry through the
mining law reform and the Colonial Office veto on any attempt to
increase the government's share of mining revenue at the expense
of the Chartered Company's royalists suggested that Pim's pessimism
was not misplaced. Ironically perhaps, the growth of settler political
power after World War II was a major factor in the adoption of a
more dynamic policy by the Northern Rhodesia Government. There
also was to be a "wind of change" in the Colonial Office as a brand

of "paternalist liberalism characteristic of the post-war years" inspired serious attempts at development planning in the colonial territories.[25]

In Northern Rhodesia, the transition from virtually complete
laissez-faire was especially difficult because private enterprise had
been accustomed for so long to act in important matters without
reference to the local government. For example, in 1936 Governor
Young objected to the terms of certain agreements between the copper
producers and Rhodesia Railways (in which incidentally the Chartered
Company then had a controlling interest). Under the terms of these
arrangements, which were to extend for a further twenty years,
Rhodesia Railways agreed to carry mining traffic at special reduced
rates and in return the copper companies agreed to rail all mining
traffic via the Rhodesia Railway system and bound themselves to use
only coal from Wankie in Southern Rhodesia and no hydroelectric
power. Young was concerned at the effect of these agreements on the
future development of alternative rail routes (e.g., via the Benguela
Railway to Lobito), but his objections were overruled by the Colonial
Office. A senior official noted: "I am not sorry that we have had no
opportunity of meddling in a business agreement."[26] Ironically,
there was to be plenty of political meddling after the expiration of
these agreements in 1956, when the Government of the Federation of
Rhodesia and Nyasaland was anxious to ensure that Rhodesia Railways
maintained a monopoly of mine traffic although the copper producers
themselves and the Northern Rhodesian Government wished to make
use of the Lobito route. Thus, it proved politically impossible prior
to independence to implement a policy based on the territory's own
requirements.

So far as the mining industry was concerned, World War II
forced both the British Government and the Northern Rhodesian
Government into greater involvement. Locally, the labor troubles
of 1940 led to the appointment of a Labor Commissioner whose office
was responsible for an increasing government interest in industrial
relations as the question of African advancement achieved prominence.
On an "imperial" level, copper production was maintained at levels
required by the British Ministry of Supply and British Government
finance was made available for mine improvements to expand production.[27]

Moreover, even under the pressure of wartime, the Colonial
Office was already giving general consideration to such questions as
future policy toward mineral royalties and mining in the colonial
empire.[28] Official feeling now tended toward the view that it was

wholly inconsistent with modern notions of development that private companies should extract from colonial territories large sums that were not the fruits of industrial enterprise but of ancient concession agreements with unknowing local rulers. Such feelings were given added weight by the election in 1945 of a Labor Government committed to the principle of public ownership at home and to a positive policy of fostering colonial development.

The Memorandum on Colonial Mining Policy published in 1946 sought to give general guidance on the principles to be followed by colonial governments in framing such policy.[29] Had these principles been applied fully at that time in Northern Rhodesia, many of the economic reforms carried out after independence was achieved would have been anticipated. The memorandum asserted that it was "of the utmost importance that the government should retain adequate control at all stages in order to ensure that mining enterprises were carried on in the interests of the Territory and for the general benefit of the community at large." To this end, it strongly upheld state ownership of mineral rights so that they should not be enjoyed "merely by limited groups of private individuals who are often not members of the community concerned." The memorandum also stated that by possession of the rights government was in a position to control the size of concessions and the rate and terms of exploitation, that the period of mining leases should not be too long, and that exclusive licences to work all minerals should never be granted. Provision also should be made for the indigenous population "to fit themselves for the highest technical and administrative posts."

Clearly, the situation in Northern Rhodesia in 1946 fell far short of these objectives. However, the first step toward reform, the recovery of the mineral rights from the British South Africa Company, already was under active consideration. The original proposal was that the rights should be purchased compulsorily by the Northern Rhodesian Government at a fixed price on the order of £5 million. This scheme came to be drastically modified in official discussion, which unearthed apparently endless complications about such matters as the assessment and payment of compensation and the income tax liability of the Chartered Company in respect of compensation payments. Moreover, unlike the United Africa Company in the similar case of Northern Nigeria, the British South Africa Company was not in any sense a willing seller. Sir Dougal Malcolm, Chartered Company President and, like Andrew Cohen on the Colonial Office side, a veteran of pre-war battles over the mining law, made it clear that the company would resist to the utmost any attempt to deprive its shareholders of the reward for "their long years of faithful and patient expectation." The Chartered Company's stand on its legal rights again received support from the Law Officers, who apparently could not be persuaded to depart from the opinion of their predecessors in 1938 that the validity of the rights could not be challenged.

However, the decisive blow to the Northern Rhodesian Government's plans to buy out the Chartered Company was the remarkable rise in copper prices in the immediate post-war years. Although this brought a useful increase of income tax revenue to government, it also meant that while official deliberation continued the value of the assets that it was proposed to acquire—that is, the mineral rights—was increasing sharply. The value of the Northern Rhodesian copper production for the year ending September 1948 showed an increase of over £7million over the previous year, and the corresponding royalty receipts of the Chartered Company increased by nearly £1 million.[30] Estimates of a fair purchase price rose to a minimum of £20 million, which was considered too great a financial burden for the Northern Rhodesian Government* to assume in view of the absence of assistance from the United Kingdom exchequer and uncertainty about future copper revenues. Thus, Dougal Malcolm's delaying tactics seemed to have succeeded once again.

However, at this time Roy Welensky, a leading "unofficial" member of the Northern Rhodesia Legislative Council and a man of equal vigor and tenacity, emerged as Malcolm's chief opponent. Welensky was determined that the Chartered Company somehow be made to disgorge the mineral rights, and he was able to turn the matter into a public political issue. In March 1949, he introduced a motion in the Legislative Council proposing the imposition of a "special tax" on mineral royalties,[31] which created a stir in financial circles in London and provoked some violent public exchanges between Malcolm and Welensky. Eventually, the two men met at Bulawayo and at last Malcolm reluctantly agreed that the matter was negotiable. The resultant talks at the Colonial Office in July 1949 involved some hard bargaining; a compromise was reached only after Arthur Creech-Jones, the Labor Colonial Secretary, made it clear that the British Government would not veto Welensky's proposed royalty tax in the event that negotiations broke down. Under the terms of the agreement formalized in September 1950 by the British Government, the Northern

---

*Northern Rhodesia Government should be considered as referring to the Colonial administration, i.e., Northern Rhodesia Legislative Council.

Rhodesian Government, and the Chartered Company, the Chartered Company was to "continue in undisturbed enjoyment, as now, of the mineral rights owned by the Company in Northern Rhodesia" until October 1, 1986,* subject to an assignment of 20 percent of the net revenue derived after October 1, 1949 to the Northern Rhodesian Government.

All three parties could derive some satisfaction from this agreement: the British Government hoped that it had seen the end of a problem that had vexed the Colonial Office for more than 20 years; Northern Rhodesia had secured a large slice of additional income without the heavy burden of compensation payments that a full scale takeover would have involved; and the British South Africa Company had the promise of 36 years of undisturbed enjoyment of an asset that was not diminished at all in real terms since the 44 percent rise in the sterling price of copper following devaluation in 1949 more than compensated the Chartered Company for the loss of a proportion of its royalty income as a result of the agreement.

Although the Northern Rhodesia Government had thus secured a more substantial share of mining revenue, a more effective degree of control over mining policy and development remained to be achieved: the mining law was still based on the antiquated 1912 Mining Proclamation. After the 1950 settlement there was no fear of effective opposition to new mining legislation, but the Chartered Company's retention of ownership of mineral rights until 1986 meant in practice that the terms of any mining legislation had to be renegotiated with the company; the result was not likely to be a root and branch reform of the mining law. A new Mining Ordinance was considered by the Legislative Council in March 1958, and the debate throws some light on the circumstances of its drafting. Mr. W.G. Dunlop, Member for Mines and Works, told the Legislative Council that the present bill was first drafted in 1955 and had been exhaustively discussed with the Chartered Company, which as holder of the mineral rights had a "vital interest" in the provisions of the mining law. He then referred to Clause 3, which vested all mineral rights in the Crown except those vested in the Chartered Company or persons deriving title from the company and gave an undertaking that "This government will continue to recognize the mineral rights exercised by the Company . . . and will not seek to invoke in any way the provisions of the new

---

*This date is now commemorated in that the postal address of Anglo-American, Lusaka, is P.O. Box 1986.

Ordinance so as to change the position in connection with such rights existing before its passage." The Chartered Company negotiators had adopted their habitual dogged defensive posture during the negotiations, although significantly they had not been able to obtain the unassailable statutory title to the mineral rights that the wording of the pre-war bill would have conferred. It is noteworthy that the "exhaustive" discussions with the Chartered Company apparently were not matched by comparable consultations with the mining companies, whose unofficial representative of the Legislative Council even asked for a postponement of the second reading of the bill as "the mining industry had not had time to consider it."[32]

The 1950's saw the opening of new mines in the Copperbelt and a vigorous prospecting campaign outside it. This campaign was inspired by the Chartered Company, which was anxious for any undiscovered mineral deposits to be identified and exploited before 1986. To this end, the company, with the Anglo-American Corporation of South Africa as its principal partner, promoted Chartered Exploration Limited, which was assigned an exclusive prospecting licence over 104,000 square miles. Subsequently, the Paramount Chief of Barotseland was persuaded, with great difficulty, to agree to open to prospecting parts of the area reserved under the 1900 and 1909 concessions.

No dramatic new discoveries were made during this period, but production figures from the existing mines gave rise to considerable satisfaction. For the year ending September 1960, total production was a record 560,000 metric tons and the Chartered Company's mining revenue after deduction of 20 percent for the Northern Rhodesian Government amounted to £11,835,000. However, the Chartered Company remained loath to put money into the territory from whence it drew the greater part of its wealth. Admittedly, during this period the company made a loan of £4 million to the Federal Government to help finance the Kariba hydroelectric project (half the liability in respect of which was later to be assumed by the Northern Rhodesian government) and lent (at a commercial rate of interest)£2 million to the Northern Rhodesia Government in 1963 for improving African housing. However, in general the Chartered Company was willing to put money only into prospecting and drilling operations where its own interests were directly involved. Lord Robins, in his statement to Chartered Company shareholders on February 7, 1962, claimed that "the Group and its friends again spent nearly£1 million last year . . . in Northern Rhodesia in the search for new mineral deposits." He went on to define the Chartered Company's investment policy: "We shall continue to seek profitable outlets, but have resisted, and will continue to resist, suggestions that it would benefit the country or its peoples to invest in failures, and squander capital for propaganda purposes." To an increasingly politically conscious African community, the Chartered Company appeared as a blatant exploiter of the country's mineral assets, a foreign "capitalist dinosaur" extracting huge sums in royalties but making a negligible contribution to local economic progress in return.

If the Federation of Rhodesia and Nyasaland had survived in the form established in 1953, it is most unlikely that any of the radical changes in the mining industry with which this book is concerned would have taken place. The legal framework of the industry would have remained in the form established by the agreement of 1950 and the 1958 Mining Ordinance. However, at the beginning of 1964 an elected African administration that enjoyed internal self-government took office in Northern Rhodesia under the premiership of Dr. Kenneth Kaunda, and full independence was obviously imminent. Clearly, Zambia's economic development in the immediate future depended on the smooth operation of the copper industry and the cooperation of the copper producers with the new Government. However, the British South Africa Company's position as "rentier" was vulnerable to attack from a Government with rather less respect for vested interests than its predecessors. African nationalist opinion had always been affronted by the Chartered Company and had never been disposed to accept the 1950 agreement as final, just as Roy Welensky once had refused to accept the "MacDonald Dispatch" of 1938.

In 1956, the African National Congress instructed lawyers in London to investigate anew the question of the Chartered Company's title to the mineral rights. An opinion was obtained that there were grave doubts about the validity of the rights, but finance was not available at that time to take the matter further. Later, Dr. Kaunda and his colleagues in the United National Independence Party made it clear that when they gained power the operation of the copper mining companies would be unaffected but noted:

> The mineral riches of the country remain . . . the in-
> alienable possession of the people. We do not acknow-
> ledge any tradition which would entitle a chief to sign
> away such possessions on behalf of his people. We re-
> pudiate all arrangements arising from the pretence that
> any such contract could be valid.[33]

The Chartered Company Board in London did little to enlist African sympathy or even to show awareness of the necessity for such sympathy. The successors as President of Sir Dougal Malcolm (who died in 1955) were Christopher Hely Hutchinson, Lord Robins, and Paul Emrys-Evans, men in the same tradition as Malcolm himself: they were not prepared to "squander capital for propaganda purposes" or to be parties as "willing sellers" to a settlement that reflected changed local political conditions more accurately than that of 1950. Moreover, until the end of the Federation of Rhodesia and Nyasaland, Lord Robins, then President of the Chartered Company, remained a strong political supporter of Roy Welensky, and the Chartered Company is alleged to have contributed to United Federal Party funds until 1962.[34]

In October 1963, shortly before the end of federation, tentative negotiations conducted through merchant banks in London took place between the Northern Rhodesian Government and the Chartered Company. A proposal that the company transfer the mineral rights to the Northern Rhodesian Government in return for twenty-two and one-half annual payments amounting to £35 million was rejected by the company "because of the uncertainty of receiving annual payments over such a long period of years, particularly after Independence when both the composition and policies of future governments could not be foreseen."[35] The Chartered Company asked for a British Government guarantee for the annual payments; the guarantee was refused, and negotiations broke down. Apparently, at the behest of Harry Oppenheimer the Chartered Company was offered a guarantee by the copper producing companies, in which case it is hard to understand why the Board failed to seize the chance for a settlement on such favorable terms before the political tide moved too strongly against the company.

Matters came to a head in mid-1964, when the Northern Rhodesia Government realized that under the constitutional instruments whereby Zambia was to achieve full independence the British Government proposed to fulfill a pledge made to the Chartered Company in the 1950 agreement: to insure that the new Zambian Government was bound to observe the provisions of the 1950 agreement. Moreover, the constitution would contain safeguards against expropriation of the Chartered Company's right without full compensation. Accordingly, the Northern Rhodesia Government, anxious to prepare its ground to meet such an eventuality, commissioned a full inquiry by legal and financial experts with a view to reexamining the validity of the Chartered Company's claims. The results of the inquiry were published as a Northern Rhodesian Government White Paper.[36] The company made its own investigations, but the results were never published in any detail. Both sides went into the legal and historical issues very fully, and both took the opinion of eminent counsel. The issues can only be summarized here; in a sense they have never been properly resolved since political considerations were decisive in the eventual settlement, as in the settlements of 1923 and 1950.

The Chartered Company's case was that its right to the royalties was firmly based on (1) the agreements made with chiefs between 1880 and 1909; (2) Northern Rhodesia legislation, including the 1958 Mining Ordinance; and (3) recognition by the British Government from 1893 onward, especially in the 1950 agreement, which expressly provided that the Chartered Company remain in undisturbed enjoyment of its rights until October 1986. Accordingly, the Chartered Company insisted that "proper compensation [be] paid in accordance with fundamental rights recognized throughout the world."

On the other hand, the Northern Rhodesia Government advisers concluded (1) that many of the original "treaties" on which the Chartered Company relied were of highy questionable validity and may have been wholly ineffective with regard to the transfer of mineral rights; (2) that even if all the alleged treaties were valid, none of them covered the vital area of the Copperbelt from whence the vast bulk of the royalties flowed; and (3) that the subsequent agreements, proclamations, orders-in-council and ordinances only confirmed the company's rights to the extent that they were originally valid. Therefore, it was argued, the rights possessed by the Chartered Company in 1964 were only those derived from the Lewanika concession of 1900, extending only over the territory properly covered by that concession. Since there was no ground for believing that any of the original inhabitants of the Copperbelt were ever subject to Lewanika, the concession was not effective to convey to the Chartered Company the mineral rights in the Copperbelt area.

Armed with such favorable advice, the Northern Rhodesian Government felt able to threaten to take over the mineral rights without compensation, although it was willing to make a small ex gratia payment. In the Northern Rhodesia Government's view, it was the British Government's responsibility to satisfy the company's claims. As Minister of Finance Arthur Wina told Chartered Company shareholders; "the case [of the Chartered Company] in law is weak; but in so far it does bear inspection it rests on agreements imposed on the country by the British Government."

As independence, scheduled for October 24, 1964, approached, the Northern Rhodesia Government made it clear that, in the absence of a settlement on its terms, it would proceed to amend the constitution and expropriate the mineral rights without compensation immediately after independence.

The end of the mineral rights saga was suitably dramatic.[37] The President of the Chartered Company, Paul Emrys-Evans, flew to Northern Rhodesia and at 3.30 P.M. on the eve of independence received an offer of £4 million, net of tax, to be contributed in equal shares by the British and Zambian Governments. Zambia's refusal to cooperate in the scheme to avoid the company's tax liability caused Mr. Evans to hesitate. He was told, in the rueful words of the Chartered Company's December 1964 circular to shareholders:

> That a decision . . . had to be made within the next eleven minutes, because the Zambian Ministers and the Secretary of State were about to leave for other engagements which would occupy them until the Independence Ceremony at midnight. Your President, faced with the alternative of expropriation without compensation, felt there was no course open to him but to acquiesce.

On December 14, 1964, a formal agreement was signed by the Chartered Company and the Zambian Government under which the mineral rights were transferred to the latter with effect from October 24, 1964, and the Chartered Company received the sum of £2 million after payment of Zambian tax. The company also received an ex gratia payment of £2 million from the British Government.

The final settlement did not mean financial disaster for the Chartered Company. Over the years, it had received an estimated £70 million net in royalties; the company had been steadily building up large reserves so that shareholders did not suffer.[38] They obtained good value for their shares in the 1965 merger of the Chartered Company and two companies in the Anglo-American group to form Chartered Consolidated Ltd., which is today one of Britain's major mining finance houses. So far as Zambia was concerned, the settlement not only brought a valuable accretion of revenue but also was an essential prelude to the mining reforms of 1969. With all mineral rights, with some minor exceptions, vested in the state, attention could now be given to questions of closer governmental control and participation in the mining industry.

NOTES

1. Accounts of the Chartered Company's initial penetration of Zambia are contained in L. H. Gann, A History of Northern Rhodesia

(London: Chatto & Windus, 1964); A. J. Hanna, The Beginnings of Nyasaland and North-Eastern Rhodesia, 1859-95 (Oxford: Clarendon Press, 1956); Richard Hall, Zambia (London: Pall Mall, 1965).

2. The text of this agreement and those subsequently signed by Lewanika are printed in T. W. Baxter, "The Concessions of North-ern Rhodesia," National Archives of Rhodesia and Nyasaland, Occa-sional Paper No. 1 (1963).

3. Minute on High Commissioner Selborne to Lord Crewe, December 6, 1909, Public Records Office CO/417/467.

4. Sir Kenneth Bradley has observed that up to that time "every successful mineral development in the world had originated with the discoveries of the small prospector." Kenneth Bradley, Copper Venture (London: RST, 1952).

5. This is made clear in, for example, the Chartered Company's letter to Robert Codrington, Administrator of North-Eastern Rhodesia, dated February 13, 1904 (Zambian National Archives).

6. Henry Wilson Fox (London Manager for the Chartered Com-pany), "Memorandum on the Proposed Northern Rhodesia Mining Law" (1909) includes a schedule of 20 separate mineral grants existing on December 8, 1909.

7. H. M. Williams, The Mining Law of Northern Rhodesia (London: Published jointly by RST, Anglo-American Corporation of South Africa, and the British South Africa Company, n.d., about 1964), p. 68.

8. Public Records Office; CO African (South) 969, p. 7.

9. Fox, op. cit.

10. Sir Theodore Gregory, Ernest Oppenheimer and the Economic Development of Southern Africa (London: Oxford University Press, 1962), p. 392.

11. Ibid., p. 393.

12. See, for example, Ibid., Chapter VII; Bradley, op. cit., pp. 78-94.

13. Gregory, op. cit., p. 416.

14. <u>Ibid</u>., p. 412.

15. See, for example, the Northern Rhodesia Government White Paper, "The British South Africa Company's Claims to Mineral Royalties in Northern Rhodesia" (Lusaka, 1964), pp. 24-25.

16. Governor Herbert Stanley in a letter to Secretary of State Amery, May 16, 1926, PRO. CO/533/350.

17. The account given consists of a brief summary of the relevant files in the Public Records Office, Northern Rhodesia Series CO 795 dated 1924-39.

18. Chartered Company to Colonial Office, October 15, 1931, CO 795 36021/31.

19. Governor Maxwell to Secretary of State Passfield, March 6, 1930 (enclosure) CO 795 35505/30.

20. Colonial No. 145 (1938).

21. Northern Rhodesia Legislative Council Debates, December 13, 1938.

22. The account given is based on the papers dealing with the mineral rights issue in the Public Records Office, Northern Rhodesia Series, CO 795.

23. Governor Hubert Young's personal letter to Secretary of State MacDonald, September 11, 1935, CO 795 45105/35.

24. Sir Alan Pim, private letter to a Colonial Office official, CO 795 45163/37.

25. The phrase is taken from David Goldsworthy, <u>Colonial Issues in British Politics 1945-1961</u> (Oxford: Clarendon Press, 1971), p. 52. For an analysis of official attitudes toward colonial economic development, see J. M. Lee, <u>Colonial Development and Good Government</u> (Oxford: Clarendon Press, 1967).

26. Minute by Sir Cecil Bottomley, October 12, 1936, CO 795 45027/6/36.

27. Gregory, <u>op. cit</u>., pp. 452-55.

28. The account of events leading up to the 1950 Mineral Rights Agreement is based on official material from the National Archives of Zambia, Lusaka.

29. Colonial No. 206 (1946).

30. The figures are taken from Sir Dougal Malcolm's statement to Chartered Company shareholders, July 28, 1949.

31. Northern Rhodesia Legislative Council Debates, March 28, 1949.

32. Northern Rhodesia Legislative Council Debates, March 1958.

33. United National Independence Party pamphlet, Lusaka, 1962.

34. Hall, op. cit., p. 150.

35. Chartered Company statement to shareholders, December 22, 1964.

36. Northern Rhodesian Government White Paper, "The British South Africa Company's Claims to Mineral Royalties in Northern Rhodesia," op. cit.

37. A colorful account of the dramatic finale can be found in Richard Hall, The High Price of Principles (Hoddes and Stoughton, 1969), Chapter 5.

38. The figure of £70 million was suggested by the Northern Rhodesian Government White Paper (Ibid.). In a letter to the Times of September 17, 1964, Chartered Company President Paul Emrys-Evans gave the following figures:

		Millions of Pounds
Gross revenue from mining rights in Northern Rhodesia from grant of charter to September 30, 1964		161
Paid to "Rhodesia" in taxes and to Northern Rhodesian Government equal to 20 percent of net revenue after 1949	79	
"Invested or spent" in Northern Rhodesia	20	
Paid in United Kingdom taxes	12	
Net exported profit for distribution, reserves, and reinvestment		50

If the sum "invested or spent" in Northern Rhodesia is regarded as part of the Chartered Company's profits, as seems reasonable, then Emrys-Evans' figures may be reconciled with those in the 1964 Northern Rhodesian Government White Paper. The net asset value of a Chartered Company 15/- stock unit in 1963 was conservatively estimated at 80/-. The book value of the mineral rights—from which a net revenue of £6.46 million was derived in 1963—was shown in the balance sheet in September 1963 at £841,293. Of the Chartered Company's book assets of £70.9 million, investments (accumulated largely out of mineral profits) accounted for £54.28 million.

3

PROSPECTING

AND

MINING ACTIVITY,

1895-1970

Alan Drysdall

THE PERIOD 1895-1922

Several centuries before the arrival of the first Europeans in central Africa, iron, gold, and copper were produced and extensively used for weapons, ornaments, and, in the case of copper, as a medium of exchange. The earliest account of this mining activity is recorded in the writings of Fillipo Pigafetta, A Report on the Kingdom of Congo, 1591,[1] and there are several subsequent references in the works of eighteenth-century Portuguese explorers and, of course, David Livingstone. Many of the major orebodies subsequently pegged by European prospectors had already been extensively exploited by local miners, and much of the early prospecting in the Rhodesias and Katanga Province of the Congo consisted of persuading them to reveal the whereabouts of these workings. The most extensive in Zambia were the excavations at Bwana Mkubwa and Kansanshi, but many others existed, including a large group in the Mumbwa District. The presence of copper at Nkana South, Chambishi, and Roan Antelope also was known, and a small pit existed at Nkana.

The Royal Charter under which the British South Africa Company was established in 1889 authorized the company to acquire and develop mineral concessions in an ill-defined area of central Africa north of the Limpopo River. Interest in the area from the mineral point of view had been stimulated by the discovery of the Witwatersrand gold field in South Africa in 1886; Cecil Rhodes also considered it essential to forestall the territorial ambitions of the Portuguese, Germans, and Boers occupying the adjacent territories, and he was undoubtedly influenced by his personal vision of a Cape to Cairo overland route. The search for gold spread northward into what was to become Southern Rhodesia, where the early prospectors met with moderate success as they systematically pegged the ancient workings, and subsequently north of the Zambezi. No significant occurrences of gold were found in what is now Zambia, but interest in the area was revived by the discovery of the rich orebodies of Katanga Province of the Congo. By comparison, the first finds in the area of the Copperbelt were regarded as disappointing: for example, in 1918 the Nkana claims were sold for £100! Nevertheless, by the late 1920's it had become obvious that the Copperbelt included several orebodies of major economic significance, and the development and exploitation of one of the most richly mineralized provinces in the world began. This development has been closely linked with extensive exploration programs, which have made Zambia one of the most intensely prospected areas in Africa.

Within ten years of the granting of the Royal Charter, the British South Africa Company had acquired mineral rights over the greater part of North Western and North Eastern Rhodesia. In addition, agreement was reached with Lewanika, the Paramount Chief or Litunga of the Barotse people, that the Western Province should be reserved against prospecting, except with his specific permission (see Chapter 2). This agreement undoubtedly restricted activity in the Western Province, but in any case the mineral potential of this area has always been regarded as limited because of a widespread cover of recent Kalahari sediments blanketing the older rocks; the problems involved in prospecting such terrain have further inhibited activity. (New approaches being tried in comparable areas of Botswana and Rhodesia may help to solve some of these problems.)

Prospecting north of the Zambezi River began in 1895,[2] and in the ten years prior to 1905 some thirty grants of prospecting rights were made, but the holders of many of these grants amalgamated their interests to form operating syndicates. The most important of these were the companies under the control of Edmund Davis, who employed T. G. Davey as Consulting Engineer, and Robert Williams (Tanganyika Concessions Limited). In 1896, prospecting of the 10,000 square miles comprising the North Charterland Concession began, but the results were disappointing and the only mine of any significance to be developed was Sasare, a gold prospect north of Petauke that produced some 12,000 ounces of gold over the period from 1904-42. Prospecting of the Big Concession between 1898 and 1903 resulted in the discovery of many copper prospects, but only Sable Antelope and Silver King were developed as producing mines (1911). In the Solwezi

District, George Grey pegged Kansanshi over a group of old workings
of Tanganyika Concessions Limited in 1908, two years after the railroad had reached Broken Hill. Following the discovery of Kansanshi,
Robert Williams became interested in the potential of what is now
Katanga Province of Congo (Kinshasa). His interest ultimately led to
the discovery of the majority of the Katanga mines that have been or
are being exploited and to the decision to extend the railroad north
from Broken Hill. (The link to the Copperbelt was completed in 1909.)
The Roan Antelope and Bwana Mkubwa claims were pegged in 1902 by
W. C. Collier and J. J. Donohue for Edmund Davis' group of companies,
and Collier is credited with the discovery of the Chambishi orebody
in the following year, although these original claims were never registered. The Broken Hill mineralized area was pegged by Davey in
1902, but development was delayed until the railroad line was completed. Broken Hill, named by Davey after the famous mining field
in New South Wales, produced the first trial shipment of calcined
zinc ore in 1906, but this operation proved unprofitable; the first lead
was produced in 1915. In 1910 a local administrator was shown the
copper-stained outcrop in the Wusikili stream at Nkana, but no claims
were registered over this surface expression of the Nkana South orebody until 1916, although in 1905 a claim apparently was pegged by an
unknown prospector in this area. Even in 1916, the low-grade oxide
mineralization was regarded as of little interest by comparison with
the orebodies that were being prospected in the Congo. The initial
unsuccessful attempt to exploit the Bwana Mkubwa deposit, which was
sited almost alongside the railroad line, also adversely affected the
assessment of the Nkana mineralization.

From 1906, there was a fall-off in prospecting activity partly
due to a recession in base metal prices but also in part attributable
to the failure to find significant deposits of gold. Interest was to
some extent revived by the introduction under new legislation in 1912
of ordinary prospecting licences, as distinct from what had in effect
been exclusive rights, but World War I and a subsequent fall in metal
prices again resulted in a reduced level of activity.

Thus, as J. A. Bancroft emphasizes, the period prior to 1922
was one of disappointment, largely due to undercapitalization and
poor communication.[3] Although a multitude of prospects and old
workings were discovered these proved of little value. The total
production of gold was less than 15,000 ounces and Kansanshi produced
some 3,000 metric tons of copper at prohibitive cost before being closed
down in 1914. Between 1913 and 1914 and from 1916-18, Bwana Mkubwa
produced at a loss 2,845 metric tons of copper in concentrates and the
Sable Antelope and Silver King produced some 4,2000 metric tons of copper

and 70,000 ounces of silver for a modest profit. Broken Hill's total production during this period was 80,000 metric tons of lead. Although coal had been discovered in the Zambezi, Luangwa, Luano, and Lukusashi valleys, it had invariably proved to be of low quality and could not compare with the major deposits being actively exploited at Wankie.

THE PERIOD 1922-45

In view of this comparative lack of success, in the 1920's the British South Africa Company adopted a change of policy that was to have far-reaching consequences: it was decided to grant exclusive prospecting rights over large areas to companies with the financial resources to undertake major prospecting programs (see Chapter 2). Of course, existing claims that had been pegged and registered were excluded from these concessions. These licences were for specified periods, although they were renewable and carried minimum expenditure obligations—generally less than £1 per square mile—and conveyed the right to prospect and peg mining locations and Special Grant areas for detailed exploration and development. The British South Africa Company retained the right to take up a proportion of fully paid-up shares in the "concession companies." This decision to issue major exclusive prospecting licences resulted in the systematic exploration of the greater part of the country, but an inevitable consequence was the discouragement of the small prospector, although it can be justifiably argued that this was a small price to pay for what was achieved. However, the Special Grant system had many disadvantages that did not become fully apparent until a much later stage and were not overcome until the introduction of the 1969 Mines and Minerals Act.

The first of the exclusive licence areas was granted in December 1922 and comprised an area of 50,000 square miles extending south of the Congo border and west of the railroad. The holder was Copper Ventures Limited, a comparatively small company founded in 1921 to promote the use of the Perkin's process in the treatment of copper ores. (Subsequently Alfred Chester Beatty, on behalf of Selection Trust Limited, took an interest in this syndicate; he also joined the board of the Bwana Mkubwa Mining Company). These concession rights were acquired by Rhodesia Congo Border Concession Limited in 1923, and in the same year the original area was increased by 2,000 square miles. As a result of various renewals, the licence remained in existence until 1940, as did most licences subsequently issued.

In 1923, Copper Ventures Limited obtained prospecting rights over a second area of 13,000 square miles in the central part of the

country; the operating company in this case was Rhodesia Minerals
Concession Limited. In the following year, Copper Ventures Limited
was granted prospecting rights in the Nkana concession, which extended
from east of Chingola to Ndola and enclosed the Nkana, Roan Antelope,
and Chambishi claims. A few weeks later, Copper Ventures Limited
disposed of the Nkana claims, which it had purchased in 1922, and of
its rights in the Nkana concession to the Bwana Mkubwa Mining Company. In 1923, an insignificant occurrence of copper-stained peaty
soil at Mufulira was noted by James Moir and Guy Bell, who were
employed by Rhodesia Congo Border Concession Limited. Initial
follow-up work was undertaken by the Bwana Mkubwa Mining Company,
but in 1926 this company ceded its rights in the Nkana concession to
the Selection Trust Group, which was at that time engaged in prospecting under option the Roan Antelope claims where sulfide ore had been
proved to underlie a capping of oxides. The Bwana Mkubwa Mining
Company, influenced by the possible significance of the sulfide mineralization at Roan Antelope, retained a one-third interest in the Nkana
concession and it was by virtue of this interest that Anglo-American
subsequently obtained a share in the development of Mufulira. By
this time it had also been recognized that the typical Copperbelt mineralization, whatever its origin, was stratigraphically controlled, and
therefore the Selection Trust geologists set out to map the concession
systematically and peg Special Grants to protect those areas underlaid
by the sub-outcrop and down-dip extensions of the potential ore-bearing
horizon.* In 1928, Rhodesian Selection Trust (RST), which was founded
in 1927 to manage Selection Trust's interests in Northern Rhodesia,
began drilling at Mufulira, and by 1931 the mine was ready to come
into production when the depression forced its closure.

In 1924, Edmund Davis persuaded Sir Ernest Oppenheimer to
take an interest in the Bwana Mkubwa Mining Company, and in the
following year, as one of the conditions of the agreement, the Anglo-
American Corporation of South Africa Limited was appointed Consulting
Engineers. In 1925, Anglo-American and Rhodesia Congo Border Concession Limited entered into a similar arrangement. Thus, from the
mid-1920's, Anglo-American and RST began to emerge as the only
two major companies on the Copperbelt. The comparatively rapid
development that followed was in no small part due to the financial
resources at the disposal of these two companies; it was estimated
that by 1963 the total investment in the Copperbelt was £ 232 million,
of which £131 million represented retained profits.[4]

---

*This approach subsequently was adopted in the Congo and led
to the discovery of the Musoshi orebody in 1935.

Three major prospecting licences covering a total of 85,000 square miles were granted in 1925 to Luangwa Concessions (N. R.) Limited, Serenje Concessions Limited, and Kasempa Concessions Limited, but in 1928 the operating companies merged as Luangwa Concessions (N. R.) Limited with Anglo-American as Managers and Consulting Engineers. An additional area totaling 50,000 square miles was added in 1930.

The exploration campaign mounted by the concession companies between 1926 and 1940 was at that time probably the most comprehensive and extensive prospecting program ever undertaken. The history of this campaign is described in detail by J. A. Bancroft,[5] and the geological results are summarized on the maps subsequently published by the British South Africa Company and in a paper by T. D. Guernsey.[6] A total of 166 geologists and 34 prospectors were employed during this period; operations reached a peak in 1931 when an average of 78 geologists were employed. From 1933-38 activity was at a considerably reduced level, and by 1940 the reconnaissance prospecting program was completed and the areas that the companies wished to retain were converted into Special Grants. The concession areas eventually totaled 203,000 square miles, of which 156,000 square miles—54 percent of the country—were prospected in detail, that is by systematic straight-line foot traverses usually spaced at quarter-mile intervals. All outcrop data were recorded, and mineral occurrences were followed up by pitting, trenching, and diamond drilling where justified. An indication of the scale of total expenditure involved is given by the figures for Luangwa Concessions (N. R.) Limited, which over the period 1926-38 spent a total of over £470,000 on prospecting some 95,000 square miles within a total concession area of 135,000 square miles. (It may also be noted that the annual average rate of expenditure was approximately 6/- per square mile).

Perhaps the most important single discovery resulting from this campaign was the finding by J. J. Beaton of the first mineralized outcrops (the River Lode) in the Nchanga area only three months after work began in the Rhodesia Congo Border Concession. In 1926, Nchanga Copper Mines Limited was registered to develop the Nchanga prospects; drilling and development continued until 1931, by which time it was apparent that a major group of orebodies had been discovered. In 1924, the copper-stained outcrops in the Chililabombwe stream north of Nchanga also were recorded by geologists of Rhodesian Congo Border Concession Limited (Williams and Babb), and follow-up prospecting between 1928 and 1931 led to the discovery of the Bancroft orebodies.

Apart from the comprehensive stocktaking of the mineral resources, which was a natural outcome of the activities of the concession companies, there were other significant results whose value has
only since become fully apparent. For example, the published maps
record only outcrop data and mineral occurrences and no attempt was
made to interpret the geological structure, but these maps used in
conjunction with air photographs now enable the geologist to compile
more comprehensive maps that have proved invaluable. The first
comprehensive geological map of Zambia was largely compiled in
this way.[7] The Geological Survey also makes constant use of this
approach in its regional mapping program, and experience has shown
that, when supplemented with further traverse data, reliable maps—
which eventually are published on a scale of 1:100,000—can be produced comparatively rapidly.

The prospecting methods used by the concession companies
were of course primitive by modern standards, and such methods
could only have located orebodies with some surface expression.
However, these methods were rigidly systematic and the probability
of any such orebodies being overlooked was therefore minimal. Other
approaches were also tried, and the first use of air photography as a
prospecting tool in Zambia was undertaken by Rhodesia Congo Border
Concession Limited, which in 1926 contracted out a flying program of
12,000 square miles in an attempt to locate copper clearings, i.e.
isolated glades with sparse vegetation resulting from a high copper
content in the soil.* In the early 1920's, geophysical (electrical)
methods of prospecting proved their value at Mtuga, a group of comparatively small orebodies in the Mkushi District southeast of the
Copperbelt, but an attempt to use the same techniques on the Copperbelt in 1926 was a failure, probably due to the fine-grained disseminated nature of the mineralization. (The mineralization in the Mtuga
area is in the form of coarse disseminated sulfides in granitic rocks
forming a persistent zone probably related to a major structure.)

---

*This program in fact constitutes one of the earliest recorded
uses of aerial photography in geology (photogeology) anywhere in the
world. The first copper clearing, or "blind dambo," to be recognized
as such was probably the very fine example at Roan Antelope, which
was shaped like a hairpin, curving around the eastern nose of the
fold and extending along the limbs.

From the point of view of actual mineral production, the disappointment of the early years continued into the 1920's. There was a continuing small production of copper from the Sable Antelope and Silver King Mines, and Kansanshi remained closed. Despite extensive prospecting and development between 1927 and 1932 and again between 1937 and 1938, Kansanshi did not resume production until 1956. After 3,490 tons of copper had been produced, it was again closed in 1957 as a result of flooding, and it was not until 1969 that it was announced that production would be resumed, probably in 1973. Broken Hill also proved to be anything but a straight-forward mining proposition. The mixed lead and zinc oxide ores sheathing massive sulfides presented complex metallurgical problems, and it was not until 1928 that the first electrolytic zinc was produced on a commercial scale. Water in the cavernous dolomitic host-rocks also proved a problem, and it was 1940 before sufficient reserves of sulfide ore had been proved to justify deepening the shafts and installing the pumping capacity required. The depression also had its effect: lead production ceased in 1929 when the accessible high-grade lead oxide ores were mined out, and zinc production ceased in 1931. However, vanadium pentoxide was recovered from the oxide ores, in particular from 1923. In 1929, the small Star Zinc prospect sixteen miles north of Lusaka shipped 21,489 metric tons of willemite ore estimated to contain some 10,000 metric tons of zinc. Production ceased early in 1930 and has never been resumed, although the area has been extensively drilled. Production at Bwana Mkubwa recommenced in 1926 from an open pit, but the mine was closed in 1931 after 22,000 metric tons of copper had been produced at a considerable loss. Again, the major problems were metallurgical.

During the latter half of the 1920's, prospecting continued at Roan Antelope, Nkana, Chambishi, Nchanga, and Mufulira. In 1923, one of sixteen shot drill-holes completed at Nkana intersected "clean" sulfide ore beneath a covering of oxides for the first time on the Copperbelt, but the possible significance of this intersection does not seem to have been fully appreciated. In 1926, a comparable intersection was made at Roan Antelope, and by the end of the 1920's it was apparent that the Copperbelt was one of the world's major metallogenic provinces. Roan Antelope commenced production in 1931, the first major mine to do so. The Nkana North orebody, which has no surface expression, was discovered in 1924 as a result of systematic pitting and drilling of a "copper-clearing." The only outcrop of the Mindola orebody was discovered in 1927, but it was not until 1931 that comprehensive prospecting and development finally culminated in bringing Nkana into production. However, the almost immediate fall in the price of copper to £27.10s. per metric ton forced the closure of Mufulira and

Nchanga prior to achievement of production.* At Nchanga, the exceptionally high-grade western orebody was discovered in 1928, but in 1931 the difficult ground and large volume of water that had been encountered ever since the beginning of underground development finally culminated in the flooding of the workings. Mufulira was reopened in 1933 and Nchanga in 1936. The depression also resulted in the temporary cessation of development at Chambishi—which was purchased by RST in 1928—and of prospecting at Bancroft.

It is not certain when it was first recognized that cobalt is occasionally present in the Copperbelt orebodies. The first production of cobalt alloy was in 1937 at Nkana, where carollite was identified as being present in the sulfide ores in the late 1920's.

During World War II, virtually no prospecting was undertaken and efforts were concentrated on attempting to maintain production from the four existing mines; the production was disposed of on an agreed-price basis to the British Ministry of Supply. With devaluation in 1949, the introduction in 1952 of a revised tax code that provided for accelerated amortization of capital expenditure on new mining development, and an increasing world demand for base metals, the stage was set for the major expansion of production that followed in the 1950's.

THE PERIOD 1945-69: AREAS OUTSIDE
THE COPPERBELT

Prospecting outside the Copperbelt was resumed in the 1950's, and for a period of some 15 years the greater part of the country— again with the exception of most of the Western Province—was once more held under exclusive prospecting licences.[8] The major licence holders were subsidiaries of the Anglo-American and RST groups, but the Rio Tinto organization also was extensively involved during this period and De Beers was actively concentrating on reconnaisance prospecting for diamonds in overlapping licence areas that covered the greater part of the country.

---

*An agreement to cut production by 25 percent came into force on June 1, 1932, following a meeting of all the major producers in New York. Thus, Roan Antelope and Nkana continued to produce at 75 percent of the previous output but Nchanga and Mufulira were closed.

During the 1950's, geochemical methods of prospecting in tropical terrains were developed, largely as a result of research undertaken in Zambia by the Geochemical Research Centre of Imperial College under J. Webb, in association with the RST and Anglo-American groups. This approach has proved very effective in the central African environment, and is today the most widely used prospecting method.

Sebembere, a prospect of the Copperbelt type near Broken Hill, is claimed by the Rio Tinto group to have been the first significant, possibly economic, mineralization to have been discovered in central Africa using geochemical methods of exploration. The most spectacular find was undoubtedly RST's discovery of the very rich Kalengwa orebody 200 miles west-southwest of the Copperbelt in the Mwinilunga prospecting area. Before the mine came into production in 1970, the ore reserves were estimated to be 653,000 short tons containing 17.25 percent copper and 225,000 short tons with 3.5 percent copper. The Lumwana group of prospects 150 miles north-northwest of the Copperbelt also were discovered by RST using geochemical methods. The ore reserves are very provisionally estimated to be some 200 million short tons with slightly less than 0.9 percent copper. Anglo-American areas outside the Copperbelt itself have to date proved less rewarding, although a number of comparatively small but promising copper occurrences have been discovered near Lusaka, again by geochemical methods (contrasting with this is the number of discoveries made on the Copperbelt, particularly in the Nchanga area).

It is relevant at this point to mention the work of the Geological Survey. The original organization was founded under a grant from Colonial Development and Welfare Funds in 1950 within the Department of Labor and Mines, and in January 1952 the Geological Survey was established as a separate department. This Geological Survey was one of the last of the British Colonial Geological Surveys to be formed, possibly because the mining scene in central Africa had been so dominated by the activities of the British South Africa Company and the Copperbelt companies that the necessity for such an organization was never appreciated.

The first priority of the Geological Survey was to begin mapping and compilation for the first geological map of the whole of Zambia, but the Department of Labor and Mines became progressively more involved in prospecting, largely due to the ever-increasing demand for industrial minerals and building materials. In 1962, an Economic Unit was established to perform these functions and also to prospect mineral occurrences that the companies regarded as not warranting large-scale exploration and development; thus, the purpose was to complement rather than overlap the field of interest of the mining

companies. In 1965, the Economic Unit also began a reassessment
of the country's coal resources, which in the same year resulted in
the discovery of the Siankondobo coal field. Southern Rhodesia's
Unilateral Declaration of Independence in November 1965 caused
accelerated development of the small Nkandabwe coal mine—which
had been discovered by the Geological Survey in 1952—and subsequently
of the Maamba mine in the Siankondobo area (1967), since Southern
Rhodesia previously had supplied all Zambia's coal (see Chapter 5).
In 1970, a 36-cubic-yard dragline and a coal-washing plant were commissioned at Maamba, and by the end of the year production was at a
rate of 75,000 metric tons of washed coal per month. As a result of
these developments, Zambia will be self-sufficient with regard to solid
fuel supplies, with the exception of coke, in the early 1970's.

The expansion of the Geological Survey during the years 1950-64
is illustrated by the figures for the professional establishment: 1951,
4; 1955, 11; 1960, 14; 1964, 18. In the immediate post-independence
years—1965-66—the rate of expansion increased appreciably. This
was undoubtedly due in part to the emphasis placed in the first National
Development Plan on rapid development of the country's resources,
in particular resources in rural areas, and also to recognition of the
need to diversify mineral production where possible as a contribution
toward diversifying the economy. The professional establishment of
the Geological Survey had risen to 38 by 1966, and fluctuated between
33 and 39 in the following years. The Department's annual budget
during the period 1965-70 averaged K660,000, reflecting some acceleration in the rate of regional mapping but more directly the increasing
involvement in prospecting. (The Geological Survey's budget for 1971
was K1.1 million.)

Since 1969, the Geological Survey has been engaged in a major
prospecting program as a joint project with a United Nations Development Fund team, in an area of 15,000 square miles west of Lusaka and
Kabwe. This program includes an extensive airborne electromagnetic
survey using a comparatively recently developed technique (INPUT),
which had not been used in central Africa at the time the project was
planned in 1966.

In 1963, the British South Africa Company established a Survey
of Minor Deposits Unit, which worked in close association with the
Geological Survey to promote and assist small workers and cooperative
mining organizations in particular. This unit examined a number of
small mineral occurrences and established two groups of cooperatives,
one to work the numerous prospects and abandoned small workings of
the Choma-Kalomo tin belt in the Southern Province and the other to

exploit the numerous mica-bearing pegmatites in the Lundazi, Serenje, and Mazabuka districts. The mica-mining cooperatives proved a failure and were wound up soon after independence; the two tin-mining cooperatives still exist in 1971, although production has always been sporadic and at a very low level.

With the advent of independence in 1964, there was a tendency for the companies to reduce the number and size of the areas held under exclusive prospecting licences and the Rio Tinto group withdrew completely. This reduction involved the extent of the areas held rather than the rate of expenditure on exploration. However, at this stage there was little outside interest in the areas that were released, mainly because their economic potential appeared to be restricted.

THE PERIOD 1945-69: THE COPPERBELT

Prospecting in the Copperbelt Special Grant areas resumed in about 1949, and as a direct result of this activity the Chibuluma orebody (which was discovered in 1939) was brought into production in 1955. This orebody has no surface expression, and the prospecting program that led to its discovery—involving systematic pitting of the sub-outcrop of the Lower Roan metasediments and diamond drilling—is a good example of the painstaking approach that is necessary in the exploration of the poorly exposed Copperbelt area.

Prospecting also was resumed at Bancroft, and this mine was eventually brought into production in 1957. However, a great deal of difficulty was encountered—water in particular proved a major problem—and the mine was shut down in 1958, partly as a consequence of a slump in metal prices. It was reopened in 1959, and production capacity has been considerably extended since despite persistent pumping problems.* However, Konkola, the most northerly shaft, was not reopened, but the next phase of major expansion at Bancroft will almost certainly involve the renewed exploitation of this orebody.

The third mine to come into production on the Copperbelt in the post-war years was Chambishi. Detailed exploration was renewed in

---

*Bancroft is currently pumping 76 million gallons of water a day, i.e. 67 tons of water are pumped for every ton of ore hoisted, and it has the unenviable distinction of being one of the wettest mines in the world.

the 1950's, and production of mixed oxide and sulfide ores from an open pit began in 1965. Current plans for expansion involve the development of an underground stage.

Prospecting elsewhere on the Copperbelt also continued. The most spectacular expansion in terms of ore mined was achieved at Nchanga, where a whole group of orebodies were brought into production in 1968, including the Mimbula and Fitula occurrences as well as the original River Lode find and a western extension of the main open pit. Nchanga itself is now a mining complex with five open pits and an underground mine producing 9.3 million metric tons of ore and over 240,000 metric tons of copper per year. Mufulira, the largest mine of the RST group, had expanded production to almost 190,000 metric tons of copper per year when disaster struck in September 1970. A catastrophic inrush of tailings from surface that caused 89 deaths and millions of Kwacha worth of damage brought production to a standstill for several weeks, and full production probably will not be resumed until 1972. Mineralization in the Special Grants around Mufulira that might conceivably prove to be economic in the future has been discovered in the Luansobe, Mutundu, and Mwekera areas and also near Mokambo, on the Congo border, and the northerly limb of the Mufulira syncline. At Nkana, significant increases of reserves have been proved, and it has to some extent been possible to postpone deep-level mining and the cutback in production that probably would follow.

At Roan Antelope, further prospecting not only proved major westerly extensions of the original orebody but also revealed significant copper-cobalt sulfide mineralization within the adjacent Baluba Special Grant. Pilot underground development was initiated in 1968, and Baluba is provisionally planned to come into full production in 1973. Further prospecting at Bancroft has indicated a major deep-level extension of the orebodies in a synformal saddle between Konkola and the southern sections; exploration of this area, where the mineralization lies at depths in excess of 2,000 feet, is still in progress. Further prospecting of the ill-fated Bwana Mkubwa orebody also has been undertaken, and production will recommence in 1971. The current situation on the Copperbelt and the history of its development is summed up in Tables 3.1, 3.2, 3.3, and 3.4.

PROSPECTING EXPENDITURE

The increases in the ore reserves (see Table 3.4) to some extent reflect the companies' exploration philosophy of concentrating on those areas with the highest mineral potential, and in particular the Copperbelt

TABLE 3.1

Summary of Mineral Production
in Copperbelt, 1930-69
(metric tons)

Year	Copper	Cobalt	Lead	Zinc	Vanadium Pentoxide
1930	6,370	—	—	19,789	99
1935	145,811	417	185	21,011	309
1940	266,619	785	293	13,401	657
1945	197,118	678	1,748	15,484	391
1950	281,150	1,774	13,904	23,078	—
1955	348,684	1,092	16,307	28,346	—
1960	568,431	10,484	14,660	30,271	—
1965	685,849	1,544	21,344	47,434	—
1969	754,212	1,798	23,006	50,163	—
Cumulative total to 1969	13,577,002	95,910	503,044	1,125,113	9,262

Sources: Mining yearbooks of Zambia and annual reports of the Government Mining Engineer.

TABLE 3.2

Copperbelt Production, 1969

Mine	Ore milled (metric tons)	Millhead Grade Copper Percent	Millhead Grade Cobalt Percent	Copper produced (metric tons)
Bancroft	1,758,000	3.37	—	50,361
Chambishi	1,018,000	2.33	—	26,585
Chibuluma	634,000	4.31	0.18	29,315
Luanshya	6,353,000	1.82	—	116,822
Mufulira	7,567,000	2.50	—	188,562
Nchanga	9,318,000	3.69	—	242,444
Rhokana (Nkana)	5,382,000	1.97	0.12	100,123
Total	32,030,000	2.70		754,212

Sources: Mining yearbooks of Zambia and annual reports of the Government Mining Engineer.

TABLE 3.3

Copperbelt Production, 1940-69
(metric tons)

Mine	1940	1950	1955	1960	1965	1969
Bancroft	—	—	—	54,994	37,087	50,361
Chambishi	—	—	—	—	2,929	26,585
Chibuluma	—	—	154	21,948	22,522	29,315
Luanshya	76,402	72,102	83,362	83,623	98,257	116,822
Mufulira	73,622	82,618	85,896	108,858	158,929	188,562
Nchanga	9,988	45,798	104,741	188,305	261,356	242,444
Rhokana (Nkana)	97,605	80,347	72,971	109,986	104,036	100,123
Total	257,617	280,865	347,124	567,714	685,116	754,212

Sources: Mining yearbooks of Zambia and annual reports of the Government Mining Engineer.

TABLE 3.4

Changes in Copperbelt Ore Reserves

Mine	Start of Mining Operations				Last Quoted Position			
	Ore Reserves (millions of tons)	Copper (percentage)	Copper Oxide* (percentage)	Date	Ore Reserves (millions of tons)	Copper (percentage)	Copper Oxide* (percentage)	Date
Baluba	–	–	–	–	59.7	2.71	trace	1970
Bancroft	83.5	3.67	0.50	1957	82.9	3.51	0.48	December 1969
Bwana Mkubwa	0.05	12.0	n.a.	1913	5.7	3.30	n.a.	1970
Chambishi	–	–	–	–	30.6	3.07	0.01	June 1970
Chibulma	6.6	5.23	–	1955	6.1	4.80	–	June 1970
Luanshya	98.0	3.44	0.17	1931	72.0	2.76	0.09	June 1970
Mufulira	105.2	4.41	trace	1933	136.4	3.27	trace	June 1970
Nchanga	130.4	4.66	2.53	1939	223.8	4.00	1.64?	December 1969
Rhokana (Nkana)	115.2	4.00	–	1932	123.9	2.61	n.a.	June 1969
Copperbelt as a whole	–	–	–	–	741.1	3.32	–	–

*The significance of the percentage of copper oxide is that it is more difficult, and therefore more expensive, to extract copper from oxide ores.

Sources: For the first set of figures, J.A. Bancroft, Mining in Northern Rhodesia (London: British South Africa Company, 1961); for the second set of figures, mining company annual reports.

Special Grants. This approach has yielded significant dividends and, in the case of Anglo-American for example, since 1960 has resulted in increases of reserves totaling 35 million metric tons contained in 10 orebodies. Four of these, Fitula, Mimbula No. 1, and Chingola "E" and block "A" were new discoveries, while the remainder were de-lineated as a result of following up indications noted prior to 1940. RST on the other hand has divided its efforts more or less equally between the Copperbelt itself and the areas RST has held outside the Copperbelt, particularly the Chisangwa and Mwinilunga exclusive prospecting areas to the west, which would be the most obvious direction in which to look for extensions of the Copperbelt-type mineraliza-tion. This approach also turned out to be profitable, and it led to the proving of major extensions of the copperbelt orebodies and also to the discovery of Kalengwa and Lumwana.

Expenditures by RST Technical Services Limited on prospecting and exploration since 1952 are listed in Table 3.5 which shows the steady rise in total expenditure to the current level of K4 million per year. Two features of particular interest are the temporary fall in expenditures on the Copperbelt areas during the "independence phase" (1963-65) and the very dramatic rise during 1969-70. Unfortunately, comparable detailed figures are not available for the Anglo-American group, but expenditures during the pre- and post-independence periods are compared in Table 3.6.

As Table 3.6 shows, in the five years following independence total expenditures on exploration by the major groups increased by some 42.4 percent. RST's expenditures increased by 44 percent, while expenditures by the Anglo-American group increased by 41 percent. (If expenditure by the De Beers organization is excluded, the figure for Anglo-American is reduced to 38 percent.) The most striking contrast between the two major groups is in the different emphasis that has been placed on the Copperbelt compared with other areas. The Anglo-American group's expenditures on the Copperbelt almost doubled in the years 1964-69 compared with the five previous years, whereas its expenditures outside the Copperbelt increased only with respect to prospecting by De Beers. On the other hand, RST's expenditures increased more or less uniformly in both the Copperbelt and the areas outside it, 55 percent and 38 percent respectively.

In 1967, the two major groups spent approximately K4 million on prospecting and exploration.[9] The Mining Yearbook of Zambia records that in 1968 RST's expenditure on prospecting was approxi-mately K3 million and that the Anglo-American group spent approxi-mately K2 million in the same year. This represents rather less

TABLE 3.5

RST Group Prospecting Expenditures, 1952-70
(thousands of Kwacha)

Year	Copperbelt	Other
1952-53	70*	530
1953-54	95*	279
1954-55	159	393
1955-56	214	409
1956-57	324*	515
1957-58	439*	696
1958-59	309*	837
1959-60	519*	1,077
1960-61	635	966
1961-62	684	919
1962-63	544	956
1963-64	348	949
1964-65	336	1,086
1965-66	611	1,048
1966-67	765	1,175
1967-68	910	1,230
1968-69	1,104*	1,545*
1969-70	1,910*	2,200*
Total	9,976	16,810

*Estimated

Source: Information supplied by RST.

TABLE 3.6

Prospecting Expenditures of Anglo-
American and RST, 1958-69
(millions of Kwacha)

| | Copperbelt | | Other Areas | |
	1958-63	1964-69	1958-63	1964-69
RST group	3.1	4.8	5.6	7.7
Anglo-American group	4.0	7.7	4.9	4.6
De Beers	—	—	0.8	1.4
Total	7.1	12.5	11.3	13.7

Source: Information supplied by the mining groups.

than 1 percent of total sales revenue, which is close to the overall
world average for major mining companies.[10] Taking into account
expenditures by the De Beers organization and the Geological Survey,
it would seem that in 1968 total expenditures on prospecting and exploration was probably on the order of K6 million. In 1969, the Anglo-
American and RST groups spent a total of K5.8 million on prospecting,[11]
and therefore total expenditure was at a slightly higher level, probably
about K6.5 million.

In his 1968 Mulungushi speech, President Kaunda severely criti-
cized the mining companies for the lack of development since 1964.
The statistics suggest that this criticism was at least in part justified,
but there were some important mitigating factors. Of the Anglo-American mines, only Bancroft showed a significant increase in production
between 1965 and 1969 (35 percent), but this was more than offset by
the falls at both Nchanga and Rhokana. In the case of Nchanga, the fall
was due to a decline in ore grades—the tonnage of ore milled increased
by 55 percent—and an increase in the percentage of oxides, resulting
in recovery problems; at Rhokana, pressure and temperature problems
as well as a fall in ore grades were being encountered with increasing
depths of mining. The RST mines showed an increase in output of 28
percent between 1965 and 1969, as against a fall of 2.4 percent in the

mines of the Anglo-American group. Of the RST mines, Luanshya, although an old mine with a limited potential for expansion, increased output by 19 percent; Mufulira, with almost twice the ore reserves of Luanshya, increased production by a similar amount and was planning a further significant increase when the disaster occurred in 1970; Chambishi only began production in 1965 and therefore showed a major increase in production by 1969; and the small Chibuluma mine increased output by 30 percent.

However, overall Copperbelt production increased by only 10 percent between 1965 and 1969, compared with 21 percent in the previous five-year period and 72 percent between 1955 and 1960, the culmination of the post-war expansion phase. It was against this background that President Kaunda announced restrictions on dividend remittance in an attempt to force the companies to reinvest profits and promised revision of the royalty system, which the companies claimed was a major factor inhibiting expansion.

The total copper content of the Copperbelt reserves is approximately 26 million short tons, i.e., 12.5 percent of the world's total reserves of 210 million short tons as recently estimated by the U.S. Bureau of Mines.[12] However, these figures are no cause for complacency: at the present rate of production and without allowing for such factors as mining losses and dilution, the Copperbelt's reserves, which are being consumed at an annual rate roughly equivalent to the total ore reserves of Chambishi, only guarantee an average life of some 22 years. Of course, many factors could influence this deceptively simple calculation, such as advances in mining and metallurgical techniques. Possibly more important is the recent replacement of the ad valorem royalty and export tax by a revised tax system based entirely on profitability. This tax, while influencing the existing mines and resulting in some lowering of cut-off grades, is designed to promote the development of comparatively low-grade mineralization that previously could not be mined economically (see Chapter 6). If achieved, this object would do more in the long run than any prospecting program to increase the ore reserves and eventually, the rate of production.

Just how essential this expansion is if Zambia is to retain its position as the world's third largest copper producer is illustrated by the following statistics abstracted from the 1969 Mining Yearbook of Zambia. Between 1967 and 1969, world copper production expanded at an average rate of 7.8 percent; Zambia's production expanded at little more than half this rate (4.2 percent), despite the recovery from the effects of Southern Rhodesia's Unilateral Declaration of Independence

and the ensuing fuel shortages. As a result, the percentage of world
copper production attributable to Zambia dropped from 13.1 to 12.2
percent. Equally important to bear in mind is the fact that, whatever
advances may be made in the technological fields and whatever tax
system may be adopted, the Copperbelt has a finite life.

LEGISLATION GOVERNING PROSPECTING AND MINING [13]

Prior to the Mining Proclamation of 1912, prospecting and mining
rights were granted by the British South Africa Company on the basis
of individual agreements, usually in the form of an exchange of letters,
that often were extremely complex. The earliest grants assigned mineral rights, and often surface rights as well, in areas to be located by
the grantee and the right to subsequently peg and work locations within
these areas. The company retained the right to participate; that is,
any minerals discovered were held on joint account with the Chartered
Company. Some of the more important areas that were pegged during
this period include North Charterland (10,000 square miles), the Big
Concession (700 square miles,[14] the so-called Rhokats blocks, and
Kansanshi.

The Mining Proclamation of 1912, which was based on the mining
law of Southern Rhodesia, introduced a more systematic approach to
the granting and registration of prospecting and mining rights, and all
previous rights were converted, with any specific provisions written
into existing Special Grants retained. (In 1934, the 1912 Mining Proclamation was incorporated into the Revised Edition of the Laws of Northern Rhodesia, as Chapter 91.) It is significant that the British South
Africa Company regarded all licences as contracts between the company and the licencees, and many of the more important provisions
regulating the activities of the holder were written into the licence
itself and were not stated in the Mining Proclamation (see Chapter 2).

Inter alia, the Mining Proclamation provided for the issue of
ordinary prospecting licences that carried the right to peg one mining
location. In 1936, a revised form of licence, valid for one year only,
was introduced, and in 1948 a further revision permitted the pegging
of more than one mining location. Development work had to be undertaken or inspection fees on a sliding scale paid in lieu to "protect" a
mining location, but because of carry-over and transfer provisions it
was possible to protect a claim over a long period by work done in
previous years or on contiguous claims. No inspection fees were
payable once a claim had been "worked for profit," and hence many

locations surrounding small, old mines continued to exist virtually in perpetuity. The British South Africa Company retained a one-third interest in all locations pegged, other than alluvial and coal claims, and could exercise this interest at the time formal permission was requested to work for profit, at which time nominal location fees also became payable (these fees were payable to the Crown, while all other fees or rents were payable to the Chartered Company). In 1948, a provision was introduced whereby the location holder could opt to pay royalty on the gross value of the mineral production and in effect escape the participation clause. The 1953 version of the licence incorporated provision for the payment of different royalty rates on copper, lead, and zinc production, but these rates were not stated. In 1957, uranium was added to this list.

The concessions or exclusive prospecting licences issued in the 1920's were in effect special grants of prospecting rights individually negotiated between the British South Africa Company and the holders. For this reason, they are both complex and variable. The holder was committed to certain minimum capital requirements, and the British South Africa Company had the right to an allotment of fully paid-up shares. The licence was for a specific area for a stated period, usually with an option to renew, and carried minimum expenditure obligations. The Chartered Company's right to participate in any resulting mining venture usually was commuted for a royalty payment provision in the agreements relating to subsequent Special Grants. In the case of copper and lead, this royalty was calculated on a sliding scale based on London Metal Exchange prices.

Special Grants of mining rights also took the form of private contracts and again varied in their detailed provisions. The Special Grant areas were regarded as consisting of blocks equivalent in size to a mining location: 2.7 million square feet in the case of base metals. Rent was payable on the whole area, and location fees were payable on any blocks being worked for profit. The areas not being worked were subject to minimum development provisions—in effect a complex minimum direct expenditure obligation—or to a rising scale of inspection fees that reached a maximum of £30 per location after five years. However, the holder could concentrate his efforts on any part of the Special Grant, and the greater part could remain virtually unexplored. Therefore, for all practical purposes the Special Grants existed in perpetuity, provided certain minimal obligations were discharged.

The Mining Ordinance of 1958, which vested all mineral rights in the Crown subject to the rights of the Chartered Company, was for all practical purposes little more than an elaboration of the 1912 Mining

Proclamation, but it did introduce administrative changes and more comprehensive mining regulations that in effect comprised a code of safe mining practice. It also required licence holders to report at regular intervals to the Government Mining Engineer. Once again, many of the conditions under which the various forms of licences and grants were held were not prescribed but were written into the actual licences and were not significantly different from those previously applicable. Moreover, all the previously pegged Special Grants continued to exist under the terms and conditions under which they were originally granted. The 1960 version of the ordinary prospecting licence included for the first time provision for acquiring Building Mineral Permits or Special Grants in respect of building and industrial minerals, and the scale of inspection fees payable in lieu of minimum development on mining locations was raised to a maximum level of £80. The British South Africa Company's one-third participation clause was dropped, provision was made for the payment of royalties on all mineral production, and in the case of copper, cobalt, lead, and zinc the complex sliding scales based on London Metal Exchange prices were set out in detail.

Following independence, the mineral rights formerly held by the British South Africa Company and the Crown were vested in the President on behalf of the Republic of Zambia. All other existing rights, including the special rights of the Litunga, were preserved. Minor modifications introduced gave rights of entry to the Director of the Geological Survey in order to map and prospect and provided for the copying of all prospecting reports to him. In the ordinary prospecting licence, the scale of inspection fees was again modified and raised to a maximum of £120 after only two years (previously five years).

In 1968, the Zambian Government enacted legislation in an attempt to force the companies to expand prospecting activity in the Special Grant areas and a new rising scale of inspection fees became applicable to sections of the grants that were not being prospected. However, it would have taken some years for the fees to reach a sufficiently high level enough to make a significant impact, and the 1969 reforms were introduced before this could happen.

Another significant development in 1968 was the announcement by the President, as part of the Mulungushi reforms, that in the future only Zambian citizens would be able to obtain Building Mineral Permits to work such materials as sand, clay, and stone. In practice, this mainly affected small-scale operators since the large quarries were for the most part protected by Special Grants. However, two years

later the President further stipulated that by the end of 1971 only
Zambian citizens or companies wholly owned by Zambians would be
licenced to produce building materials.

The 1968 Mulungushi speech foreshadowed the 1969 invitation
to the major mining companies to sell to the Government a 51-percent
share in the operating mines and included the statement that new mining
legislation would be introduced with effect from January 1, 1970. Thus,
the Mines and Minerals Act of 1969[15] is an integral part of the sweeping
reforms announced by President Kaunda in his Matero speech, when
he stated inter alia (1) that all rights of ownership or partial ownership in minerals must revert to the State; (2) that the Litunga's special
rights would be terminated; (3) that the State would retain the right to
take up a 51-percent share of the equity in any future mine and would
pay its share of pre-production costs; (4) that Special Grant areas in
which no prospecting activity had taken place since independence
would revert to the State; (5) that other Special Grants would be converted to prospecting and exploration areas and existing mines would
be protected by mining licences, valid in the first instance for 25 years;
and (6) that an operator working under a tribute agreement would himself have the right to apply for a mining licence.

These reforms were embodied in the 1969 Mines and Minerals
Act, which came into effect on January 1, 1970. This act adopted an
entirely new approach to prospecting and mining activity in Zambia,
particularly insofar as any form of licence conveys statutory obligations as well as rights. The act also gives practical effect to the
spirit of the reforms, i.e. to attempt to balance the natural desire of
the Government to have a controlling interest in the exploitation of
the country's most important natural resources and the legitimate
profit motive of the companies that provide the technical expertise
and much of the required capital. At the same time, provisions have
been made to promote the conservation and best use of Zambia's
mineral wealth.

All mineral rights—that is rights of ownership, searching for,
mining, and disposal of minerals—are now vested in the President on
behalf of the Republic of Zambia. All preexisting mining rights were
extinguished by the introduction of the act, but it included provision
for the immediate granting of mining licences to protect the producing
mines. These licences were valid for six months and were then renewed under the conditions laid down in the act for up to 25 years.
Memoranda of understanding with the Anglo-American and Roan Selection Trust groups guaranteed these companies the first option to acquire prospecting and mining rights over agreed areas that represented

approximately 12 percent of the ground they formerly held under prospecting licences.16 Although the Government considered that the original areas were excessively large, almost completely tying up the most promising parts of the country, the intention was not to inhibit prospecting but rather to pressure the companies to concentrate their activities. The companies for their part indicated their intention of maintaining the level of expenditures on prospecting insofar as it was practical to do so.

The Anglo-American and RST groups also agreed to surrender all Special Grants in which no prospecting had taken place since 1964 and certain others that had been prospected but were not considered by the groups to include mineralization likely to prove economically viable in the immediate future. Most of the Copperbelt Special Grants were redelineated and scheduled as mining licence areas in the act. The others were trimmed down and scheduled in the memoranda of understanding referred to earlier or were surrendered.

Under the 1969 Mines and Minerals Act, the minerals for which licences may be issued are divided into four major categories: (1) building minerals (sand, clay, gravel, laterite, limestone, etc.); (2) industrial minerals (nonmetallic minerals such as graphite, gypsum, mica, and talc, and sands and clays when used for industrial purposes); (3) reserved minerals (mineral oils, gas, diamonds, emeralds, gold, the platinum group, and radioactive minerals); and (4) all other minerals.

The various forms of mining rights are: prospecting licences, exploration licences, and mining licences. Licences in respect of reserved minerals differ only insofar as they include conditions relating to the disposal of any reserved minerals ultimately mined. (The rights referring to building and industrial minerals are somewhat different; prospecting licences, mining licences, and mineral permits.) The serial nature of the licence system permits the applicant to proceed in a logical manner through prospecting and exploration phases until an orebody has been proved, in which case he has the right to apply for a mining licence. Once a prospecting licence has been issued, the issue of subsequent exploration and mining licences is obligatory, provided that the holder has discharged his obligations, can show reasonable evidence of mineralization, and proposes an acceptable plan for the next stage. (The right to obtain subsequent licences is safeguarded by a right of appeal to a Mining Affairs Tribunal.)

All prospecting licences include a condition giving the State the option, through Mindeco, to acquire up to 51 percent of the equity in any company formed to exploit any orebody discovered (see Appendix

D). The State will of course pay its share of the prospecting and exploration costs involved in the discovery of the orebody and the development of the mine.

An applicant for a prospecting licence must show that he has the financial resources and technical competence to carry out his proposed program of operations, which must accompany his application. Obviously, this program must be consistent with the size of the area applied for and the group of minerals for which it is intended to prospect, and the funds and personnel available must be adequate. The program also should take into account any previous work done in the area concerned. The applicant must state the groups of minerals in which he is interested and, provided that his program proves that the proposed prospecting methods could be reasonably expected to locate any economically significant occurrences of such minerals, all the minerals referred to in the application will be included in the licence (provided of course that there is no overlap with existing exploration, mining, or prospecting areas for the same minerals).

In the drafting of the 1969 Mines and Minerals Act, four possible approaches to ensure that holders of mining rights maintained an acceptable level of activity were considered: (1) a limitation to the period of time for which any particular right is valid (2) minimum expenditure obligations, (3) penalties if the holder fails to conform to an approved program, and (4) an obligation to surrender a proportion of the area after a given period of time. The solution adopted embodies all four approaches. A prospecting licence is valid for a maximum of four years and there is no right of renewal, although the holder may apply for a new licence over the whole or any part of his original area. An exploration licence is valid for up to three years with the right of renewal for a further two years, provided that the progress achieved is satisfactory and the program for future operations is adequate (in special circumstances, the period of renewal may be longer than two years). A mining licence is granted in the first instance for a maximum period of 25 years (15 years in the case of industrial minerals), depending mainly on the reserves proven, and it may be renewed for a similar period provided that the applicant can show that ore reserves remain to be exploited and submits a satisfactory program. The minimum expenditure obligations stipulated in the act are defined as direct expenditure and have been set at a low level as far as prospecting is concerned in order to encourage the use of new reconnaissance techniques over extensive areas. Except in the case of prospecting licences for industrial or building minerals, there is no provision for payment of any form of rent since it was considered preferable that funds set aside by a licence holder for prospecting or mining be spent on such items as actual field activities.

The annual minimum expenditure obligations are as follows:

Prospecting Licence

Building and industrial minerals: K15 per square mile.

Other minerals: K25 per square mile.

Exploration Licence

Initial grant

First year: K2,000 per square mile.

Second year: K4,000 per square mile.

Third year: K6,000 per square mile.

Renewal period: K10,000 per square mile per year.

Strong emphasis is placed on the requirement that any applicant for any form of licence shall submit a program of his intended operations. This program is one of the more important criteria used in assessing applications, and in effect the issue of a licence means that the program is approved. The licence holder must then proceed to prospect or mine in accordance with his program or any approved amendments; and if he fails to do so, he will be in default and liable to forfeiture. He must submit quarterly reports to demonstrate that he has conformed, and so that all relevant information is safeguarded for future reference. This information remains confidential for the period of validity of the licence concerned. Within six months of the termination of any right, a comprehensive final report and an audited account of expenditures must be submitted. Except in the case of a renewal of an exploration licence, the geological information embodied in this final report is not regarded as confidential, and therefore data relating to areas that may be the subject of an application for some other form of licence must be excluded.

No limitation is placed on the size of prospecting areas. However, these are limited in practice, partly by the minimum expenditure obligations but more effectively by the program of operations, since every applicant must prove that he has the financial resources and technical staff available to carry out his program effectively. There is no stipulated requirement that a prospecting licence holder must at any stage reduce his area by a minimum proportion; such a restriction was considered unnecessary in view of the comparatively short maximum period of validity of a prospecting licence, after which the holder in effect reduces his area to one or more exploration areas.

Exploration areas are limited to a maximum of ten square miles but, if an applicant can outline geological evidence indicating that a more extensive orebody may exist, he may apply for more than one adjacent area. This provision ensures that very large areas cannot be held for long periods with all the work confined to one small portion, as exploration would have to proceed in each of the adjacent areas according to approved programs.

The holder of a prospecting or exploration licence has the right to obtain one or more mining licences, subject to any conditions written into the original prospecting licence. At this stage, the State must exercise its option to participate if it intends to do so. As in the case of applications for prospecting and exploration licences, applications cannot be rejected on the ground that the proposed program is unsatisfactory unless reasonable opportunity has been given for amendments to be proposed and accepted; as noted earlier, the holder of any licence also has a right of appeal to a Mining Affairs Tribunal in the event of a refusal to issue a subsequent licence.

A mining licence holder must report his production monthly and submit an annual report of his activities. He also must submit annually a proposed program of future operations and, at intervals of two years, a geological report describing the exploration undertaken, in particular the current position regarding ore reserves.

In taking over the mineral rights, the State has had to assume responsibility for ensuring the best use and conservation of the mineral resources. Thus, the Chief Mining Engineer is obliged to call upon the holder of a mining licence to cease using wasteful mining or metallurgical practices if he considers that the use of such practices is not justified by circumstances. However, his decision is subject to appeal by the holder to the Mining Affairs Tribunal. A further provision to promote optimum development lies in the right of the Minister responsible for mines to direct that neighboring operations be coordinated or merged if he considers that this would result in more efficient working.

1970 AND THE FUTURE

As the 1969 Mines and Minerals Act and the take-over of the operating mining companies have only been effective for a very short period of time, it is still too early to assess the possible long-term effects. In the short term, the possibility of obtaining prospecting rights in areas adjacent to the Copperbelt and on the Copperbelt itself undoubtedly captured the attention of mining interests in many parts of the world; however, this interest was to an extent tempered by the effect of the 51-percent takeover (insofar as it affected confidence in capital investment in Zambia generally), the state participation clause to be incorporated in all future licences, and the tax situation.

In the first three months of 1970, the Chief Mining Engineer and the Director of the Geological Survey Department were inundated with inquiries relating to the new act and requests for geological information concerning the areas that had been relinquished by the Anglo-American and RST groups. These inquiries stemmed from companies based in North America (Canada and the United States), Western Europe (Britain, France, and Italy), Eastern Europe (Czechoslovakia, Yugoslavia, and Roumania), Asia (Japan), and South Africa. It is a measure of the interest shown that the majority of interested companies sent senior technical personnel to Lusaka to examine the great mass of available data. It is also a measure of the degree of cooperation and goodwill that existed between Government and the local companies that the bulk of this information was provided on very short notice and that the companies supplemented it by answering individual inquiries in detail.

Interest of course centered on the Copperbelt; Mokambo was regarded by many as the most promising area since economically significant mineralization had been to a large extent proved by an extensive diamond drilling program. (More than 90,000 feet of drilling had been completed on this property by RST.) Information concerning areas adjacent to the Copperbelt and its possible extension to the west—the former Chisangwa and Mwinilunga areas—was also very much in demand, and there was some interest in the more widely scattered possibilities that had been prospected in some detail and where mineralization of possible economic potential had at least been demonstrated to exist (e.g., Sebembere). The majority of the inquirers were concerned with the prospects for copper mineralization, but some also were interested in the potential for other metals. For example, Somiren, an Italian company, ultimately applied for a prospecting licence for radioactive minerals over a large area west of the Copperbelt and south of Katanga, and this company has since flown an extensive airborne spectrometer survey.

The impression gained was that the majority of the companies and organizations concerned were favorably impressed by the Mines and Minerals Act, particularly insofar as the rights and obligations of

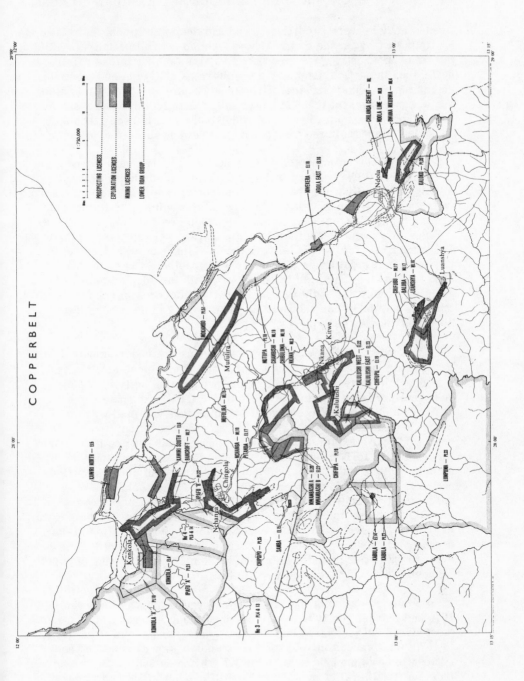

COPPERBELT

licence holders were precisely stated and the commitment as to State participation was made clear. Those who did not follow up their initial interests apparently were discouraged by the tax provisions relating to new mines in particular and by possible rates of return on investment, rather than by other considerations (see Chapter 8). There was also some disappointment that the known mineralization in the areas released was in no way comparable to that which had recently been taken up by Japanese interests in the Congo under somewhat similar circumstances.

This phase culminated in the issue of a group of new licences in April 1970. The holders included Suico, a consortium of Mitsui Mining and Smelting Company and Continental Ore Corporation; Somiren (with separate licence areas for copper and uranium), an Italian company in the ENI group; Geomin, a Roumanian organization; and Sidco, a Yugoslav group. In addition, certain options were granted to Equitex Petroleum Limited. A decision regarding Mokambo was deferred, but this former Special Grant ultimately was granted as an exploration area to Geomin. This was in conformity with the adopted policy of granting exploration rather than prospecting licences in respect of those areas where considerable previous work had been done; Sebembere was another example.[17]

Of course, at this stage all these groups are undertaking only preliminary phases of their programs, and it will be some time before it is possible to assess whether or not prospecting activity actually has been increased significantly. In this regard, of course a great deal will also depend on the extent to which RST and Anglo-American maintain their levels of activity. To date, the operating mines have continued active exploration in their licence areas, and both the Anglo-American and RST groups have continued to prospect not only the remaining 12 percent of their original concessions but also the exploration areas they have pegged within them. This should lead to final assessment in the near future of the economic potential of several promising prospects. De Beers has also continued prospecting, again in greatly reduced prospecting areas centered on exploration areas pegged over occurrences of previously discovered kimberlite. However, to date no diamonds other than extremely small stones of purely academic interest have been recovered.

Some indication of the level of prospecting activity achieved in 1970 and planned for 1971 can be obtained from the proposed expenditures listed in the applications for prospecting and exploration licences. In 1970, total expenditure by all licence holders on prospecting and exploration was planned to be some K3 million—a substantial reduction from the 1969 level of more than K5 million—but in 1971 the figure is

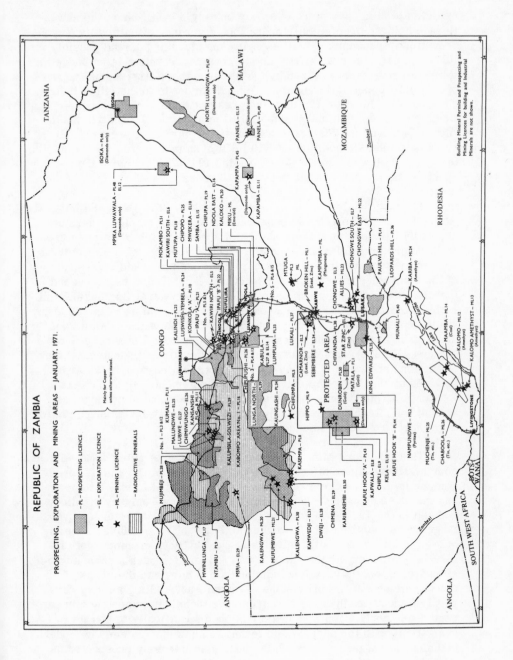

REPUBLIC OF ZAMBIA

PROSPECTING AND EXPLORATION AND MINING AREAS — JANUARY, 1971.

— PL — PROSPECTING LICENCE

— EL — EXPLORATION LICENCE

— ML — MINING LICENCE

— RADIOACTIVE MINERALS

Mainly for Copper unless otherwise stated.

Building Mineral Permits and Prospecting and Mining Licences for building and Industrial Minerals are not shown.

85

expected to rise once more to approximately K5 million as the new
licence holders become fully operational. An indication that an apparent
reduction in expenditure by the Anglo-American group (and possibly
RST as well) is at least partly due to conservative long-term budgeting
in licence programs is given by a statement in the first annual report
of Zambia Copper Investments. This statement is to the effect that
Zamanglo Exploration Limited (the prospecting arm of the Anglo-
American group, originally established jointly with the British South
Africa Company as Chartered Exploration Limited) is provisionally
planning a total expenditure of K10 million on prospecting areas outside
the Copperbelt over the five-year period 1971-75, i.e. more than was
spent by the company in the previous 13 years.

Thus, the major immediate effects of the 1969 Mines and Minerals
Act as far as prospecting is concerned have been twofold. There undoubtedly has been an intensification of activity which is now centered
on the more promising areas and prospects, leaving other large areas
open for reconnaissance. There also has been a marked diversification
of the companies involved in prospecting. It is of interest to record
that this diversification has been reflected elsewhere; Zamanglo Exploration Limited recently announced that the shareholding in the company
would be split between the original holders and Japanese (Mitsui and
Mitsubishi Trading Companies), French (Bureau de Recherche Géolo-
gique et Minière), and Italian (Somiren) companies. Undoubtedly, the
attraction here was the opportunity to obtain an interest in the areas
retained by the Anglo-American group, supplemented by the use of
Zamanglo Exploration's technical facilities and local knowledge, as
against the alternative of establishing a new locally-based organization
to prospect a recently abandoned area.

The Mines and Minerals Act has had two other immediate, although
comparatively minor effects. First, the interest of the small-worker
community has been revived, although this has still to prove to be of
any major significance. The British South Africa Company's policy,
adopted in the 1920's, of issuing exclusive prospecting licences over
large areas inhibited small-worker activity until the 1960's, when the
Survey of Minor Deposits Unit was set up partly to promote their interests. However, by that time it was too late for such a change to be
effective, as only a very few individuals had survived the years of
discouragement. The provisions of the new act, calling as they do for
proof of adequate financial resources and technical competence in support of any application, are again designed specifically to attract organizations with the backing and technical know-how to employ modern
techniques on a large scale. In a country as intensely prospected as
Zambia, where there seems little possibility of any significant surface

indications of base metal mineralization having been overlooked, this was the only reasonable approach. However, the individual can meet these requirements provided he is prepared to tailor his ambitions to his resources, and it is a possibility, although a remote one, that small-working may once more become a significant part of the mining scene in Zambia, as it is for example in Chile.

The second comparatively minor effect relates to the provisions regarding programs and reporting of progress. As a result of these provisions, it is already apparent that Government and Mindeco can keep a close watch on the future plans and progress of all involved in mining and prospecting. Moreover, the reporting procedures also ensure that a great deal of valuable information is safeguarded for the future.

There can be little doubt that the immediate effects of the Mines and Minerals Act have been beneficial. However, the extent to which development will ultimately follow must depend largely on Government maintaining the balance between its interests and those of the companies concerned. Only time will show whether or not a climate can be established in which long-term development will flourish.

NOTES

1. Fillipo Pigafetta, A Report on the Kingdom of Congo, 1591 (Reprinted, New York: Negroes University Press, 1969). Originally published in 1881 by John Murray, London.

2. A comprehensive summary is given in J. A. Bancroft, Mining in Northern Rhodesia (London: British South Africa Company, 1961).

3. Ibid.

4. G. W. H. Relly, "Address" at the Open Day of the CIPEC inauguration conference, (Lusaka, June 1967).

5. Bancroft, op. cit.

6. T. D. Guernsey, "A Summary of the Provisional Geological Features of Northern Rhodesia," Colonial Geology and Mineral Resources, No. 1, 1950, pp. 121-51.

7. W. H. Reeve, "The Geology and Mineral Resources of Northern Rhodesia," Bulletin of the Geological Survey of Northern Rhodesia, No. 3, 1963.

8. G. J. Snowball and J. H. Carter, Exclusive Prospecting Areas and Special Grants in Zambia (to be published as an Economic Report of the Geological Survey of Zambia).

9. Relly, op. cit.

10. F. C. Kruger, "Mining, a Business for Professionals Only," Mining Engineer, XXI, 1969, pp. 83-88.

11. D. R. de Vletter, "Significant Changes and Developments in Zambian Mineral Industry," Geologie en Mijnbouw, XLIX, 1970, pp. 339-42.

12. A. D. McMahon "Copper, a Materials Survey, "U.S. Bureau of Mines Information Circular 8225.

13. A comprehensive historical account of legislation governing prospecting and mining is given in H. M. Williams, The Mining Law of Northern Rhodesia (London: British South Africa Company, Anglo-American Corporation of South Africa Limited, and the RST Group of Companies).

14. The complex history of the Big Concession is described in M. Cikin and A. R. Drysdall, The Geology of the Country of North-West of Mumbwa (The Big Concession); Explanation of Degree Sheet 1426 South-East Quarter, Report of the Geological Survey of Zambia, No. 26 (in press).

15. See A. R. Drysdall and E. J. Langevad, "Zambia's New Mines and Minerals Act," Mining Magazine, CXXII, 1970, pp. 266-77; and, by the same authors, "The Mines and Mineral Act 1969 and the Mineral Tax Act 1970," Economic Report of the Geological Survey of Zambia, No. 26, 1970.

16. Cf. Ibid. for maps showing these areas.

17. To overcome certain legal complications, prospecting licences that were valid for only three months but carried the right to apply for exploration licences were issued.

4

GROWTH SINCE INDEPENDENCE[1]

At Independence in late 1964, Zambia inherited an economy with very limited supplies of capital in the physical sense but with an effectively unlimited supply of capital in the monetary sense. This money came from the acquisition of mineral royalties on the eve of independence (see Chapter 2), and from the ending of the Federation of Rhodesia and Nyasaland, during which revenue from the copper mines was used to develop Southern Rhodesia. As it happened, the copper price moved unsteadily upward after 1964, so that, despite very rapid increases in government spending, there was an excess of revenue over the total of capital and current spending in 1969, as there had been in 1964 and most of the years between. At the same time, export earnings rose sufficiently to give a surplus on the balance of payments current account in 1969 for the fourth time in five years, during which period foreign exchange reserves rose substantially.

The ending of the Federation of Rhodesia and Nyasaland also gave Zambia an opportunity to protect its industrial sector for the first time.

Under these conditions, the economy grew rapidly. But at the end of 1969 a great many of the structural problems inherited in 1964 not only remained but in some cases had grown worse. Table 4.1, for example, shows the relative rates of growth of different sectors of the economy.

89

TABLE 4.1

Growth in Gross Domestic Product
at Current Prices, 1964-68
(at factor cost; millions of Kwacha)

	1964	1968	Percentage Change
Mining[a]	230	389	+69
Agriculture[b]	53	66	+25
Manufacturing	28	76	+171
Construction	20	63	+215
Government administration	21	46	+119
Trade	46	115	+150
Other	76	177	+133
GDP at factor cost[a]	474	932	+97

[a]The figures for mining and total GDP at factor cost include royalty and export tax, which were charged on production and therefore are theoretically indirect taxes but in practice have the same effect as profits taxes. For further discussion of this point, see Charles Harvey, "Inflation in a Very Open Economy: Zambia 1964-69," Eastern African Economic Review, Vol. III, No. 1 (June, 1971), Appendix 2.

[b]The figures for agriculture include both marketed production and farmers' consumption of own products. They conceal the departure of many expatriate farmers, an increase in productivity of those remaining, the formation of some new sectors such as sugar and day-old chick production, and a rising trend in the marketed output of Zambian farmers. The estimates of farmers' consumption of own products are extremely vague.

Source: Monthly Digest of Statistics (Lusaka: Central Statistical Office, 1971).

Despite the very high rates of growth achieved in all the non-mining sectors except agriculture, the proportion of GDP accounted for by mining alone fell from 49 percent to 42 percent, and in 1969 (for which official figures were not available by March 1971) a higher copper price, plus virtual stagnation in the rest of the economy, meant that the proportion of GDP attributable to mining had climbed back to 46 percent. In addition, the annual rate of growth decreased steadily from 1964 to 1968 as follows: 1965, +30 percent; 1966, +25 percent; 1967, +12 percent; 1968, +9 percent. Furthermore, a large part of the increase can be attributed to the rising copper price. Although this leaves the country better off in real terms, it cannot be relied upon for future growth and may of course reverse itself. Finally, prices rose internally, by some 30 percent, so that real GDP only rose by about 50 percent.

The enormous increases in spending underlying the growth shown in Table 4.1 were led by Government spending, and particularly by Government capital spending (see Table 4.2).

Other factors contributing to the large increases in spending were the excess liquidity of the commercial banks at independence, coupled with the absence of any official control of increases in advances, and rapid increases in earnings especially after the large increase granted to the African copper miners in 1966. In addition to these increases in demand, there were severe constraints on increases in supply, not only because of the shortage of skilled man-power and lack of spare capacity in industry but also because the Southern Rhodesian Unilateral Declaration of Independence created a transport crisis that slowed up or prevented the delivery of imports. Given these circumstances, it may be considered remarkable that prices rose by only 30 percent or so between 1964 and 1968.

The highest annual rate of inflation occurred in the second half of 1967 and the first half of 1968, when it was over 15 percent. Although this very high rate of increase was almost certainly the result of earlier wage increases, increases in cost of imports, and physical constraints on imports and these effects had temporarily worked themselves out by the second half of 1968,[2] the Government reacted with the first serious counterinflationary measures since independence. The first set of economic reforms, announced at Mulungushi in April 1968 (see Chapter 5) gave the Government effective control over commercial bank lending, which was vigorously used. In the budget of January 1969, Government spending was cut back sharply (see Table 4.3), and there were some small increases in tax rates. The following year's budget reinforced this trend, with the result that growth was

TABLE 4.2

Changes in Spending, 1964-68
(at current prices; millions of Kwacha)

	1964	1968	Percentage Change
Private consumption	250	471	+88
Government current expenditure[a]	59	124	+110
Government capital expenditure[b]	28	190	+579
Private capital formation[b]	48	76	+58
Net change in stocks	-19	+51	-
Domestic expenditure	367	912	+149

[a] Government current expenditure is taken from the National Expenditure Table (Table 56) in the Monthly Digest of Statistics and thus excludes such items as transfer payments. Total current spending by Government rose by a similar percentage, 113 percent.

[b] Gross fixed capital formation is not broken down in the National Expenditure Table into public and private sectors; the figures for Government capital expenditure are taken from Government spending figures and those for private capital formation are residuals.

Sources: Monthly Digest of Statistics and Annual Estimates of Revenue and Expenditure (Lusaka: Central Statistical Office, 1971).

almost completely halted, except in the price of copper. Furthermore, the whole force of the cutback in government spending fell on the capital budget, thus endangering future as well as present growth.

Table 4.3 shows how total government spending in 1970 was actually below the level of 1968, despite the continued increases in current spending. Not only did the economy cease to grow but employment also stagnated and employment in construction, hardest hit by the greatly reduced capital budget, actually fell. Any chance of reaching the development plan target of 100,000 new jobs by 1970,[3]

TABLE 4.3

Government Spending, 1968-70
(millions of Kwacha)

	Actual 1968	Estimated 1969	Actual 1969	Actual 1970
Current spending	216	190	223	242
Capital spending	190	127	144	150
Total	406	317	367	392

Source: Monthly Digest of Statistics and Annual Estimates of Revenue and Expenditure (Lusaka: Central Statistical Office, 1971).

which already had been rendered unlikely by the rapid rise in wages, faded completely (see Table 4.4 for figures on wages and employment, 1964-69). Inflation did slow right down—it was less than 2 percent in 1969 and probably no more in 1970—but this was bought at high cost, much higher than was necessary. However, criticism of over-reaction by the Government to an inflation that had in any case slowed down before most of the tough measures were introduced is only possible using statistics that were not available at the time.

The 1971 budget planned for a 20 percent increase in total Government spending, indicating that growth would probably be resumed in the short term. However, more than 80 percent of the increase was budgeted for current expenditure, reinforcing the trend against the capital account evident since 1968.

ECONOMIC STRUCTURE: EXPORTS

Despite the rapid growth in sectors of the economy other than copper mining (see Table 4.1), Zambia remains utterly dependent on copper. Although by African standards Zambia's manufacturing sector is large—as large for example as that of Kenya—the country still relies almost entirely on copper for exports and thus for the imports that keep the manufacturing sector, and virtually everything else in the modern sector, in being.

TABLE 4.4

Wages and Employment in Zambia, 1964-69
(percentage change)

	1965	1966	1967	1968	1969
Increase in African earnings[a]	+12	+12	+39	+18	n.a.
Increase in African employment[b]	+10	+9.5	+6	+3	+.5

[a]Earnings figures for 1967 and 1968 are for fourth quarter only.
[b]Employment figures are yearly averages except for 1969, which compares June 1969 with June 1968.

Source: Monthly Digest of Statistics (Lusaka: Central Statistical Office, various issues).

One of the main strategies of development since independence has been to reduce dependence on copper. However, so far this approach has taken the form of import substitution rather than development of alternative exports. Indeed, other exports actually have diminished in relative importance (see Table 4.5) and have shown no real sign of growth.

The increase in copper exports proceeds, and thus the increase in copper's proportion of exports by value, is mainly the result of increasing copper prices. Only in 1969 did the volume of copper exports, at 747,000 metric tons, exceed the 1965 figure of just over 680,000 metric tons, and one of the reasons for the high 1969 figure was the smelting of concentrates stockpiled during the fuel shortages of 1966 and 1967.

The policy of import substitution has begun to work, in a limited way. From 1964 to 1968, import volume rose by 80 percent while gross domestic expenditure rose by 98 percent. For some of this time, there were physical constraints on imports, mainly because of the transport crisis following Rhodesia's unilateral declaration of independence. However, toward the end of 1968, the oil pipeline from Dar-es-Salaam was completed, which increased the capacity of the Dar road for other imports. Slightly earlier, greater use began to be made of the Benguela

TABLE 4.5

Zambian Exports, 1964-69
(millions of Kwacha)

	1964	1965	1966	1967	1968	1969
Copper	297	343	461	434	516	725
Other minerals	16	17	18	17	15	23
Other visible	23	20	15	19	13	19
Total	336	380	493	470	544	767
Copper as a percent- age of the total	88	90	93	93	95	95

Source: Monthly Digest of Statistics (Lusaka: Central Statistical Office, various issues).

Railway from Lobito to Angola (see Chapter 5, Table 5.2). At least in 1969, the problem eased, as shown by the small fall in total imports in 1969 (from K325 million to K312 million).

Opportunities for import substitution were many at independence. The Federation of Rhodesia and Nyasaland was a common market with its main growth points at Salisbury and Bulawayo in Southern Rhodesia, and before the Federation both territories were part of what amounted to a customs union with South Africa. Independence thus gave Zambia its first chance to protect infant industries. Of course, the big question is how many of these small, high-cost, import-dependent infants will take root, grow up, and become capable of exporting. Although reduction of dependence on imports in itself reduces the economy's dependence on copper, imports undoubtedly will continue to grow (in part to service the new industries), and thus new exports must be found.

The size of Zambia's internal market—4 million people of whom perhaps one-quarter live in or near towns and 350,000 have wage-earning jobs—precludes large-scale and thus competitive manufacturing in all but a few fields. An application to join the East African Common Market was submitted by Zambia at the end of 1967, but discussions on Zambia's application were suspended immediately after the military takeover in Uganda.

In any case, with the experience of membership in the Federation, the initial Zambian approach was one of caution. The economic advantages of membership in the East African Economic Community depend on the extent to which the trade diversion costs of accepting the East African common external tariff are minimized and on the increased possibilities for Zambian exports to establish markets in East Africa. There already is an increased flow of goods from East Africa (Kenya in particular), which arose following the use of alternative routes and Zambia's attempt to disengage from Southern Africa. Possibilities do exist for Zambian mine-based industries to establish markets in East Africa and, as a member of the enlarged Community, Zambia should be able to secure its share of investment in Community-based industries. However, the inability of the current partner states in the East African Economic Community (Kenya, Uganda, and Tanzania) to rationalize their investment policy for Community-based industries prevents much optimism with regard to investment allocation.*

Congo (Kinshasa) would in many ways be a more logical partner for Zambia, but for many reasons—linguistic, cultural, political—this idea has not been actively pursued. Because of the uncertainties of the future for the East African Community after the military takeover in Uganda, it could be that new economic groupings will arise in Eastern Africa. Only in a common market with a powerful investment allocation policy does land-locked Zambia stand much chance of developing manufactured exports, except in industries based on local raw materials (including of course the processing of agricultural products) and industries that service the mining industry, in some of which Zambia has a real comparative advantage.

The other possibility is agriculture, which undoubtedly has a vast potential. In addition, if successful, agricultural development would reach through to the largest and poorest section of the population. In 1969, Zambia imported K30 million worth of food per annum and exported K3 million of tobacco (down from K5 million in 1961-64)

---

*For example, in East Africa there are two oil refineries, two tire plants, two fertilizer plants, and at least four steel mills. Most of these plants have the capacity to meet the requirements of the entire East African Economic Community market.

and small amounts of timber and groundnuts. The development of agriculture since independence is a confused picture because of the departure of many large-scale expatriate farmers who dominated the sales figures in several crops. Clearly, the first priority is supply of the rapidly growing home market, which in itself would be a considerable feat. If and when export surpluses appear, the marketing problem, in a world increasingly riddled with quota agreements for agricultural exports, is considerable, and the price and growth prospects are poor in many items. In the words of Arthur Lewis:

> There is a booming demand for cereals, for meat and for some kind of fruit and vegetables. But these are not what the underdeveloped countries mainly export. They export coffee, tea, cocoa, sugar, cotton and rubber, all of which are a drag on the market. The only agricultural export from underdeveloped countries which is doing well is vegetable oils.[4]

In Zambia's position, any agricultural export, however slowly growing, will reduce to some extent the dependence on copper. And Zambia, which is in a position to create its agricultural structure nearly from scratch at least as far as export sectors are concerned, can avoid getting into the depressing position of many agricultural exporters. Export surpluses in most products may be a long way in the future, but the opportunity exists to concentrate on products whose surpluses will be marketable.

OTHER ASPECTS OF DEPENDENCE ON COPPER

Inevitably, copper provides the bulk of the Government's tax revenue directly; from 49 percent to 61 percent according to the price of copper in the last few years. Indirectly, it provides far more, since the above figures do not include income tax on the salaries of copper company employees, not to mention government employees paid out of copper taxation and the indirect taxes paid by both groups. These, and other figures such as some 40 percent of GDP,* 15 percent of employment, and 25 percent of the wage bill are merely alternative ways of expressing the dominance of copper in Zambia.

---

*This figure conceals some ambiguities in the measurement of national income; see Table 4.1.

However, one aspect of copper's importance is worth elaborating briefly. Wages on the mines are much higher than elsewhere in the economy. In part, this is a product of the history and strength of the mining unions; in part it may also reflect the very high price of copper since independence and the political vulnerability of the mining companies before nationalization, both of which greatly weakened resistance to wage demands.

The African miners' union was one of the basic strengths of the independence movement; and one of the things that gave it strength was the sense of grievance over the huge differences between white and black miners' wages and over the lack of opportunities for African promotion. Of course, in part the income differences reflected relative skills, but in part they did not; in any case, the total dominance of the top jobs by expatriates who were also the ruling class, and the discrimination practiced in every field (not just in employment), made it inevitable that after independence a large settlement would be necessary to narrow the gap. Since mining wages set the pace in the economy (although, as already mentioned, they were considerably higher than other wages), it was also inevitable that wages in other sectors would follow. Wages in other sectors also must have had some momentum of their own—for much the same reasons as wages in mining—but it was the Brown Commission award in 1966[5] that really opened the floodgates and produced huge rises in earnings throughout the economy in 1967 (see Table 4.4).

The vast gap between wages of local people and expatriates, and the extent to which this gap has narrowed, can be seen in Table 4.6. The position since 1964 is partially obscured by Zambianization of many posts previously held by expatriates, which has pushed up the average wage in both groups without altering the overall average (except to the extent that Zambians' total emoluments are less). Insofar as it also narrows the gap, this process is of course relevant to the comparison.

Although African employees, mining and nonmining, have had a faster rate of growth in earnings, the original gap was so large that it has widened in absolute terms. This probably does not matter as much as one might expect, partly because a high rate of growth in earnings is itself satisfying and partly because barriers to promotion (and acquisition of skills) have been removed in the major industries. Indeed, at present the "barriers" are negative in large firms, in the sense that the drive for Zambianization is very strong; the situation may be different in small firms, especially at the management level (see Chapter 1). It is interesting that the Brown Commission wage

TABLE 4.6

Wage Differentials in 1964 and 1968
(Kwacha)

Average Wages	1964	1968	Percentage Change
All Africans	382	789	+106
African miners	732	1,248	+70
All non-Africans	3,294	5,150	+53
Non-African miners	4,875	7,604	+56

Source: Monthly Digest of Statistics (Lusaka: Central Statistical Office, various issues).

round in 1966 successfully bought industrial peace for longer than expected: only in 1970 did a second major round start.[6]

COPPER AND EXPORT INSTABILITY

Zambia is a classic case of export dependence on a single commodity with a highly volatile price. In 1970, for example, the monthly average copper price was as high as K1,250 (729) per metric ton in March and was down below K750 (437) per metric ton by the end of the year. Since a change of K10 per metric ton in the price of copper, if sustained for a year, alters export earnings by about K7 million, such earnings undoubtedly have been unstable.

But Zambia is also a classic case of a country that has gained more than it has lost from export instability. At K750 per metric ton, the copper price is still high enough to pay for the 1969 level of imports, including invisibles, expatriated profits, and expatriate savings remitted abroad. In other words, fluctuations in export proceeds above the level needed to give balance of payments equilibrium are uncomfortable to live with but cause little real hardship. They merely alter the rate of growth of the reserves. The balance of payments is threatened only if the fall is expected to continue and, provided the

country has adequate reserves, no steps need be taken in the short
term if the price falls below the balance of payments equilibrium point.
As it happens, the period since independence has seen the price of
copper almost continuously above that equilibrium point, and frequently
very far above it, so that the reserves have built up rapidly. At the
end of 1970, they were probably up to a year's imports (including
invisibles), and the country also has borrowing powers at the International Monetary Fund.

Copper price fluctuations in themselves have almost no effect
on the economy in the short term; they are reflected in government
revenue, profits remitted abroad, and profits retained in Zambia.
Since nationalization, the picture is very little changed if one includes
compensation payments in the category of profits remitted abroad.

When tax revenue fluctuates, it is usually difficult for government
to alter its spending plans quickly, up or down. Current spending is
almost impossible to reduce quickly in normal circumstances; that
is, unless government is prepared to reduce civil service salaries
or not to use capacity available from earlier capital spending, such
as schools and hospitals. Rather more surprisingly, it is almost as
hard to alter the rate of change of current spending upward, especially
if, as in Zambia, lack of skilled personnel forms a major bottleneck
so that many posts in government are unfilled anyway. Only if salaries
or subsidies are increased—which can be done more or less at the
stroke of a pen—can the growth rate of current spending be increased
quickly. This is not to say that current spending does not sometimes
increase upward very rapidly: rates of increase in the first two or
three years after independence were between 20 percent and 30 percent. But rapid acceleration is nearly as hard as rapid braking.

The second point about government spending is that it should
not be altered in response to changes in revenue from copper. A rise
in the copper price increases the country's capacity to import but not
its capacity to spend locally. Since almost all government spending
has some local content, its level should be determined according to
the internal capacity of the economy. This assumes, of course, that
no balance of payments constraint is operating, as has been the case
in Zambia throughout most of the period since independence. In any
case, provided that reserves and credit facilities are adequate, there
is no foreign exchange constraint in the short term even if the copper
price falls below the point of balance of payments equilibrium.

Profits remitted abroad clearly have no impact on the Zambian
economy. In the past, when the mining companies were able to keep

a large part of their sales revenues in London and elsewhere abroad, the money probably never even entered the country. Since nationalization, the companies are required to remit all sales proceeds to Zambia, which caused the banking system to be highly liquid in 1970* and forced the Treasury Bill rate down below 2 percent while the Bank Rate remained at 5 percent. But the Bank of Zambia has ways of controlling the expansion of bank credit even when the banks are highly liquid, so that this change has made little difference.** All it means is that the copper mines must sell their foreign exchange earnings to the Bank of Zambia as soon as they are received. The Bank of Zambia then invests this foreign exchange in London and New York and earns interest on it. In short, part of the reserve holding function of the country used to be performed by the privately owned copper companies and has now been fully transferred to government; there need be no impact on internal demand.

Profits are retained in Zambia mainly to finance capital expenditure for expansion by the mines. The mining companies are so large, and investment in the expansion of production takes so long to come to fruition, that investment spending must be based on long-term planning and especially on a long-term view of the copper price. Therefore, it is unlikely that short-term price movements have much effect on investment spending; their main effect is on expectations. Clearly, short-term price changes may alter long-term price expectations and thus investment plans; in an extreme case, a sufficiently large or sustained fall in the price could induce a belief in a fall in the long-term average price and result in cancellation or postponement of investment plans, even if half-completed.

There also may be some psychological effect of short-term price movements on government. It is much harder to resist demands for higher spending when the budget is running a large surplus, even

----

*In mid-1970, commercial bank balances at the Bank of Zambia and its head offices abroad were roughly twice what was required by legal reserve ratios.

**The Bank of Zambia can refuse permission to borrow to non-Zambian companies through powers granted at Mulungushi (subsequently, at Matero, a Zambian company was redefined as a company more than 50 percent Zambian-owned) or it can raise the legal reserve ratio or, in the case of parastatal companies, it may try and control their spending by direct means.

if the surplus is caused entirely by a high copper price and thus
releases no additional internal resources to government. (It also may
be harder to resist mining wage demands at such times.) Equally, it
takes strong nerves to maintain spending plans in the face of a steadily
falling copper price, even before it falls below the point of budget and
balance of payments deficit, and even when the country has large
reserves.

The whole Zambian economic structure contrasts very strongly
in this respect with export economies dependent on volatile peasant
crops, e.g., cocoa in Ghana. If the price of such commodities rises—
unless the extra money is creamed off by a marketing board—individual
incomes rise and can be spent. In Zambia, the foreign mining companies may have created a high-income enclave with relatively few
linkages and a damaging demonstration effect; however, in the field
of profit distribution the same isolation from the population does
insulate the economy from short-term disruption as the copper price
fluctuates.

The problem caused by having to depend so heavily on a volatile
copper price is in the difficulty of making plans at all, whether for
investment in mining or in capital spending by Government. On the
one hand, planning may be based on too optimistic an assumption; in
such a case, if the copper price falls too low to keep a mine or a
school open, capital spending may turn out to have been wasted. On
the other hand, one can argue that it is pointless to pile up "unnecessary" reserves in London and that the money must be spent now to
increase self-sufficiency, to educate the people, and to accomplish
objectives before the population has doubled and the copper ore
reserves have been exhausted. Neither argument is conclusive; in
the meantime, further expansion of the economy demands increasing
export earnings. Since in the short term these can only come from
copper, whether in the form of a rising price or rising output, diversification recedes ever further into the future.

THE ROLE OF GOVERNMENT
OVERSEAS BORROWING

Another aspect of export instability and the vulnerability of the
economy is the extent to which Government has committed future
export earnings for repayment of foreign borrowing, and the extent
to which borrowing powers already have been used and thus are not
available for future use.

The outstanding external debt at the end of 1969 was K111 million, of which K56 million remained from the external liabilities inherited at independence and the remaining K55 million had been raised since independence. Against this, the Government has lent some K6 million abroad directly, and another K5 million of sinking funds are invested in London. In round figures, then, net external debt at the end of 1969 was K100 million, which is under two months' export earnings at a copper price around K750 (£437) per ton.[7] In 1970, two big new loans were announced: the Chinese loan of K287 million for the railroad to Dar-es-Salaam, shared by Tanzania and Zambia with a ten-year grace period, no interest, and twenty years to pay; and a World Bank loan of K29 million to build the Kariba North Bank power station.

Why does Zambia borrow when many of the loans could have been met out of current balance of payments surpluses and all could be paid off using perhaps one-fifth or one-quarter of the reserves? The quick answer, that it pays to borrow from the World Bank at 7 percent and invest in London at 9 percent, is not really satisfactory. The London rate is temporary and runs some devaluation risks, whereas the repayment commitments stretch into future years. One reason for the borrowing is that Zambia is buying management. In the case of the World Bank loans, for example, borrowing helps to prevent badly planned projects from being started and provides continuing project supervision. The Chinese loan brings Chinese technicians (engineers and surveyors) and enables the participation of the Tanzanian Government, which does not have a balance of payments surplus or large reserves. Interestingly, Zambia has lent Tanzania K1.9 million at 1 percent with 15 years to 1986 to repay. So Zambia has become an aid donor.

A second reason for Zambia's borrowing is to increase the reserves, or to rather maintain them, against falls in the copper price; in short, the country is buying liquidity. This is a legitimate use for loans in Zambia's vulnerable position, but one wonders how many lenders realize the use that is made of their loans.

A third reason is to enable longer-term planning to take place independently of movements in the copper price and such natural disasters as that at Mufulira, which will reduce the reserves unless the price moves up sufficiently to compensate the loss in copper production. Borrowing also gives a ministry limited independence of the capital budget and thus may allow it to increase its share of capital spending and to escape cuts in times of financial stringency. The economic logic here is weak, and there are signs that government does in fact control this sort of expenditure in terms of overall spending targets.

Although these reasons for borrowing are valid in themselves, the dangers of external borrowing remain. In particular, bilateral loans are invariably tied, and the cost of equipment financed in this way may be high immediately as well as high in the long run in terms of spares and replacements and the unnecessarily wide variety of equipment in the country. Even multilateral loans have biases toward imports and foreign contractors, because of World Bank insistence on international tender.[8]

Management can be bought in other ways than by borrowing from the World Bank; indeed, rapid visits from World Bank employees, however well qualified, are probably not the best form of supervision. Thus, the soundest reason for borrowing has been the need to add to the reserves. Whatever their right level—and this is always impossible to decide—they are undoubtedly a great deal higher than they were, relative to trade as well as in absolute terms. The need to add to the reserves is correspondingly reduced; it would be nice to think that as a result Zambia will borrow less.

CONCLUSION

This chapter has considered the key aspects of the relationship of growth, the copper mines, and economic management. Briefly, the economy is fairly well insulated from short-term movements in the copper price but still is utterly dependent on copper price in the long run. It is not possible at present to foresee the time when alternative exports will be significant and, although imports are increasing less rapidly than domestic expenditures, they will continue to grow so long as the economy grows.

Part of the problem of diversifying the economy comes from the high salaries paid on the mines and, more generally, the high salaries demanded by expatriates and their Zambian successors. The very prosperity created by copper has enabled the modern sector to give a very high standard of living to the few, and the ability of the economy to import has enabled it to neglect agriculture on which most people still depend. Again, the high price of copper has sustained a high rate of exchange for the Kwacha, making it harder for indigenous industry and agriculture to compete with imports and move into exporting. Devaluation, the obvious weapon, will be successful only if the government is willing and able to force a drop in real wages on urban workers, especially copper miners. If the copper price did remain low in the long term, the country would of course be poorer and would have to face lower standards of living. Even if Zambians accepted this, and ultimately they would have to, at salaries much lower than at present the country would be unable to recruit the expatriates who are still needed to run the present size of the economy: for example, over 90 percent of secondary school teachers are non-Zambians.

What is needed is a lot more time. It remains to be seen, in subsequent chapters, whether the takeover of copper and its consequences have increased Zambia's chances of obtaining this necessary time.

NOTES

1. The first section of this chapter is derived in part from two earlier papers by Charles Harvey: "Financial Constraints," in C. M. Elliott, ed., Constraints on the Economic Development of Zambia (Nairobi: Oxford University Press, 1971), and "Inflation in a Very Open Economy: Zambia 1964-69," Eastern African Economic Review, Vol. III, No. 1 (June 1971).

2. For detailed support for this statement, see Harvey, "Inflation in a Very Open Economy: Zambia 1964-69," op. cit.

3. First National Development Plan 1966-70 (Lusaka: Office of National Development and Planning, 1966), p. 5.

4. W. A. Lewis, Some Aspects of Economic Development (London: Allen & Unwin, 1969), p. 8.

5. See Commission of Inquiry into the Wages and Conditions of Service in the Mining Industry in Zambia (Lusaka: Government Printer, 1966). The report also contains an excellent summary of earlier commissions of inquiry into mining wages and conditions.

6. For a discussion of the two-way relationship between wages and inflation in Zambia, see Harvey, "Inflation in a Very Open Economy: Zambia 1964-69," op. cit.

7. Financial Report for the Year Ended 31st December, 1969 (Lusaka: Government Printer, 1970), Appendixes 4 and 5, pp. 157-73.

8. For a Chilean example of this, see K. B. Griffin, Underdevelopment in Spanish America (London: Allen & Unwin, 1970), p. 130.

Mark Bostock

INTRODUCTION

Zambia became an independent Republic within the Commonwealth within one year of the dissolution of the Federation of Rhodesia and Nyasaland on December 31, 1963, and thirteen months before the Unilateral Declaration of Independence by the Smith regime of Southern Rhodesia.

Membership in the Federation had been grossly expensive in terms of economic cost. Arthur Hazelwood states:

The federal arrangements engineered massive fiscal re-
distribution from Northern Rhodesia to Southern Rhodesia
and Nyasaland. The removal of all restrictions on trade
between the three countries and the institution of a common
protective tariff stimulated development in Southern Rhodesia which was, on balance, a disadvantage to the other
territories. Therefore, Southern Rhodesia gained and
Northern Rhodesia lost on both accounts.[1]

With independence coming so soon after the dissolution of the Federation, Zambia inherited a system that can only be described as laissez-
faire in the sense that there was a minimal number of controls affecting
economic activity (for example, exchange control and import licensing).

The management of the economy was essentially in the hands
of expatriates, many of whom had been employed by the Federal

Government, and the economy was dominated by the foreign-owned mining groups. The industrial sector was oriented toward servicing the mining sector, and the mine-based enterprises were not geared to exporting, despite their comparative advantage relative to neighboring economies.

In the agricultural field, which only accounted for about 11.5 percent of GNP in 1964, 1,000 or so European farmers supplied the bulk of the urban economy's food requirements.

In the field of communications, Zambia inherited a system that was very much oriented toward the former Federation. Of particular importance in this respect was transport, which over the years Zambia had not been able to develop independently of Southern Rhodesia. This had been effectively precluded by the operation of the various railroad agreements, which culminated in the agreement between the Governments of Northern and Southern Rhodesia of December 10, 1963, which provided for the continuation of the railroad as a unitary system after the dissolution of the Federation. The agreement ensured that Zambia achieved an equal measure of ownership and control of Rhodesia Railways vis-á-vis Southern Rhodesia, as well as an equal financial responsibility for meeting liabilities despite the uneven distribution of assets. In addition, provision was made for the free movement of rolling stock and locomotives and the construction of new lines.[2]

Therefore, at independence Zambia was an integral part of the Southern African economic matrix. With its whole economy dependent on the mining, processing, and exporting of copper to overseas countries, there seemed little immediate prospect that Zambia would extract itself from this cobweb. Although political control had been secured on October 24, 1964, the new Zambian Government in no sense had an effective control over the management or the operation of the economy.

However, it should be mentioned in passing, that President Kenneth Kaunda's Government had reached an agreement on mineral royalties with the British South Africa Company, albeit a few hours before independence. This arrangement secured for Government the mineral rights over almost the whole country (see Chapter 2). However, the mining rights previously granted by the Chartered Company, including Special Grants held in perpetuity, continued to be held by two mining groups. Thus, the mining companies ensured their predominance in the mining field and, by retaining exclusive prospecting licences over the more promising mineralization areas of Zambia, prevented new mining investors from gaining a foothold in Zambia.*

Southern Rhodesia's Unilateral Declaration of Independence on November 10, 1965, provided an impetus for Zambia to disengage from Southern Africa. However, considerable economic costs were to be incurred and the train of events set in motion a whole range of policy measures that have had an irrevocable effect on the management and operation of the economy. The changes were announced in the form of major policy statements. Between independence (in October 1964) and 1971, there have been three such speeches: the Mulungushi speech on April 19, 1968, "Zambia's Economic Revolution"; the Matero speech on August 11, 1969, "Towards Complete Independence"; and a speech on November 10, 1970, "This Completes Economic Reforms: Now Zambia is Ours."

The most significant aspect of these "economic reforms," together with their implementation, is that Zambia and Zambians have secured nominal control over a large portion of the country's economic activity (amounting to probably 75 percent of GNP). Therefore, it may be said that by January 1, 1971, Zambia had achieved economic independence in the limited sense that majority holdings in all the large enterprises had been acquired from foreign interests (the mining companies, insurance companies, transport companies, industrial enterprises, retail shops, building societies, and banks) and severe limitations had been introduced on the extent to which non-Zambians could engage in commerce. But although ownership may have shifted to the State, operational control still remained in the hands of the expatriates and, in many cases, in the hands of the former owners of the enterprises taken over by the State. The private interests retained management control through various types of contracts.

These reforms must be seen in their historical context to assess their effect on the economy. This chapter will therefore be concerned in particular with looking at the mining and industrial sectors, in terms

---

*One potential venture that may have been hampered by the entrenched mining rights was the financing and construction of the Zambia-East Africa Railway; interest possibly could have been created among overseas finance houses if the Zambian Government had been able to grant mining concessions to consortiums involved in the construction and financing of the railroad.

of State control and participation, to establish the background to
President Kaunda's announcement on August 11, 1969.

> I have . . . decided that I shall ask the owners of the mines
> to invite the Government to join in their mining enterprises.
> I am asking the owners of the mines to give 51 percent of
> their shares to the State.[3]

THE EFFECTS OF THE UNILATERAL
DECLARATION OF INDEPENDENCE

Prior to November 1965, Zambia maintained a trade and payments
system that was virtually free of restrictions in respect of current
transactions. Authorized dealers were empowered to sell foreign
exchange for several categories of payments for current transactions,
while for categories not covered approval was freely granted by the
Bank of Zambia (the Central Bank, established 1964). On the import
side, only a few specified commodities required individual licensing;
all others were free if originating in the sterling area or were admitted
under open general licence if originating elsewhere. In June 1965,
the Exchange Control Act came into force, and six months later in
December 1965, as part of the machinery created to implement the
UN Security Council's resolution on Rhodesia, licences were required
for all imports from all countries. Immediately after Southern Rhodesia's Unilateral Declaration of Independence (UDI) exchange control
regulations were introduced to restrict payments to Rhodesia, and
payments to certain of the jointly-owned services. These restrictions
covered payments to all the former Federal Common Services: the
Central African Power Corporation, Central African Airways, and
Rhodesia Railways. With regard to the latter, the restriction was
subsequently lifted to allow payment for freight charges to be paid
to Rhodesian Railways through continental European banks.

Until the Mulungushi speech, on April 18, 1968, non-resident
companies were permitted to remit profits and dividends abroad,
subject to the production of appropriate documentary evidence. These
companies also could repatriate capital brought into the country,
together with increases in that capital arising in Zambia from their
operations; special restrictions applied to Rhodesia after the UDI.

During this period, the Government's industrial policy, as outlined in a White Paper, was aimed at promoting import substitution
industries, labor-intensive modes of production, the training of
Zambians, and rural location of industry.[4] It did this through

customs legislation (tariff protection), through income tax (pioneer industry status that granted a maximum tax holiday of five years), and through the operations of a company wholly owned by Government, the Industrial Development Corporation of Zambia Limited (Indeco). The Government secured control of Indeco in August 1964 when arrangements were concluded for the purchase of shares held by the Anglo-American group, the British South Africa Company, the Commonwealth Development Corporation, and the RST group. During this period, Indeco was responsible broadly to the Ministry of Commerce and Industry "but, being a Corporation set up in terms of the Companies Ordinance and having its own Board of Directors, it is largely autonomous in the fulfillment of its functions."[5]

Indeco's objectives at this stage were specific and included the promotion of Zambian business; the issuing of loans; liaison between Government and the private sector; the promotion of investment; the holding, management, and financing of Government investment in industry; and the holding of shares in and/or management of certain industries (iron and steel, fertilizers, bags and sacks, cement, sugar, textiles, copper processing, leather processing, and building materials).

In short, it was Government's policy during this early stage to develop State enterprise the hard way by confining the role of Indeco to that of promotion of joint ventures in many sectors, rather than that of forced participation. In the Chairman's statement for 1965, A. S. Sardanis said:

> The implementation of the Government's policy of accelerating the industrial development of the nation by participating in the establishment of certain large-scale and key industries was entrusted to us, and we were given the task of promoting, financing and managing the Government's interests in industry.[6]

The preoccupation with developing new industries with varying degrees of State participation was short-lived, although this role has continued to be a part of Indeco's activities.

Arising from the UDI, Indeco was required to establish a major road transport organization to link the Tanzanian port of Dar-es-Salaam to the Zambian rail line and to construct an oil products pipeline from Dar-es-Salaam to Ndola. In May 1966, Zambia Tanzania Road Services Limited was set up (with Indeco and the Tanzanian Government each holding 35 percent equity and the balance held by Italian interests) to transport copper to the port of Dar-es-Salaam in

Tanzania and to bring in vital petroleum products on its homeward run. Tazama Pipelines Limited, established in December 1966 (Indeco 67 percent, Tanzanian Government 33 percent), was charged with building the petroleum products pipeline, which was completed in September 1968. The successful implementation of these two projects began a new era for Indeco.

The effect of the UDI on Zambia was dramatic. A full system of import and export licensing was introduced on December 6, 1965, following the UN Security Council Resolution imposing economic sanctions on Rhodesia. This control was introduced to keep a close check on the type and quality of goods imported into Zambia from Rhodesia, to ensure the optimum application of sanctions, to divert traffic onto alternative traffic routes, and at the same time to ensure the priority of freight space to essential goods. Therefore, this policy fundamentally affected the traditional links of trade and business and obviously had a specific effect on the costs—transport, higher cost sources, and financing the import pipeline. At the same time, there was a UDI-induced boom for both foreign-controlled and resident-expatriate-controlled companies operating in Zambia (this distinction is important in the Zambian context because of the predominance in the business community of persons who, although resident in the country, are not Zambian citizens).

While these boom conditions prevailed, the controls introduced as a result of the UDI had a significant psychological effect on these companies, in particular on the expatriate companies that over the years had developed or retained close links with the south. This effect of the UDI must be seen in political terms, since the time horizon of the nonresident companies was reduced significantly. The economic outcome were attempts to secure an increased rate of return in the quickest possible time and to secure avenues for remitting profit and capital in the realization that they would not be able to continue their operations in Zambia indefinitely. To a large extent, the actions of these companies were responsible for the Mulungushi takeovers of April 18, 1968. (Estimates based on remittances of annual dividends by the Zambian mining companies and the published balance of payments accounts show that remittances by nonmining companies increased by 84 percent in 1966, increased by 15 percent in 1967, and fell by 59 percent in 1968 when the Mulungushi reforms were introduced.[7]) However, before looking at the Mulungushi take-overs, consideration should be given to the UDI-induced cost changes.

In order to put the following discussions in some kind of perspective, it should be noted at the outset that by 1970 Zambia had to a large extent managed to secure the main objective of import licensing, in that imports from Southern Rhodesia were reduced from K62 million in 1964, accounting for 40 percent of total Zambian imports, to K22 million or 7 percent of total imports by 1969 (at a time when Zambia's imports doubled). Over 90 percent of 1969 imports from Rhodesia were coal from Wankie and electricity from the jointly owned Kariba Dam. By 1971, Zambia will be self-sufficient in coal; by 1975, after the commissioning of both the Kafue project and the Kariba North Bank Hydroelectric Project, the country will be in a position to reduce its imports from Rhodesia still further (see Table 5.1).

Zambia has not been as successful with transport routing (see Table 5.2). In 1964, virtually all Zambian traffic used the Rhodesia Railways system (which remains jointly owned in law although assets were divided on a de facto basis on June 30, 1967), and in 1968 61 percent of total trade continued to use the system or was imported through Rhodesia (49 percent if trade with or through South Africa is excluded). This inability to reduce the flow of traffic through Rhodesia reflects the inadequacies of alternative routes to absorb the capacity required of them. The Zambian Government was obliged in October 1968 to agree with the Rhodesian authorities to move 25,000 metric tons of copper per month via Beira or Lourenco Marques in return for a guarantee that Zambian traffic would not be discriminated against. The situation will change with the completion of the Zambia-East Africa Rail Link; this K287-million project is scheduled for commissioning in 1975 and, if there is sufficient handling capacity at the port of Dar-es-Salaam, Zambia will then be able to reduce its dependence on transport routes through Rhodesia. Thus, during the ten-year period following the UDI, Rhodesia has continued and will continue to have a significant leverage over Zambia in that alternative transport routes have been of insufficient capacity to meet the substantial requirements of Zambia and in that there has been dependence on the import of energy from Kariba.*

_____

*The situation in February 1970 illustrated this problem. It was reported that Zambia had not shipped 25,000 metric tons via Rhodesia, which immediately retaliated with a 50 percent surcharge levied on all Zambia imports using Rhodesia Railways. Since the whole transport system is geared to moving copper, any disaster such as that at Mufulira Mine which meant an estimated 200,000 metric tons reduction in production from late 1970 to 1972, has an immediate disruptive effect.

TABLE 5.1

Rhodesia's Share in Zambia's Imports, 1964-69

	1964		1965		1966		1967		1968		1969	
	Millions of Kwacha	Per-centage	Millions of Kwacha	Per-centage	Millions of Kwacha	Per-centage	Millions of Kwacha	Per-centage	Millions of Kwacha	Per-centage	Millions of Kwacha	Per-centage
Total imports (fob)	156.4	100	210.7	100	246.1	100	306.4	100	325.1	100	311.8	100
Rhodesia	61.7	40	71.1	34	46.4	19	32.2	11	22.6	7	21.8	7
of which:												
Coal	2.4		2.9		2.3		3.8		3.5		3.7	
Electricity	8.5		8.8		9.4		13.9		15.0		15.9	

Source: Annual Statement of External Trade (Lusaka: Central Statistics Office, 1965-71).

114

The political situation that resulted from the UDI led to immediate restrictions on traffic flows between Rhodesia and Zambia. On
December 18, 1965 the Rhodesian authorities prohibited the export of
petroleum products and stopped the movement of railroad tank-cars
into Zambia. This interference, in denying transit transport facilities
to Zambia, was contrary to the Inter-Governmental Agreement of
1963, which provided for the continuance of the unitary system following the dissolution of the Federation. The situation was further
confused in May-June 1966, when the movement of locomotives and
rolling stock across the Rhodesia-Zambia border was restricted on
a one-for-one truck exchange basis. Concurrently with these disrup-
tions, the Zambian Government blocked the transfer of railroad funds
to Rhodesia, to which Rhodesia responded by requesting payment in
advance. The cumulative effect was to force the mining companies
to declare force majeure because of their inability to move exports.
At the same time, a serious fuel supply shortage developed during
the latter half of 1966, necessitating a forced cutback of 25 percent
in copper production from October 1, a cutback that was increased
to 33.33 percent from November 6, 1966. Full production was resumed
again in June 1967.[8]

In this chapter, the UDI-induced cost increases are considered
only in relation to the mining industry. Table 5.3 shows that between
1964/65 and 1968/69 the operating costs per metric ton of copper
sold (excluding capital expenditure) increased from K342 to K620, or
81 percent. The main components of this increase are listed in
Table 5.4.

When the Zambian copper companies announced early in 1966
that their selling price for electrolytic copper would be the three
months forward sellers wirebar quotation on the London Metal Exchange, the Zambian Government announced that an export tax would
be levied with effect from April 25, 1966 (see Chapter 6). The change
in the price base led to an immediate increase in sales revenue from
£336 (K576) per metric ton to £624 (K1,070) per metric ton.

Table 5.3 shows that during the period under review, because
of the increased revenue per metric ton of copper sold in each year
royalty payments and export tax constituted the most important single
increase in costs. Table 5.4 shows that this amounted to 40.3 percent
of the K278 per metric ton total increase in costs. Although the increase in wages (see Chapter 4, Table 4.4) had nothing to do with the
Rhodesian situation, the effects of increased transport costs and fuel
costs have been most significant. These two components of cost have
accounted for a 9 percent increase in cost of sales (delivered to buyer)
over the period 1964/65 to 1968/69.

TABLE 5.2

Zambian Import/Export Routes, by Weight
(thousands of metric tons)

| | Fiscal Year | | | | Calendar Year | |
	1963/64	1964/65	1965/66	1966/67	1968	1969
IMPORTS						
Via Ports	222	249	426	562	814	834
Dar-es-Salaam (Tanzania)	—	—	93	240	425	570
Lobito (Angola)	5	9	48	114	127	115
Beira/Lourenco Marques (Mozambique)	218	240	285	208	262	149
From Countries	1,401	1,561	1,930	1,219	1,375	1,273
Rhodesia	1,244	1,386	1,651	879	858	860
Congo	4	6	31	36	24	6
South Africa*	153	169	248	304	431	351
Malawi*	—	—	—	—	62	56
Miscellaneous	—	—	—	—	18	13
Total	1,623	1,811	2,255	1,781	2,207	2,120
Percentage of total via Rhodesia	99	99	92	78	68	64
EXPORTS						
Via Ports	692	686	667	657	690	806
Dar-es-Salaam (Tanzania)	—	—	8	147	230	244
Lobito (Angola)	—	—	30	143	154	114
Beira/Lourenco Marques (Mozambique)	692	686	629	367	307	447
To Countries	96	105	159	200	142	60
Rhodesia	n.a.	n.a.	22	13	39	11
Congo	5	9	46	73	44	9
South Africa*	91	96	87	82	50	32
Malawi*	—	—	4	33	9	8
Miscellaneous	—	—	—	—	2	4
Total	789	791	826	856	834	869
Percentage of total via Rhodesia	99	99	89	54	47	56

*Malawi includes traffic using South African Ports and Beira.

Source: 1968 and 1969 from Zambian trade statistics; 1963/64 to 1966/67 based on financial years ending June 30. See R. M. Bostock, "The Transport Sector," in C. M. Elliott, ed., Constraints on the Economic Development of Zambia (Nairobi: Oxford University Press, 1971).

TABLE 5.3

Mining Industry Costs, 1964-69

	1964/65	1965/66	1966/67	1967/68	1968/69	1969 July-Dec
Copper production (metric tons)	643,221	682,408	537,110	649,428	699,870	465,057
Copper sales (metric tons)	667,081	682,823	545,387	651,337	685,825[a]	530,766[a]
Sales revenue per metric ton (Kwacha)	501	574	788	802	862	1,127
Cost per metric ton of sales (Kwacha)						
Income tax	67	70	78	77	81	138
Capital expenditure[b]	30	28	40	39	62	70
Cost of sales (delivered buyer)[b]	342	409	593	574	620	714[c]
Royalty payments	78	117	105	98	96	114
Export tax	—	2	108	88	94	170
Cost of sales (excluding royalty and export tax)	264	290	380	388	430	431
Cost of transport (exports)	47	55	62	63	64	66
Selling costs, administration, interest, etc.[d]	19	31	30	26	30	28
Cost of sales at mine of which:	198	203	287	300	335	336
Wages	106	116	158	138	132	138
Fuel costs	6	7	15	15	14	14

[a]Includes sales of 18,821 metric tons smelted on toll outside Zambia and 2,042 metric tons in concentrates exported in 1968/69, and 36,034 metric tons of concentrates sold in 1969 (July-December), this resulting from stockpiling of concentrates during the previous years of fuel shortage.

[b]Capital expenditure includes capital expenditure for new mine capacity and nonexpansion capital, which is not a meaningful distinction due to different accounting procedures of the two mining groups. Therefore, the cost of sales excludes any provision for replacements.

[c]No provision has been for changes in stock valuation arising from the Heads of Agreement, signed 24-12-1969.

[d]Selling, general, and administrative expenses including certain supervisory costs of mining; based on RST data.

Sources: Mining company annual reports, Copper Mining Year Books, and RST "Explanatory Statement for Shareholders," June 30, 1970.

TABLE 5.4

Mining Industry Cost Increases, 1968/69 on 1964/65

	Increase	Percentage Increase	Percentage of Total Increase
Sales	18,744 metric tons	3	
Sales Revenue/metric ton	K361	72	
Cost per metric ton			
Cost of sales (delivered buyer)	K278	81	100.0
Royalty	K18	23	6.5
Export Tax	K94		33.8
Cost of sales (excluding tax and royalty)	K166	63	59.7
Cost of transport (exports)	K17	36	6.1
Selling expenses	K11	58	4.0
Cost of sales at mine	K137	69	49.3
Wages	K26	25	9.4
Fuel costs	K8	133	2.9
Other	K103	120	37.1

Source: Table 5.3

In 1965, the total Zambian requirement of coal (1 million metric tons) originated from Wankie, Rhodesia, representing about one-third of the colliery's output. (The Wankie Colliery Company Limited is administered by the Anglo-American group, which also has a substantial equity participation). The mines were the single largest consumer of Wankie coal, accounting for 580,000 metric tons. The cost of Wankie coal was K6.36 per metric ton (CIF copper mine), which remained constant until November 1966 when the colliery increased prices by more than 100 percent. With the division of the unitary railroad system on July 1, 1967, Zambian customers had to pay higher railroad charges because the tariff basis was altered. This situation was further aggravated by the fact that in April 1968 the Rhodesian authorities introduced a surcharge of K2.20 per metric ton for the short distance of railage in Rhodesia and by the increase in the Zambia Railways tariff in April 1969. Because of the transport bottleneck and the increasing dependence on local coal, the mines were unable to take advantage of bulk purchases. The net effect of these changes was to increase the cost of Wankie coal to the mines by 285 percent per metric ton in 1970; this explains the importance placed by Zambia on developing its own coal resources.

Although the unwashed local coal has a reduced thermal efficiency around 84 percent that of Wankie, the mines have used an increasing amount of local coal. In 1970, 41 percent (in Wankie equivalent) of their requirements were met by the local coal. Although the cost of local coal to the mines has remained constant at K11.02 per metric ton, the railage charges have been increased, and in 1970 local coal in Wankie equivalent cost 312 percent more than the traditional low-cost Wankie source. The real cost increase caused by the switch to local coal cannot be measured solely in these terms. In particular, the furnace life of the smelter has been greatly reduced and maintenance costs have been increased. Moreover, the refractory lining of the furnaces requires replacing more often, and the material cost for this is substantial. This problem was eased early in 1970 with the commissioning of a washing plant that has increased the thermal efficiency of the local coal.*

---

*Wankie coal has a rating of 12,500 BTU. The initial Zambian coal came from the Nkandabwe mine with a thermal efficiency of 10,500 BTU. Maamba coal at 11,000 BTU replaced Nkandabwe and with the installation of the washing plant the thermal efficiency is 12,000 BTU.

Transport costs of copper exports have played an important part in the total increase in unit costs. This has arisen mainly through the use of alternative routes. Traditionally, all copper was exported on the Rhodesian Railways routes at a rate of K36.05 per metric ton. By 1969, 38 percent was exported via Dar-es-Salaam at a cost of K46.30 per metric ton. Although the Rhodesian Railways rate has increased so that the Dar-es-Salaam rate now is only marginally more expensive, the weighted average for transporting copper from the Copperbelt to an African port was around K45.90 per metric ton in 1970, representing a 27 percent increase in cost on 1964. Additionally, higher port charges at Dar-es-Salaam and greater transport time have increased even further the real cost incurred by the mining companies.

As Table 5.4 shows, there is a substantial residual cost increase of K103 per metric ton, representing 37.1 percent of the increase in cost of sales (delivered buyer). There is no available quantitative data to isolate specific cost components within this residual. However, one important factor must be the increased mining costs at Nchanga, which accounts for some 30 percent of total Zambian production, arising from the fall in ore grade from 5.4 percent in 1964/65 to 3.65 percent in 1969. Nchanga Consolidated Copper Mines Limited annual reports show that the increased cost per metric ton of finished production amounted to K66.13 in 1967/68 on 1966/67, an unqualified additional increase in 1968/69, and a further K29.76 per metric ton during the period March-December 1969.

In addition, the rising landed cost of imports in general also has played its part and probably accounts for a significant part of the residual cost increase. This increase has arisen because the government's routing policies have necessitated a search for new sources of supply. South Africa has been the traditional supplier of mining equipment to Zambia; it is a low-cost supplier because of its proximity and the size of its own mining industry. However, no South African goods can be imported via Dar-es-Salaam due to the sanctions policy adopted by the Tanzanian Government. This has had the effect of increasing import costs, financial charges, and freight costs since 1967/68.

Clearly, most of the UDI-induced cost increases that have affected the mining industry are irrevocable, given the Zambian Government's policy toward Rhodesia and South Africa. Even though unprecedentedly high copper prices prevailed during the period 1964-69, the effect of these cost increases has been dramatic. The increase in costs relative to other producers reduces the industry's competitiveness and

ultimately its viability, especially in a situation of falling prices when
international action to establish a floor price might be necessary.
Moreover, the effects of high production costs on the raising of capital
for development and on Government revenue also must be considered.
The latter is particularly relevant where revenue is based on profits
as opposed to the prevailing LME prices. Finally, a situation must
arise whereby the mining companies, because of rising unit costs,
are forced to raise their cut-off grades, thus reducing the mineral
reserves of the country. In terms of the State's participation in the
mining companies, these price considerations clearly had an important effect on the price to be paid as compensation to the owners.

THE MULUNGUSHI SPEECH

As mentioned earlier, although the UDI-induced costs had a
significant impact on the mining industry and the economy as a whole,
boom conditions prevailed in Zambia for both foreign-owned and expatriate-controlled nonmining companies after the introduction of import/
export licensing. The profits boom that occurred in the period 1966/
67 meant that these companies were able to repatriate a high proportion of their profits and still earn adequate funds for reinvestment to
keep their businesses running (although not to fund expansion). Some
companies went further and took advantage of their position as first-
class risks (reinforced by the profits boom) to obtain local bank finance
that enabled them to expatriate a substantial proportion of their capital
reserves, paying scant regard to the resulting financial structure of
their companies. The Bank of Zambia Annual Reports show that Commercial Bank Advances increased by 94 percent in December 1965 on
December 1964, a further 16 percent during 1966, 76 percent in 1967,
and only 8 percent in 1968. Therefore, a large part of the "artificial"
profit arising from the immediate post-UDI situation was not reinvested
in Zambia and the opportunity was taken to export large amounts of
capital. This action, unprincipled from a Zambian viewpoint, played
an important part in the formulation of the Mulungushi speech of
April 19, 1968.

The Mulungushi speech introduced several measures especially
designed to prevent exploitation by foreign- and expatriate-controlled
companies.[9] The measure announced by the President included the
following:

1. Regulations governing local borrowings by expatriate-controlled companies were to be the same as those that applied to foreign-
controlled companies, that is, they were to be tied specifically to the

amount of capital brought into the country. A Zambian enterprise was deemed to be that in which 100 percent of its members were nationals.

2. A limitation was to be introduced on remittances abroad for all foreign-controlled companies. Dividends could be remitted only if they "did not exceed 30 percent of the equity capital of the company," provided that the 30 percent did "not exceed half of their profits."*

3. The State intended to invite certain companies to offer Government a 51 percent interest in their enterprises. Most of the 27 companies selected were chosen to curtail excessive profits: "They operate price rings because of the buoyant demand and the difficult supply position. They do not make enough effort to move away from unacceptable sources of supply and outdated management philosophies. They still maintain personnel and training policies which are not in accord with the Nation's present needs. They are failing to re-invest a sufficient proportion of their profits for general expansion and development." The companies selected were in the construction industry where "prices have soared to astronomic heights"; in the transport sector to "rationalise and co-ordinate the activities" of the transport companies "to direct them to co-operate in the national interest"; in the retail/wholesale sector, including all five retail chain stores (one of these companies was Zambian) as a measure of control and a check on inflation; in the brewing industry because of monopoly position and "excessive profits"; and a few miscellaneous companies.

4. Legislation was to be introduced to safeguard approved foreign investments. Although this was never implemented, it was Government's original intention to provide any company with a guarantee that dividends and interest on foreign capital could be remitted, that no expropriation would occur for a set number of years, and that any nationalization thereafter would be at a fair valuation with the method laid down in the "certificate." (For new mining ventures, safeguards were introduced with the issue of the new prospecting licences: see Chapter 3 and Appendix D).

---

*As a result of this limitation, Zambian Anglo-American Limited increased the capital of the company from K15.38 million to K30.24 million in shares of K1 each by a one for one capitalization issue in December 1968. The dividends in 1967/68 amounted to 76 percent of equity capital. Likewise, Roan Selection Trust Limited increased its issued share capital from K43.69 million to K87.99 million by a bonus issue.

5. Expatriates would be granted retail trading licences only in restricted areas: the urban centers. In addition, road service licences were to be restricted to companies in which 75 percent of members were Zambian. Likewise, building mineral permits also were limited to Zambian enterprises.

6. Finally, the President indicated his disappointment at the "virtual lack of mining development since Independence" and stated that the mining companies "could have embarked upon further expansion if they chose to devote part of their profits for this purpose." He went on to note that "instead of re-investment they have been distributing over 80 percent of their profits every year on dividends." He announced that the royalty system would be changed and that the amount of dividends to be remitted would be limited to only one-half of profits: "the other half they must utilize for further development."

The effect of the Mulungushi speech was an immediate reduction in the rate of growth of bank lending, which in 1968 was only 8 percent higher than in previous year, compared to a 76 percent increase in 1967. Certainly, with the introduction of dividend restrictions increased capitalization of many companies did take place in order to accomodate their local borrowing capacities (based on a one for one ratio of equity to total local borrowing)* and to enable the continued remittance of dividends overseas.[10] At the same time, the magnitude of exchange irregularities was not reduced, which necessitated further measures that were incorporated in the Matero speech (see below).

The basis for the takeover of the 27 companies by Indeco was a "fair value represented by the book value." At Mulungushi, the President said "there is no such thing as business goodwill in paying for future profits as far as I am concerned." Indeco quickly reached agreement with most of the companies listed at Mulungushi on the

---

*The Bank of Zambia 1968 Report pointed out that, since the Zambian sector accounted "for about 15 percent of the total bank credit," the Mulungushi restriction on local borrowing for all non-Zambian companies, including the Indeco 51 percent companies "provided the Bank with a powerful instrument of regulating, though indirectly, the total volume of bank credit." The report further stated that, although the avowed intention of this measure was to divert the credit away from the non-Zambian sector to the Zambian sector, the measure lended itself "to being used as an instrument for regulating the volume of credit, at any rate, in the short run."

price to be paid for Government's 51-percent share. During 1968/69, the total value of Indeco's share of fixed assets taken over amounted to K26.8 million. Thus, Indeco's emphasis was changed and by the end of 1968 it held direct participation in 32 companies of various sizes (20 were added in 1968), increasing Indeco's net assets from K35.6 million on December 31, 1967, to K108.1 million on March 31, 1969.

The arrangements entered into by Indeco with the private companies followed a stereotyped pattern. The private parties tended to retain 49 percent of the equity and at the same time entered into management/consultancy and/or technical "know-how" agreements with the State-owned company. The remuneration for these contracts was in the form of a fixed payment supplemented by a percentage on turnover or gross profits payable overseas. The conditions in many of these contracts were such that operational control tended to remain in the hands of the former owners, especially in cases where preemptive rights were granted, such as overseas purchasing with the retail trading companies. In return, the management contractors were obliged to retain or supply expatriates to fill managerial or technical posts.

In short, since Government had failed to indicate its objectives (both commercial and noncommercial) in operational terms, the management contracts were in no way designed to meet these. For example, there was no incentive for effective Zambianization built into the fees payable to the contractors. However, it was imperative for Indeco to conclude deals quickly to ensure the continuation of the companies, and this necessitated retaining the expatriate staff in view of the lack of skills—particularly managerial skills—available in Zambia. Indeed, the attractiveness of many of these contracts—in terms of fees (not subject to Zambian tax or exchange control regulations) and implicit security of tenure for a specific time period—led several other companies to voluntarily negotiate for Indeco participation in their ventures.

THE MATERO SPEECH[11]

In the Matero speech of August 11, 1969, President Kaunda again spoke of "unscrupulous people who, in collusion with their suppliers overseas, inflate the prices of merchandise and in this way build fat accounts for themselves overseas while the nation is suffering from foreign exchange drain and from inflated prices." To counteract these continued trends, he announced that "where there are state companies operating in a particular field" he proposed "to confine the importation of the goods they handle to the state companies

themselves." Although this would be straightforward for many products, the President realized that it would be more difficult for a
whole range of consumer goods. He therefore announced that "a
National Import Agency in association with the four State Trading
enterprises" would handle the major items in this field. Thus, import
monopolies for State manufacturing and trading companies were proposed to check price inflation and exchange control evasion. At the
same time, the President announced his intention to relax the restrictions on remittances of profits and dividends and local borrowing for
companies in which Zambian participation exceeded 50 percent.

While reemphasizing Government's interest in welcoming foreign
capital, President Kaunda indicated that Indeco was willing to consider
"any major business proposition either in operation or at the planning
stage" and "to consider participation." Six major industrial projects
were announced: an oil refinery (Indeco 50 percent with ENI); the
National Oil Marketing Company (with Agip, a subsidiary of ENI, and
Indeco each with 50 percent); a car assembly plant (with Fiat 30 percent
and Indeco 70 percent); an integrated iron and steel plant (Indeco 100
percent); a glass project; and an agricultural implements project.

A major section of the Matero speech was devoted to the mining
industry. It will be recalled that at Mulungushi disappointment with
the slow rate of new mining development was expressed. The mining
companies defended this situation, with some justice, in terms of the
royalty system, which they said inhibited new development. But at
Matero the disappointment was expressed even more strongly, amounting almost to a postulation of conspiracy. A referendum on June 17,
1969, had approved constitutional changes (among others, permitting
compulsory purchase without compensation in the case of absentee
landlords, for example). This enabled the President to announce that
all existing private rights of ownership or partial ownership of minerals
would revert to the State and that the grants in perpetuity made by
the British South Africa Company would be cancelled. The new Mines
and Minerals Act became effective on January 1, 1970. In addition
to the reform of mining grants, the system of royalty payments (and
export tax) was abolished (see Chapter 6).

After announcing impending State participation in the mines
President Kaunda said:

> I wish to remind the owners of the mines that, according
> to the Exchange Control regulations, they can only remit
> 50 percent of their profits outside the country. I wish to
> point out to them that it is to their advantage to offer 51

percent of their shares to the Government in that as a result and in line with what I have announced earlier their
remittance of dividends will no longer be subject to exchange control. I also wish them to know that Government's business record is excellent and the companies,
which have associated themselves with Indeco in line with
last year's Mulungushi reforms, are perfectly happy and
satisfied with Indeco's business-like approach, in both
concluding the negotiations and subsequently in managing
the enterprises under its control. This year again I intend
to leave it to Indeco to negotiate the value and terms of
payment but again I want to make it clear that what Indeco
will pay is a fair value represented by the book value. At
the same time I want to make it clear that Government has
no money to pay as a deposit against these shares; I also
cannot afford to release part of the mineral tax as the income tax is badly needed for our development program.
Indeco, will therefore, have to negotiate payment out of
future dividends bearing in mind the advantage the shareholders will derive from associating with the State.

The full details of the new mining deals are complex and are
given in Appendix A and elsewhere in the text. Suffice it to say at
this stage that, in addition to participating in the mining companies
within the Anglo-American and RST groups, Government announced
its intention that all new large mining ventures would be controlled
by the State (see Appendix D); that, as stated above, all the mining
and mineral rights would revert to the State; and that changes were
to be introduced in taxation. Thus, the Matero speech spelled out the
basis for a comprehensive package for the mining industry. For the
first time since independence, the Government announced its future
plans for the industry, thereby reducing the increased uncertainty
that had arisen in the minds of the mining groups, especially since
the Mulungushi speech.

Following President Kaunda's announcement that it was Government's intention to participate in the two mining groups, the Zambia
Industrial and Mining Corporation Limited (Zimco) was set up as a
holding company. It had two wholly owned subsidiaries: (1) Mindeco
Limited, to hold Government's interest in the two newly formed state
controlled mining companies, Nchanga Consolidated Copper Mines
Limited (NCCM) and Roan Consolidated Mines Limited (RCM); and
(2) Indeco Limited, to hold (as before) Government's interest in other
fields.

With the further growth in Indeco Limited, the corporation rationalized the 70 or so companies in its control into divisional groupings. Previously, the various individual companies, in many cases because of their management contracts, were not in any way accountable to Indeco central, the parent company. Therefore, the purpose of the rationalization was to promote, and in certain cases to control, the management of individual companies and at the same time to float some of the shares on the stock exchange (whose establishment was announced at Mulungushi). As a result of the acquisition of a 51-percent interest in the mining companies, the net asset value of Zimco on January 1, 1970, exceeded K600 million ($840 million). Through this octopus, the government had a majority equity interest in the mining sector and in a significant part of the manufacturing, transport, and retail sectors.*

CONCLUSION

The Zambian "economic reforms" did not end with the announcement that the State would participate in the copper mining companies. On November 11, 1970, President Kaunda announced, inter alia, the State's intention to participate in the two main commercial banks, to take over all the building societies, and to transfer all insurance business to the State-owned insurance company. He also announced a further list of companies in which the State wanted a 51-percent interest.[12]

Thus, during the period 1968-70 the State secured "control," either indirectly or directly, over a large part of the country's economy. At the same time, an elaborate system of State participation, supported by State import monopolies, had been established and extensive controls had been developed following independence. The controls included

---

*On January 7, 1971, the President announced measures for the decentralization of Zimco. From April 1, 1971 Zimco was abolished as the holding company of Indeco Limited and Mindeco Limited but retained its legal identity for purposes of the bond redemptions. At the same time, it was announced that several Indeco holding companies would be transferred to the relevant ministries and the Permanent Secretaries of these ministries were appointed executive chairmen of the relevant holding companies.

import/export licensing, price control, exchange control on overseas remittances of profits, control over local borrowing by foreign-owned companies, and control over employment of expatriates through the issue of work permits (introduced in 1964). Indeed, by 1970/71 there were few aspects of the operation of a foreign company that Government did not directly control. It could be argued that in these circumstances there seemed little point in direct State involvement to the extent of 51 percent, especially since local management skills and know-how simply were not available. Therefore, the newly formed State companies were dependent on management contracts with the former owners for operating the enterprises. From the viewpoint of the private sector, the opportunity of a monopoly position in manufacturing or trading, a remunerative management contract, and a mechanism for overcoming bureaucratic controls provided incentives for inviting the State to participate, despite the limitations of negotiating a price based on book value for the assets taken over.

With regard to the mining companies, the Mulungushi reforms of April 1968 were of great significance in paving the way for a takeover by the State. The arrangements for State involvement in the 27 companies enabled Indeco to establish a mechanism for securing a controlling 51 percent interest and to pay for this out of future profits. In addition, the establishment of a management contract ensured the continuity of management; the need to retain technical management skills and know-how to a large extent determined the type of deal entered into by Indeco. The State's participation in the mining industry followed in the same way. If Government, through Indeco, had not had the experience arising from the Mulungushi reforms, the arrangement with the mining companies might have taken a different form.

As a result of the pragmatic evolution of the State's intervention policy, controlled both by events and by manpower shortages, the fundamentals of the policy have become obscured. This failure to define the extent and objectives of State involvement could prove costly in economic terms, especially if there is no mechanism for management accountability in State ventures. This means that the institutional framework created by the various "economic reforms" must be developed at the same time as an adequate policy for harnessing the immense productive power acquired for the social benefit of the country.[13]

NOTES

1. Arthur Hazelwood, ed, African Integration and Disintegration (London: Oxford University Press, 1967), p. 249.

2. "Agreement between the Government of Southern Rhodesia and the Government of Northern Rhodesia relating to the Rhodesia Railways," (December 10, 1963). With the development of the copper mining industry in the 1930's, an opportunity was created for Rhodesia Railways to secure valuable traffic provided that it was not diverted on the contiguous railway to Lobito in Angola. Because of the availability of this alternative route, the various agreements, the first of which was signed with the Zambian copper companies in 1936, ensured the flow of copper traffic via Beira and Lourenco Marques. See R. M. Bostock "Transport Sector," in C. M. Elliott, ed., Constraints on Zambia's Economic Development (Nairobi: Oxford University Press, 1971).

3. Kenneth Kaunda, "Towards Complete Independence," the Matero speech, August 11, 1969 (Lusaka: Zambia Information Services, 1969), p. 36.

4. Ministry of Commerce and Industry, White Paper Outline of the Government's Industrial Policy (Lusaka: Government Printer, January 3, 1966).

5. Ibid., p. 5.

6. Indeco Limited, Sixth Annual Report (1965), p. 4.

7. See Monthly Digest of Statistics (Lusaka: Central Statistical Office, various issues).

8. See annual reports of the mining companies.

9. Kenneth Kaunda, "Zambia Towards Economic Independence," Mulungushi speech, April 19, 1968 (Lusaka: Zambia Information Services, 1968). All direct quotations in this section are from the Mulungushi speech.

10. See Charles Harvey, "Financial Constraints," in Elliott, ed., op. cit.

11. Kaunda, "Towards Complete Independence," op. cit. All direct quotations in this section are from this speech.

12. Kenneth Kaunda, "Take Up the Challenge," speeches made to the United Independence Party National Council, Mulungushi Hall, Lusaka, November 7-10, 1970 (Lusaka: Zambia Information Services, 1970).

13. In 1969, President Kuanda stated that "he was not interested in the quarrel between the ideologies of East and West as to who should own the means of production . . . . Our common aim should be a ban forever on the exploitation of man by man . . . . For us, and indeed for the people to whom we owe everything. When we speak of the State participation in the ownership of the means of production, we are doing so in the full knowledge that this is but a transition. The State can be overbearing. The State can very easily become oppressive for the State can lose the way . . . . We hope that the time will come when everything in Zambia will be owned by the common man." See "Report of the Second National Convention on Rural Development, Incomes, Wages and Prices in Zambia" (Lusaka: Zambia Information Services, 1969).

6

**TAX REFORM
IN THE
MINING
INDUSTRY**

Charles Harvey

INTRODUCTION

The takeover of the mines was used as an occasion for reforming mining taxation, something that was long overdue and had been officially promised by President Kaunda in the 1968 Mulungushi speech.[1] The old tax system badly needed changing since it created wrong incentives in the fields of investment and production. It also had some curious and undesirable effects in the distribution of profits between the various mines and between the mines and Government.

It may seem odd at first to be discussing the question of taxation and incentives when the Government had already acquired 51 percent of the mining companies' shares and thus would appear to have the right to dictate policies on investment, the mining of marginal ores, training and promotion, and indeed any other policy issue it choose. As is explained in Chapter 7, despite its majority ownership the Government cannot in fact control the mines directly, having agreed to allow the management contractors to decide all important matters affecting the mines.

In fact, the Government never really had any option but to continue to control the mines indirectly, as before. Even if the management contractors had been willing to release control of commercial policy, the Government did not have enough people with enough knowledge and experience of the industry to do the job. The Government seems to have recognized this fact since otherwise there would have been no need to reform taxation and President Kaunda would not have said, when announcing the new tax system, that he had "met the mining companies' demands 100 percent"[2].

Nor is it necessarily desirable for the Government to control the mines directly, even if the personnel can be found to do it. It is arguable that the parastatal sector is best left to be run on commercial lines by commercial managers rather than controlled by civil servants. In short, it may be better to endure the imperfections of the profit motive and the market place than to suffer the imperfect application of social criteria by civil servants. If there is a clear divergence between social and private objectives, then the Government can pay direct subsidies to compensate for loss of profit.* Countries with adequate supplies of skilled manpower often prefer to control parastatal companies in this way, even those that are wholly owned by the government.

The exact working relationship that develops will doubtless be some sort of compromise, and it will be interesting to see if Government will be able to resist the temptation to try to increase its role in direct management as it acquires the personnel and thus the ability to do so. Those familiar with the history of the British Government's changing relationship with its nationalized industries know how much this is a matter of evolution and, to some extent, the personalities of the leading men involved. The point remains that taxation's influence upon management decisions is important now and probably will still be important when Government has acquired the manpower resources to control the industry directly.

THE OLD TAX SYSTEM

The faults of the old tax system have been described many times before, but a brief repetition here is necessary in order to be able to compare it with the new system.[3] The old system contained three separate taxes: royalty, export tax, and income tax. Up until independence in 1964, royalty was paid to the British South Africa Company, its transfer to the new Government being finally negotiated a bare three hours before the lowering of the British flag (see Chapter 2).

---

*The existence of private shareholders imposes an obligation to compensate for noncommercial activity, although there are many government policies that reduce profits, such as taxation itself or the diversion of trade routes, which are not so compensated.

Given that for many years the royalty had been a source of political discontent, it is perhaps understandable that the new Government was at first unwilling to change a formula that had clearly been so very profitable to the British South Africa Company. But the formula was for 13.5 percent of the "price" of copper, less K16, per long ton produced. (Originally the deduction was £8, but this was changed to K16 in November 1967 when Britain devalued.) The royalty was thus a tax on production and ignored cost. The price used was the monthly average of eight prices on the London Metal Exchange (cash and forward for four types of copper) at the <u>time of production,</u> an average that frequently bore little relation to the prices reported as actually received by the companies.

The reduction of K16 was intended to eliminate royalty when the price of copper was low, and in 1930 or 1940 would have succeeded in accomplishing this intent. Thus, the formula exacts no taxation at a price of less than K118.52 per long ton, a figure that bears little relation to modern costs of production but was highly significant in the 1930's: between 1934 and 1939, the average value of electrolytic copper produced varied between K63.34 and K120.64, taking £1 = K2 for comparison.[4]

As a tax on production, the royalty increased the cost to the mines of each ton of copper produced and thus made it unprofitable to mine all sorts of ore because of such factors as quality, position, and grade. Some lower-grade ores that were not mined in the past because of the royalty may never be mined because it would only have been possible or profitable to mine them at the same time as higher-grade ores. Furthermore, as an additional cost to the mines, the royalty could of course prevent the development of an otherwise profitable mine by reducing or eliminating the potential profits. Any tax reduces the rate of return on an investment, but a profits tax cannot eliminate a profit, whereas the royalty could (see Table 6.1 below).

The royalty also was inequitable between mines in that it could and did take a higher proportion of the profits of less profitable mines than it took of the profits of more profitable mines. Although both major mining groups in Zambia contain both high- and low-cost mines, the individual mines also had other shareholders, who were differentially and unfairly treated by the royalty.

All criticisms of the royalty as a tax apply, although to a slightly lesser extent, to the export tax. The export tax was 40 percent of the price per long ton of copper above K600, no export tax being payable when the copper price was below K600. It was introduced in April 1966 when the producers' price was dropped, in order to try to obtain for the Government a large share of the ensuing windfall profits. Just before it was abandoned, the producers' price was K576 (£336) per long ton, and the yearly average LME price for 1966 was K943 (£550) per long ton. The export tax was moderately successful in its main objective. However, it was charged on exports, and thus effectively on production since virtually all production is exported. Furthermore, it took no account of cost, so it simply added to the bad effects of the royalty.

Income tax was charged on profits, after the deduction of royalty and export tax, at a rate of 37.5 percent on the first K200,000 of profits and 45 percent on the remainder. Because of the large profits made by the mines, the effective rate of income tax was almost exactly 45 percent (which is the figure used in the remainder of this book). The differential rates of tax produced a number of irritating absurdities in the payment of inter-company dividends, but these were minor in absolute amount (although of great arithmetical complication). The 37.5/45 percent system was at least a great improvement on the pre-1968 arrangements under which different mines paid different rates of profits tax: the low-cost mines paid a high rate and vice versa, after paying the same rates of royalty and export tax.

Table 6.1 shows the theoretical percentage of profits paid in total under the three old taxes, at various costs and prices per long ton, and indicates some of the absurdities of the whole system of copper taxation. First, low-cost mines in general paid a lower proportion of their profits in tax. Second, tax could amount to more than 100 percent of profits. This was a real and not a hypothetical problem for a high-cost mine like Bancroft, which made a loss of K9.18 per long ton in 1967 after paying K102.60 per long ton royalty and K94.79 per long ton export tax.[5] (Bancroft did on occasion have some royalty remitted, after the event, as did Broken Hill for the same reason; the objections to this procedure are that it still left the mine with a zero profit and that remittance of royalty was not certain beforehand.) Third, tax could theoretically be charged on a mine making no profits at all before tax. Although this never in fact happened, it was becoming an increasingly real possibility as costs rose very rapidly after independence; this was one of the factors that made it almost certain that a change in the system would have to take place. Fourth, the percentage of profit paid in tax actually decreased as the copper price rose for the higher-cost mines.

TABLE 6.1

The Old Tax System for the Copper Companies:
Percentage of Profit Paid in Tax at Various
Prices and Costs per Long Ton

Price Per Ton	K300	K400	K500	K600
K500	59.1	73.2	*	*
K600	56.9	61.9	80.8	*
K700	61.3	66.6	77.6	118.5
K800	64.0	68.7	76.6	92.3
K900	65.7	69.8	76.0	86.4
K1,000	66.9	70.6	75.7	83.3

Note: The reduced rate of income tax, 37.5 percent, on the first
K200,000 of profits has been ignored; it makes very little difference
to the figures because of the size of the copper mining companies.
The table also ignores the effects of different rates of capital spending.
The table is correct as shown if one assumes that "costs" include
the part of capital spending allowed to be set off against income tax
and that the percentages shown as tax are a percentage of net profits.

*Some tax would be payable although no profits were made.

Source: Compiled by author.

TAX REFORMS

The first of the major changes in taxation announced in Matero
was that the new system would be based entirely on profits and would
thus meet most of the above criticisms. In fact, President Kaunda
said: "Instead of royalties and instead of the export tax I ask the
mining companies to pay 51 percent of their profits in the form of a
new mineral tax which I intend to introduce. The mineral tax, which
replaces the royalties and copper export tax, is based on profit and

in this I have met the mining companies' demands 100 percent."[6] In addition to the new mineral tax, the companies will continue to pay income tax of 45 percent on their profits after payment of mineral tax, giving a rate of tax on profits of 73.05 percent.

A flat-rate profits tax of 73 percent clearly removes most of the anomalies shown in Table 6.1. All mines will now pay the same percentage of profits in tax; tax can no longer amount to more than 100 percent of profits, nor can it be charged on a mine making no profit at all; and the percentage of profits paid in taxation will be constant as the copper price changes, since marginal and average rates of tax are now identical. The new marginal rate, 73 percent, is virtually unchanged from the old one, which was 74.42 percent for rises in the copper price above K600 per long ton (at copper prices below K600 per long ton, export tax was not operative; so that marginal tax rate was only 52.42 percent).

The other major tax change announced at Matero was to allow all capital expenditure to be set against profits in the year in which it is made and to allow capital expenditure as a deduction against both mineral tax and income tax. Previously, there was a system of capital allowances that varied according to the category of expenditure and could only be set off against income tax, not against royalty or export tax. So the amount of capital spending that is effectively paid by the Government is now 73 percent compared with 45 percent previously, and in addition the tax relief is available immediately instead of being spread over a number of years. The capital allowances under the old system are shown in Table 6.2.

Capital spending in copper mining varies greatly in its composition from one project to another, so there is no typical profile of capital allowances. However, the change from the old to the new system can be illustrated, at least for a period of moderate expansion, by using the assumptions of Table 7.7 in the Statistical Appendix to Chapter 7, where capital spending and allowances that would have been available had the takeover reforms never occurred have been estimated for an expansion of production from 700,000 metric tons to 800,000 metric tons between 1970 and 1975. The new and old capital allowances are compared in Table 6.3.

Even if expansion ceased after 1975 in the example illustrated in Table 6.3, in which case allowances under the old system would begin to be greater than under the new, the difference between the two systems is so great in the early years that it is clear that the new system is considerably more advantageous to the mining companies.

TABLE 6.2

Capital Allowances in Copper Mining
Before Takeover
(percent)

	Initial Allowance	Annual Allowance
1. Industrial buildings	10	10
2. Low-cost housing	10	5
3. Commercial buildings	—	2
4. Prime moving machinery	20	30
5. Other machinery	20	20
6. Other mine development	—	5

Notes: Annual allowances for all types of buildings (lines 1 to 3) were on a straight line method; other annual allowances (lines 4 to 6) were on a declining balance method. Theoretically, the mines could choose to depreciate on an agreed life-of-mine basis, but this method was never chosen since it was invariably less advantageous.

Source: Abstracted from various Tax Acts.

SUPPOSED ADVANTAGES OF THE OLD SYSTEM

The old system was supposed to have some advantages, the most important of which was to give Government a large share of rises in the copper price. Table 6.1 demonstrates some of the absurdities that this introduced; the new system achieves neatly enough the same high marginal rate without the inequitably high average rates on the least profitable mines. Very small increases in the average rates paid by the more profitable mines will be sufficient to give the Government roughly equal amounts of revenue because the largest mines (Nchanga and Mufulira) also have the lowest costs per ton.

Similarly, because the big mines have low costs, the new system also will produce slightly less variation in Government revenue than before. At low copper prices, when the high-cost mines would have

TABLE 6.3

Comparison of Old and New Capital Allowances
(millions of Kwacha)

	1970	1971	1972	1973	1974	1975
1. Estimated capital spending	42	17	28	28	26	19
2. Estimated capital allowances	20	17	20	20	20	18
3. Tax saving, old system	9	8	9	9	9	8
4. Tax saving, new system	31	12	20	20	19	14

Note: The allowances in line 2 include estimated carry-over from capital spending in earlier years (see also notes to Table 7.7). The present values of lines 3 and 4, discounted at 10 percent, are K41 million and K96 million respectively.

Source: Lines 1 and 2 taken from lines 7 and 8 of Table 7.7 in the Statistical Appendix to Chapter 7; line 3 is 45 percent of line 2; line 4 is 73 percent of line 1.

138

suffered penally high rates of tax, the relief offered under the new system will again be offset by the higher rates paid by the low-cost mines. Only if the copper price fell below the costs of all mines, including the big low-cost mines, would the old system have been theoretically more effective in producing some government revenue. In other words, royalty was supposed to guarantee the government some yield from copper taxes even in bad years, and thus to force on the copper companies some of the reserve-building functions of government. In practice, whenever royalty payments forced a company into making losses after tax, the government rebated enough royalty to eliminate the loss. (This happened to Bancroft and to Broken Hill which, although not a copper mine, paid a royalty to government.)

In the Zambian economy, dependent on a single commodity with a highly volatile price, the reserve-holding function of government is extremely important. Pushing a very small part of that function on private companies was both undesirable and unreliable in theory, as well as pointless if in any case it was not enforced. Under either tax system, "temporary" falls in the copper price below balance of payments equilibrium must be paid for out of the reserves if the government is to maintain its spending program. The problem is in knowing what is temporary. In practice, falls usually must be assumed temporary at first and run on the reserves; depending on the size of the reserves and thus on how long they last, a prolonged price fall must eventually lead to a cutback in government spending, perhaps with devaluation. The latter is a relatively weak weapon because of the fairly small local value added in copper and the difficulty of forcing a loss of real wages on the powerful mining union. Expatriates in mining (still nearly 6,000 and vitally important) probably would be able to force a compensatory wage rise because of their international mobility and the world shortage of high-skill copper and other metal mining workers.

The point here is that these problems would face government under either tax system. There was never really any serious question of forcing loss-making mines to pay royalty; under every other circumstances, the new system is slightly less volatile in revenue production than the old. No system can significantly reduce the extreme vulnerability of the government to changes in the price of copper, especially if it is eager to have a share of high profits when they are being made. The only stable system would be one in which the government extracted no revenue at all from the mines, so that high earnings were offset by high income paid abroad. The absurdity of this idea makes the obvious (but important) point that huge revenues from copper, however unstable, are much better than no revenues at all.

As it happens, luck has been with Zambia because exceptionally high prices since 1964 (plus various constraints on spending[7]) have allowed a large build-up of reserves. Some of these reserves will be needed to pay for the loss of production in 1971 and 1972 from the disaster at Mufulira Mine; a rough estimate suggests the reserves could suffer by about K150 million. But the underlying financial strength of the country is well illustrated by its ability to meet this loss and retain substantial reserves. Some further idea of the origin of this financial strength can be gathered from the fact that the copper price fell from about £750 (K1,286) a metric ton to about £440 (K754) a metric ton between March and December 1970, yet this price was still high enough to give a small balance of payments surplus on current account in a normal— that is, full production—year (see Chapter 7, especially Table 7.4).

Some other minor advantages were attributed to the old tax system. One was that royalty and export tax were paid throughout the year, while income tax was paid a year in arrears. To avoid transition problems and maintain this advantage, the new mineral tax will be paid throughout the year, on the basis of the copper price and estimated costs, with an end-of-year adjustment.

A second minor advantage that weighed heavily against tax change in Government circles was that royalty and export tax were based on the published LME copper price and on production and export volume, respectively. This avoided any possibility that the companies might manipulate their costs and sales to avoid tax and exchange control. The system was rigidly applied despite the fact that the companies often paid tax on the basis of sales prices very different from those they actually received because of the long period between production, export, and sale.

It seems unlikely that significant manipulation took place, or would have taken place if taxes had been profit-based before the take-over, despite the high level of Zambian taxes. First, the companies' stake in Zambia was so large (valued at over K400 million at the time of the takeover) and the investment so profitable despite the high taxes that it would have been foolish to risk it. Second, most costs were fairly well known and few were paid to overseas subsidiaries. Third, sales were mainly by contract at prices based by a published formula on the LME price. In any case, profits could always have been based on LME rather than sale prices if the Government was suspicious of this part of the company accounts. The sheer size of the companies, and the size and reputation of their auditors, would have meant that a very large number of people were in the know and kept quiet.* In any case, since the new tax system is entirely profit-based, the government has either recognized these arguments or believes that government-appointed directors will be a sufficient additional safeguard against manipulation of accounts contrary to the national interest.

WEAKNESSES OF THE NEW SYSTEM

The principal weakness of the new system is that 73.05 percent is a very high rate of tax by any standard. There is no inherent reason why new mining investment should have to earn a higher pre-tax rate of return than other investment in Zambia in order to earn the same rate of return after tax. In fact, the reverse is more likely to be the case. Mining is a high-risk industry, so that a higher prospective rate of return than in other industries is required to attract new investment. A similar argument could be applied to the position of mining in Zambia as opposed to mining in the rest of the world. Central Africa in general, and Zambia in particular, are regarded as high-risk areas and therefore a higher prospective rate of return is needed to attract investment in competition with parts of the world regarded as less risky. Although the number of countries with substantial copper deposits is obviously limited, there are alternatives, and there are also alternatives for prospecting activity. In principle, any new mining development is desirable even if it pays no tax at all. The whole question of taxation and new mining development is dealt with at length in Chapter 8; it is sufficient to mention here that the problem has been recognized by Government but that attempts to deal with it have been inadequate. Briefly, the government has legislated that if the return on equity falls below 12 percent, tax will be rebated to restore a 12 percent return. For various reasons, this has small incentive effect.

A second criticism of the new system is that no attempt has been made to differentiate between very high (or windfall) profits, and

---

*A fourth reason, based on purely subjective judgement, is that the top management in the companies had real sympathy with Government and its aspirations. Remarkably, they were eager for tax reform but did not press for a reduction of the total burden. No doubt, this position was based on a recognition of mutual self interest; it may indeed be no more than an enlargement of the first point above.

"normal" profits. In other words, there has been no attempt to replace the export tax, insofar as it tried to tax "excess" profits. Although the export tax was wrongly formulated, the intention has some merit; it could still have been realized by a tax with high and rising marginal rates for high and rising rates of profit, either per ton or as a rate of return on equity. Since the rate of return on equity is sensitive to gearing, profit per ton expressed as a percentage of cost, probably would be the best measure of profitability. A low rate for low profitability would have the advantage of reducing the disincentive effects of Zambia's high tax rates, whereas high rates on highly profitable operations have little disincentive effect since high profits are in any case being made. Before the event, the prospect of such high profits would be only too attractive a possibility, tax or no tax.

A third criticism is that the new tax incentive to expansion is geared entirely to capital spending and thus has the effect of making capital cheaper than all other inputs. The rest of the tax system compounds this effect. In general, import duties tax industrial inputs, especially capital equipment, very lightly or not at all, while duties on consumer goods are relatively heavy. Since the prices of consumer goods affect the cost of living, and this tends ultimately to be reflected in wages, import duties have the effect of making labor expensive relative to all other inputs. In addition, the employer's contribution to the National Provident Fund, based on wages, has the effect of a tax on labor, whatever its principal intention.

Many other features of the Zambian economy make labor unattractive relative to capital, but these are partly or wholly outside the government's immediate ability to control. The tax system before the takeover was wholly within the government's range of possible actions. As shown in Chapter 7, the government has agreed as part of the takeover agreements not to change the tax laws as they affect the mining companies, at least not so as to increase the total tax paid, while compensation is being paid. Although theoretically it would be possible to negotiate a change in the form of allowances in order to remove the bias toward capital spending or even introduce a positive bias in favor of labor, in practice it would be extremely difficult to show that any new system could not under any circumstances result in increased tax burdens, unless the Government sugared the pill with a significant tax cut. Therefore, it may be argued that Zambia is stuck with the present tax system for the duration of the takeover agreements.

It also can be argued that mining technology does not allow much substitution between capital and labor, but R.E. Baldwin has given a great deal of evidence to show that the relative cost and effiency of African labor, expatriate labor, and capital equipment has indeed caused significant changes in their relative utilization in the past. At the same time, he shows that, although at times of relatively low African wages and high African labor efficiency technical processes in the mines fell behind other copper producers in the sense of not using the latest labor-saving technology, the mining companies were able to catch up when African wages rose.[8] This is an important point, since one of the reasons given by the Government for not changing tax incentives in favor of labor is the fear of becoming permanently backward in technology.

However, as a second best solution the new system is already a vast improvement on the old. It has removed the inequities and illogical aspects illustrated in Table 6.1, and it even has marginally reduced the instability of Government revenue. Finally, it has removed the uncertainty surrounding the tax system, which was caused by the system's own shortcomings and increased by the announcement of impending change in the 1968 Mulungushi speech. This reduction of uncertainty, together with the establishment of partnership on an equity base, should do much to improve the general investment climate, which is a necessary prerequisite for growth, however attractive the other financial details.

This chapter has dealt with only some of the implications of the new tax system. The question of further improvement in the system, especially that of coping with the continuing disincentive effects of the very high rate of tax, is considered at length in Chapter 8, where a new system is proposed. Most of the other implications cannot be separated from consideration of the whole package of measures that make up the takeover deal, and so are discussed in the following chapter.

NOTES

1. Kenneth Kaunda, "Zambia Towards Economic Independence," the Mulungushi speech, April 19, 1968 (Lusaka: Zambia Information Services, 1968), p. 45.

2. Kenneth Kaunda, "Towards Complete Independence," the Matero speech, August 11, 1969 (Lusaka: Zambia Information Services, 1969), p. 35.

3. An earlier critique, written in 1968, and some proposals for a new system (which were not adopted) can be found in Charles Harvey,

"Taxation in Zambia," in C.M. Elliott, ed., Constraints on the Economic Development of Zambia (Nairobi: Oxford University Press, 1971).

4. W. J. Barber, The Economy of British Central Africa (London: Oxford University Press, 1961), p. 127; for details of costs since 1964, see Chapter V.

5. Bancroft Mines Limited, Annual Report (1967).

6. Kaunda, "Towards Complete Independence," op. cit., p. 35.

7. See Harvey, op. cit.; Charles Harvey, "Inflation in a Very Open Economy: Zambia 1964-69," Eastern African Economic Review, Vol. III, No. 1 (June 1971).

8. R. E. Baldwin, Economic Development and Export Growth: A Study of Northern Rhodesia, 1920-1960 (Berkeley: University of California Press, 1966), Chapter 4.

7

THE

TAKEOVER

Mark Bostock

Charles Harvey

INTRODUCTION

The terms of the takeover are summarized in some detail in Appendix A; the legal constraints mutually imposed by the Government and the companies are discussed in Appendix B; and the changed structure of the companies with their principal shareholdings are shown in Appendix C. This chapter will provide some comment on the arrangements in terms of the various objectives of Government and, to a lesser extent, the companies.

First, for the reader who has not read Appendixes A and B (although this is strongly advised), the arrangement is briefly summarized:

1. <u>Company structure</u>. The Government created a new State company called Mindeco, the Mining Development Corporation, to hold its shares in the mining companies. Mindeco is in turn wholly owned by Zimco, the Zambian Industrial and Mining Corporation. Also wholly owned by Zimco is Indeco, the old holding company for industrial and trading assets (see Chapter 5). The Government actually took over only the mining companies operated by the Zamanglo (Zambia Anglo-American) and RST Groups and involved in mining and processing.* In the case of the Anglo-American group, these were

---

*Because of the corporate structure of the mining industry (see Appendix C), the takeover of the mining companies meant that

amalgamated into a single company, Nchanga Consolidated Copper
Mines (NCCM). In the case of RST, the companies were amalgamated
into another company, Roan Consolidated Mines (RCM). Mindeco has
a 51 percent holding in NCCM and RCM.

2. Payment. Mindeco's 51 percent shares in NCCM, valued at
K126 million (U. S. $176 million), are being paid for by issue of 6 per-
cent Zimco loan stock to be paid off in installments every 6 months
over 12 years. Payment for Mindeco's 51 percent share of RCM,
valued at K84 million (U. S. $118 million) is by issue of 6 percent
Zimco bonds to be paid off in installments every six months over 8
years. (Hereafter, both loan stock and bonds are referred to as Zimco
bonds.) Payment is guaranteed by the Government, which expects the
payments to be met out of Mindeco dividends. These payments come
to annual figures of K13.5 million (U. S. $18.9 million) for RCM and
K14.8 million (U.S. $20.7 million) for NCCM. The agreements specify
that payments shall be made in U. S. dollars, protecting shareholders
from devaluation of the Zambian Kwacha.

3. Acceleration of payment. If two-thirds of the Mindeco dividend from either company comes to more than the annual compensation
payment, then the difference must be applied to additional redemptions
after 1971/72. Such accelerated redemption does not reduce the
obligation to meet additional half-yearly payments, except insofar as
it brings forward completion of payment. All repayments, including
the 6 percent interest, are free of Zambian tax and exchange control.

4. Management contracts. Management contracts have been
given to the former controlling companies and are held by Anglo-
American (Central Africa) Limited and RST Management Services
Limited. The two companies are not directly owned by the 49 percent
private shareholders, although there is an indirect interest (see
Appendix B). The fee for management is .75 percent of turnover and
2 percent of profits after mineral tax but before income tax.

5. Agreements. The vital features of the various documents
relating to the running of the new companies are that all essential
decisions, especially decisions on investment and financing of investment, must be approved by separate majorities of the "A" Directors

----

Government also took a 51 percent interest in the three copper refineries, Mines Air Services, the Copperbelt Power Corporation,
and Ndola Lime Company.

(Government) and the "B" Directors (representing 49 percent minority interest) and that the companies must be run so as to "optimize production and profit." Breach of these agreements, including breach of the management contracts, makes all the Zimco loan stock and bonds due and payable immediately.

6. Sales, purchasing, and recruiting contracts. The former parent companies have exclusive sales contracts for .75 percent of sales and exclusive contracts for overseas purchases. These can be transferred to agents with the approval of NCCM and RCM. In addition, the parent companies have expatriate recruiting contracts for 15 percent of each recruit's first year's gross emoluments. All these contracts include an obligation to give staff seconded from RCM and NCCM training and experience, at the mining companies' expense.

7. "Frozen Law." The Zambian Government has agreed that Zambian law as in force on December 31, 1969, shall continue to apply while the Zimco bonds are outstanding. .This includes very specifically the tax and exchange control rules applicable to the companies and the new legislation envisaged by the agreements themselves.

8. Non-mining assets. Nonmining assets have not been taken over and have been allowed to be externalized—to Bermuda in the case of Anglo-American and to the United States in the case of RST. Such assets include cash forcibly retained in Zambia under pre-Matero exchange control regulations: K17.9 million (U. S. $25 million) in monthly installments to December 1971 for RST and K27.5 million (U. S. $38.5 million) in monthly installments to June 1972 for Anglo-American. However, it is also part of the agreement that out of these externalized funds RST and Anglo-American will make available K15 million (U. S. $21 million) and K12 million (U. S. $16.8 million) respectively for reinvestment in new mines or the expansion of existing ones.

9. Taxation. Taxation of existing mines has been changed as described in Chapter 6; taxation of new mines and the tax arrangements for exploration and development expenditure are considered in Chapter 8. Briefly, there is a 73 percent tax on profits, and capital expenditure can now be written off freely.

10. Government participation in new mines. Government has an option to take a 51 percent share in all new mines. If it takes up this option, it will pay its share of exploration and development expenditure (see Appendix D).

11. Exploration rights. RST and Anglo-American have given up large areas over which they held prospecting rights, and all present and future rights are for limited periods during which there are minimum expenditure requirements. In addition, no mining licence can again be granted in perpetuity; they are now granted for limited periods (25 years with option of renewal for the same period).

12. ICSID affiliation. The Zambian Government has agreed to join the International Centre for the Settlement of Investment Disputes (ICSID), an institution affiliated with the World Bank. Virtually all substantial disputes between "A" and "B" Directors and any breach of the agreements must be referred to ICSID.

LEGAL CONSTRAINTS

As part of the takeover deal, the Government has accepted a number of restrictions on its freedom of action. In total, these restrictions appear to amount to a considerable reduction in the independence of the Zambian Government. In part, however, the loss of freedom is more apparent than real, and in part the restrictions are necessary to achieve the Government's various objectives.

Thus, the Government has undertaken not to increase the rate of taxation on the mining companies above its present level of 73 percent. For example, if the company income tax were raised from 45 percent to 50 percent, the mining companies would have to be exempted. However, it is the principle of this restriction rather than its practice that is onerous, since the existing 73 percent is such a high rate of tax; in addition, part of the post-tax profit accrues to Mindeco and thus the public sector, provided the copper price is high enough. In practice, a problem is more likely in deciding if, when, and by how much to reduce the tax rate in order to encourage new mining investment than in not being able to increase it (see Chapter 8).

The promise not to impose any exchange controls on the various overseas payments of the companies is also a necessary part of the arrangement. The Government could hardly have agreed to pay compensation for the shares taken over without at the same time promising to allow these payments to be made. Regarding the sending of dividends overseas, one is discussing a mere 13 percent or so of total profits whose remission probably is essential if any shareholder goodwill at all is to be retained; in any case, the forcible retention of post-tax profits would once again raise the awkward problem of a build-up of foreign-owned assets. In the period between the 1968

Mulungushi speech, when restrictions on dividend remission were
introduced, and the Matero speech 18 months later, large sums were
accumulated out of unremittable mining profits. One of the reasons
that these funds were not being spent was that mining investment in
particular cannot get under way that quickly. But in addition some
funds were not being committed to investment because of the very
uncertainties concerning tax and ownership that were resolved at
Matero.* Thus, an optimistic view of the new situation would be that
increased investment should now take place, to which the mining
companies should be willing to commit retained profits. Therefore,
the remission of the remaining profits, post-tax and post-retention,
should be smaller than before even though they can all be freely
remitted abroad (for further elaboration of this point, see following
sections, especially Tables 7.2 and 7.6).

        The question of additional investment in expansion is thus crucial.
Formal control of such investment is to be exercised by a combination
of the "B" Directors, representing the private sector shareholders,
and Adam Smith's invisible hand. The "A" and "B" Directors voting
separately must approve—that is, the "B" Directors have a veto
over—all expansion plans and appropriations out of profit for capital
expenditure or expenditure on exploration or prospecting. The "B"
Director veto must not be "unreasonably withheld having regard to
the interests of RCM (and NCCM) and to the interests of the shareholders."[1] At the same time, the "B" Directors have a specific
directive to run the companies on commercial principles, and they
are specifically required not to approve any undertaking for which
the companies cannot raise money on "commercially competitive
terms."

        It thus appears that the "B" Directors need not approve any
plan that is not sufficiently attractive to appeal to outside capital.
Insofar as the Zambian capital market is not big enough to finance
mining projects, this means that the criteria applied to investment
in Zambian mining by foreign financial sources can be used by the
" B" Directors in assessing the commercial viability of new projects.
The prospective rate of return must therefore include any additional
risk premium required by overseas lenders, as opposed to local ones.

----

        *Capital spending did increase in 1968 and 1969, as shown in
Chapter 5, Table 5.3; see the following section for a possible explanation.

The control over post-tax profits is completed by a provision that all profits not appropriated for capital, prospecting, or exploration spending or needed for working capital, must be paid out as dividends. Therefore, the companies cannot build up revenue reserves. This function must be performed by Government out of tax revenue, and by Mindeco or Zimco if they wish out of any part of dividend income that remains after making compensation payments.

Therefore, the "B" Directors control the level of development spending (although they must not unreasonably veto commercially viable projects), appropriation from profit for development spending, and the level of dividends (as a result of the control of appropriation from profit for development spending). To the extent that the "A" Directors, whom we are assuming to be basically in favor of as much expansion as possible (see below), can show that new projects are viable and can encourage the search for viable new projects, the "B" Directors have an obligation to go ahead. If they do not agree to appropriate profits for such projects, they must presumably agree to borrow the necessary funds, and repayments on such loans will in due course reduce the level of dividends. Meanwhile, expansion should increase profits and thus dividends: the timing of the two opposing influences determines the flow of dividends. Thus, control over dividends by the "B" Directors is not absolute.

Other areas of "B" Director veto simply fill in the details of the commitment to commercial principles and prevent the use of profits for any nonmining activities. In other words, the "B" Directors cannot be forced to use mining profits for investment in, for example, agriculture or manufacturing if the "B" shareholders would prefer to have their money out of Zambia as dividends. Undoubtedly, they would so prefer.

Although in the past the mining companies did invest outside mining and refining, of course the Government has other means of encouraging diversified development and other funds than the small part of 49 percent of post-tax mining profits that might be involved. What is more, there is no inherent reason why the mining companies should be better at manufacturing or agriculture than Indeco.

Finally, the Government has guaranteed the Zimco bonds with its "full faith and credit," and will be in breach of that guarantee not only if it fails to ensure that payments of interest and principal are met but also if it fails to abide by any of the provisions discussed in this section, for example if it raises the overall rate of tax, applies "unfrozen" law to the companies, or tries to get around the "B" Director veto.

Although it is normal practice for loan agreements to make the entire loan due and payable immediately upon breach of <u>financial</u> conditions, this penalty is unusual for breach of <u>nonfinancial</u> conditions. Nevertheless, this is what has been done. The penalty for being in breach of agreement is that all the Zimco bonds become immediately due. The sheer size of the sum involved—the diminishing balance on K208 million—makes nonsense of this provision. Nobody can seriously expect Zambia to hand over such a sum in a single payment, at least not until the balance has diminished enormously. In fact, it is entirely possible for the foreign exchange reserves to fall so far that such a payment would be impossible.

The importance of the provision is to ensure that any dispute between the Zambian Government and the private shareholders or their representatives, the management companies, is not a private affair that can be ignored by the rest of the world. Whether such a dispute concerned nonfinancial or financial matters, the whole financial world immediately would be made aware of it because the Zimco bonds would be declared due and the dispute would be taken to the ICSID. Even if this sequence of events were not followed, its threat would be present.

The implications are clear. ICSID is an institution sponsored by the World Bank and with a wide international membership. Other investors in Zambia—including the World Bank itself and the IMF—whose money could very well be needed to bridge a period of low copper prices would be unlikely to ignore any refusal by Zambia to abide by a ruling of ICSID. In other words, the mining companies have successfully ensured that their own private agreement is an inseparable part of the whole complex of Zambia's international financial relations.

Zambia has always been dependent on its international borrowing powers because of the instability of its export earnings, even if this dependence has been potential rather than actual in recent years. As a result, Zambia's reputation for financial rectitude, whether in deals with private or with official lenders, has always been important. What the mining companies have done is to formalize this situation further by ensuring that Zambia earns as much disapproval as possible from as many people as possible for breach of these particular agreements.

Such provisions add greatly to the value of the agreements to the private shareholders. Clearly, the value of the new arrangements depends not only on the financial payments agreed upon but also on control of future profitability. Thus, it was essential for the private shareholders to ensure both that they got their share of the cake, in their hands and not in a deep freeze in Zambia, and that they continued to control the size of the cake so that their share would be worth having.

The penalties that the Zambian Government can impose are less powerful. Inadequate provision of management services can lead to a premature ending of the contracts, but this weapon would be usable only if there were some alternative group that could offer comparable services. The local knowledge needed to run the Zambian mines means that such alternative services are not available. Only in the long term, when trained and experienced Zambians are available, can the Government think of doing without the present management services. In the unlikely case that Zambia chooses to take a dispute with the companies to ICSID, it is not easy to see what sanctions that body could impose, except that failure to abide by a ruling on the part of the companies would remove the ICSID weapon from their armory.

COMMITMENT TO EXPANSION

In his Matero speech announcing the takeover of the mines, President Kaunda said, at first quoting from his 1968 Mulungushi speech of the previous year:

"First of all, I want to say to the mining companies that I am very disappointed at the virtual lack of mining development since Independence. Apart from very small developments at Kalengwa and Mimbula Fitula and some further development at existing mines, we have seen nothing. The companies claim that the royalty system has been against new development. Nevertheless I think they have not done enough towards further development of the country in which they make their great profits. Let me also say that I do not agree with the mining companies that royalties have been the obstacle to the development of the industry. I have been following their accounts and I know very well that they could have embarked upon further expansion if they chose to devote part of their profits for this purpose. Instead of reinvesting they have been distributing over 80 percent of their profits every year as dividends."

I am afraid, having gone into the matter very thoroughly
in my capacity as Minister of Mines, I now hold even
stronger views that I did last year.[2]

Thus, one of government's main criticisms of the mining companies was the lack of expansion, and one of the main government
objectives in introducing the Matero reforms, including the takeover,
was to induce further expansion. The government is now claiming
success in this objective. In a speech in November 1970, President
Kaunda said:

What is more important than the financial deal we obtained
for the mines is the influence we have brought in their expansion program despite the fact that they have been under
our control for a very short period of time. When the
mines submitted their production forecasts for the period
1970-75 before they came under our control last year, they
estimated that their production by 1975 would rise to
[793,000 tonnes].* Under our control the expansion plans
have been revised and accelerated and the production is
expected to reach 967,000 tonnes by 1975, an increase of
nearly 200,000 tonnes. When Mufulira Mine is rehabilitated
its production will rise from 165,000 metric tons before the
disaster to 190,000 metric tons per annum. A decision has
been made to open up the Baluba Mine which will produce
22,000 metric tons by 1973 and 51,000 metric tons by 1975.
Kalengwa Mine will be producing at the rate of 17,000
metric tons per year. Kansanshi Mine will be opening
soon and it is expected to produce at 18,000 metric tons per
year by 1972. Bwana Mkubwa will be producing 15,000
tonnes per year. Plans are in hand to re-open the Konkola
Number 2 shaft which will be producing initially 5,000
metric tons rising to about 18,000 metric tons by 1980. The
The most interesting new development is the one which is be
being proposed at Nchanga. So far a great deal of copper
was being lost in the tailings at Nchanga Mine but we have
now decided to establish a very large leaching plant which
will enable us to treat the Nchanga ores more efficiently

---

*The President actually said "780,000 metric tons," but to be
consistent with the known figures he must have meant 780,000 long
tons, or 793,000 metric tons (or tonnes). All other measurements
in extract are in metric tons.

and at the same time retreat the tailing dumps which have
accumulated over the years. This will increase the production of the Nchanga Mine by 55,000 metric tons per year to
a total of nearly 300,000 metric tons. The overall mining
development I described above represents a combined expenditure between the two mining companies under Mindeco
of at least 300 million Kwacha over the next 5 years. This
is an unprecedented level of investment in mining in
Zambia and it has been achieved by our own efforts.[3]

The companies would undoubtedly dispute the implications of
this statement. In the first place, as we have already argued strongly
in Chapter 6, the old tax system was a real hindrance to the exploitation
of low-grade ores. In addition, much of the expansion in production
announced since Matero would have taken place with or without the
takeover.

Even without the complication that the tax change and the takeover were announced simultaneously, so that it is extremely difficult
to disentangle their separate influences, it is clear that there probably
will never be complete agreement. The situation is further complicated
by the timing of the earlier plans to expand to 793,000 metric tons
by 1975. These plans were drawn up soon after the 1968 Mulungushi
speech, in which the President announced that the tax system would
be reformed. He did not say at that time when reform would take
place, but the mining companies, stung by criticism of lack of investment, may have drawn up new plans on the assumption that the tax
change would be soon and that it would be in a direction more favorable
to investment. There was no lack of tax reform plans at that time,
and all were based more heavily on profits, which is what was required and what eventually occurred.

One imagines then that there must have been a number of expansion plans waiting, as it were, for the removal of various uncertainties, including the question of tax reform. At the same time, other
factors affecting investment decisions, independent of the Matero
reforms, continued to be important: for example, the copper price
cost changes and technical progress.

Certainly, the logic of the takeover arrangement as we have
seen it thus far is that government has not gained "control" of the
mines since the "B" Directors must approve all expansion plans.
Furthermore, they have no obligation to do so unless the project is
commercially viable. Assuming that this framework is indeed the
one in which decisions have been made, then any new investments

must have been induced by the tax changes plus the removal of uncertainties about tax, exchange control, and ownership. In addition,
the fact that Mindeco must find 51 percent of the cost of expansion
may have made some expansion more viable, as well as reducing the
companies' share of the risk to 49 percent. The government's ability
to apply informal pressure to the companies has, if anything, been
slightly reduced by the formal spelling out in the agreements of the
rights of the "B" Directors and their commitment to commercial
principles and by the removal of the takeover threat itself. This
possible disadvantage must be set against the additional informal
contact through the boards of directors.

One is left then, with a variety of possible interpretations: (1)
that the takeover directly induced a commitment to expansion that
raised the production forecast for 1975 from 793,000 metric tons to
967,000 metric tons; (2) that such expansion as was induced by the
package deal was induced by changes in taxation and exchange control
and thus would have taken place without 51 percent government participation; (3) that all the expansion would have taken place anyway,
the time between various announcements being simply the normal
passage of time before commitments become firm, and the timing of
the takeover in relation to these commitments a coincidence; and (4)
that some part of the expansion to 793,000 metric tons was dependent
on tax reform or other changes and would never have taken place
without it.

Somewhere within this range of possibilities one can try to
identify expansion projects that seem to have been "Matero-induced."
Unfortunately, this leads to yet another complication, since adding up
all the known expansion projects gives total production by NCCM and
RCM together of only 899,000 metric tons by 1975 (see Table 7.1).

Known increases after 1975 are another 29,000 metric tons at
Baluba, probably in 1976, and a very large further increase of over
90,000 metric tons at Nchanga, because of the technical breakthrough
in the treatment of tailings. But after 1975 production at Luanshya,
Chibuluma, and Kalengwa is expected to fall off; in general, fore-
casting becomes too speculative to have any value for the late 1970's.

Of the increases shown in Table 7.1, those at Baluba (22,000
metric tons), Kansanshi (18,000 metric tons), and part of the increase
at Nchanga (perhaps 35,000 metric tons) can most confidently be
attributed to the takeover, including all its ramifications such as tax
reform. In addition, it may be that the extra 22,000 metric tons to
be produced by Rhokana at the new Mindolo extension also can be

TABLE 7.1

Identifiable Production Increases
to 1975, by Project
(thousands of metric tons)

	Actual Production 1970	Estimated Changes					Estimated Production 1975
		1971	1972	1973	1974	1975	
NCCM							
Nchanga	240	+5	+25	+25	--	--	295
Bancroft	50	--	--	--	--	--	50
Rhokana (including Mindolo)	100	--	+5	--	+17	--	122
Kansanshi	--	--	--	+18	--	--	18
Bwana Mkubwa	--	+15	--	--	--	--	15
Total	390	+20	+30	+43	+17	--	500
RCM							
Mufulira	165	+25	--	--	--	--	190
Kalengwa	--	+17	--	--	--	--	17
Chambishi	24	--	--	--	+12	+12	48
Chibuluma	24	--	--	--	--	--	24
Baluba	--	--	--	+22	--	--	22
Luanshya	98	--	--	--	--	--	98
Total	311	+42	--	+22	+12	+12	399
Total RCM and NCCM	701	+62	+30	+65	+29	+12	899

Note: These forecasts ignore the effect of the disaster at Mufulira in 1970. Loss of production (in thousands of tons) has been estimated at 40 in 1970, 110 in 1971 and 50 in 1972. In addition, the allocation of increases to each year is not definite in all cases; in particular, it has not been publicly stated when the increases at Nchanga will take place.

Source: Mining company reports.

described as Matero-induced. In other words, we estimate that (in round figures) 100,000 metric tons of projected production increases are Matero-induced.

If production does in fact reach 967,000 metric tons in 1975, as opposed to the 899,000 metric tons that can be forecast from known projects, then presumably this additional increase also will be attributable to the takeover.* For the moment, we have chosen to compare expansion to 899,000 metric tons under the new tax and exchange control rules with expansion to 800,000 metric tons under the old rules. The full implications of this comparison are spelled out in detail in Tables 7.7, 7.8, 7.9, and 7.10 in the Statistical Appendix to this chapter. In the following sections, we compare the two situations in their effect on the balance of payments, the public sector's revenue position, and the growth of the economy. Alternative assumptions about the impact of the takeover can of course be fed into the same framework. In general, the greater the expansion induced, the higher the short-term cost as that expansion is paid for and the higher the long-term gain as exports increase and generate more tax revenue, foreign exchange, and thus growth potential.

THE BALANCE OF PAYMENTS

If one accepts the argument that an expansion of production was one of government's main objectives, it still remains to calculate how much this expansion has cost the country. An expansion of copper exports is effectively the only short-term way of continuing to expand the economy without reducing the foreign exchange reserves; both import substitution and noncopper export promotion may gradually reduce dependence on copper, or rather reduce the amount by which copper exports must be expanded, but cannot of themselves allow significant growth in the short term. Therefore, it might be argued that the government must accept almost any cost to achieve it. But the victory would be a hollow one if the balance of payments cost on

---

*Some of the differences between the government's forecast of 967,000 metric tons and the aggregated company forecasts of 899,000 metric tons in 1975 may be in production by other companies, for example at Mkushi, but it is unlikely that this can account for the whole difference. And the influence of the takeover on such expansion is indirect at most.

capital account turned out to be greater than the gain on current account. Even if one holds that the takeover was entirely a political move, it is still of interest to assess the economic consequences.

In this section, these economic consequences are examined on the assumption that the takeover induced a revision of production plans from a target of 800,000 to 899,000 metric tons in 1975. (The working out of the implications of this and the other assumptions we have made is shown in detail in Tables 7.7, 7.8, 7.9 and 7.10 in the Statistical Appendix to this chapter. Basically, we have made a comparison between (1) changes in the balance of payments that would have occurred after January 1970 if production had expanded to 800,000 metric tons by 1975 and if the takeover changes had not been made and (2) changes in the balance of payments that would have occurred if production had expanded to 899,000 metric tons by 1975, with post-takeover tax and exchange control rules. The viewpoint is from January 1970; that is, the view of the parties to the takeover negotiations, and it thus ignores all subsequent events. This seems the logical way to analyze the economic effects of the takeover in its own terms. The most important relevant events that have occurred since January 1970, notably the very high average copper price in 1970 and the disaster at Mufulira in September of that year, will be discussed briefly below but are not considered for the moment since they were not known at the time of the negotiations.

The price of copper we have used is K750 (£437.50) per metric ton because it is roughly the price projection used by government at the time of the takeover. In addition, it is roughly the price that would have given balance of payments equilibrium on current account in 1971/72 (see the following section, on growth). A higher level naturally will leave both parties to the agreement better off. Although Zambia will have to make higher compensation payments and allow larger overseas remittance of dividends, sufficient money will by definition be available. In the event of very high copper prices, the takeover affects the rate of increase of the reserves, but in such a situation the importance of such chances is diminished. A lower price is discussed later.

The large increases in production must be financed. Immediately before the takeover, the mining companies were forced to retain 50 percent of post-tax profits in Zambia and therefore finance of capital spending was no problem. There is a certain perverse logic in suggesting that all expansion should continue to be financed from retained profits, since all capital spending is to be allowance for tax

TABLE 7.2

Changes in the Balance of Payments
Caused by the Takeover Deal
(millions of Kwacha)

	1970	1971	1972	1973	1974	1975
1. Increase in export proceeds	- -	+1	+12	+61	+73	+74
2. Decrease in remittable dividends	+3	+1	+1	+11	+16	+18
3. Compensation payments	-14	-28	-29	-28	-28	-28
4. Externalization of nonmining assets	-13	-26	-7	- -	- -	- -
5. Balance of payments, excluding foreign loans	-24	-52	-23	+44	+61	+64
6. Foreign loans, net of interest and capital repayments	+9	+13	+14	-3	-10	-9
7. Balance of payments, including foreign loans	-15	-39	-9	+41	+51	+55

Note: If the profits of the management contract are remitted abroad, an additional K1 million should be deducted from lines 5 and 7 for each year.

Source: Tables 7.7 and 7.8 in the Statistical Appendix to this chapter; these tables include detailed assumptions and explanations.

159

in the first year. In fact, it is clear that neither party intended this, since otherwise there would have been no need to negotiate the K27-million reinvestment of externalized funds by the external holding companies. In Table 7.2 showing changes in the balance of payments caused by the takeover deal, we have assumed that a figure amounting to some 6 percent of current costs, or some 10 percent of gross operating profit, will be retained for capital spending. This figure approximates the old concept of capital spending for the maintenance of production. The concept was a slightly spurious one, being manipulated at times to create an impression of greater spending for expansion, but it seems reasonable to suppose that some profit will be retained for this purpose.

Other financing assumptions are that K5 million gross new borrowing can be supplied each year by local financial institutions and that Mindeco and the companies must find their respective shares of the remaining capital needs. The company share of borrowing is assumed to come from abroad. Although it is probable that local financial markets could produce more than this and that in some years after 1973 Mindeco would have surplus funds, it seems likely that the mining companies will be pressed to borrow abroad when they can, so as not to compete for credit with other local companies that may find foreign borrowing more difficult or impossible.

Mindeco does not have a clear incentive to maximize profit retention by the mining companies for capital spending, since this reduces dividends. If dividends were too low to make the minimum guaranteed compensation payments, Mindeco would simply have to borrow to pay compensation instead of borrowing to meet its share of capital spending. Mindeco does have an incentive to keep dividends below the point at which compensation payments would be accelerated, since this would increase its total commitments in the short term.

Table 7.2 shows that the balance of payments benefits begin to exceed the costs only in 1973. Only in 1974/75 do the discounted present values of balance of payments excluding and balance of payments including foreign loans become positive, using a 10 percent discount rate. To 1975 only, the balance of payments excluding foreign loans has a net present value of K24 million and the balance of payments including foreign loans has a net present value of K42 million. Benefits continue positive after 1975. In 1975, the amounts of borrowing outstanding under our assumptions at the end of the year would be: local financial institutions, K11 million; Mindeco, K34 million; and foreign sources, K28 million.

TABLE 7.3

Changes in the Balance of Payments
Caused by the Takeover Deal, Under
Various Capital Financing Assumptions
(millions of Kwacha)

	1970	1971	1972	1973	1974	1975
Variation A						
1. Balance of payments (net)	-13	-36	-6	+45	+57	+55
Variation B						
2. Balance of payments (net) excluding foreign borrowing	-24	-52	-23	+44	+61	+64
3. Foreign loans net of repayments of interest and capital	+7	+22	+24	-6	-15	-14
4. Balance of payments (net) including foreign loans	-17	-30	+1	+38	+46	+50

Note: Variation A is the extreme assumption that all capital spending is financed from profit retentions. Variation B assumes that Mindeco retains half of the dividends that remain after meeting compensation payments as a reserve, lending the other half to the mines, and that the remainder is borrowed abroad. In both variations, gross new borrowing of K 5 million per annum is again assumed to be available from local financial institutions. As in Table 7.2, approximately K1 million should be deducted from lines 1, 2, and 4 for remission abroad of the management profits.

The net present values discounted at 10 percent are: Variation A, K 56 million; Variation B, line 2, K 24 million; and Variation B, line 4, K 48 million.

Source: Tables 7.7, 7.9, and 7.10 in the Statistical Appendix to this chapter, which include detailed assumptions and explanations.

Innumerable alternative financing assumptions can be made. To illustrate that they make surprisingly little difference, Table 7.3 shows the effects of two alternative financing assumptions.

Not surprisingly, financing all capital spending out of profits proves to be the most favorable to the balance of payments; this amounts to "borrowing" as much as possible from a fund that would otherwise mostly have gone out of the country. (The alternative is for 49 percent to go out as dividend and some additional sum to go out as accelerated compensation.)

Because of the innumerable assumptions made in arriving at these figures, only orders of magnitude are really significant. Nevertheless, it is significant that in all these examples the rate of return in balance of payments terms is greater than 10 percent (ignoring benefits after 1975), so that the government appears to have " bought" expansion, and the economic independence and political advantage it thinks the deal has given, at no real cost to itself. The foreign exchange reserves in 1970 were large enough to finance the early negative effects, and at no time have they earned more than 10 percent in overseas capital markets. Moreover, these calculations are based on an assumption that by 1975 only 100,000 metric tons of additional output were induced by the takeover package, which is probably near the lower end of the possible range of assumptions.

Of the factors not so far mentioned, rising costs could most easily wreck these calculations from Zambia's point of view. We have assumed them constant at their 1969 level of K431 per metric ton, plus an additional K5 per metric ton because of the new management and sales contracts, at a copper price of K750 per metric ton.[4] As is shown in detail in Chapter 5, although costs increased very rapidly in the pre-takeover period, a number of special and hopefully nonrecurring factors contributed to this. An alternative way of looking at the figures is that most of them could be regarded as being in constant 1970 prices if costs and the copper price were to inflate at the same rate. Only those figures fixed in money terms, notably the minimum guaranteed compensation payment of K28 million per year, would diminish in real terms.

If the copper price falls below K750 per metric ton, the induced changes in the balance of payments show surprisingly little change— but of course the early negative figures would be superimposed on balance of payments deficits. This factor, as well as the Mufulira disaster, illustrates the danger to Zambia of making no provision for deceleration of compensation. It also raises the question of whether

Zambia should press ahead with plans to expand output when there is already a risk of oversupply and low copper prices. In fact, if Zambia acts alone, even in a position of excess supply of copper, it does not seem likely that any reduction of Zambian exports could push the price of copper up sufficiently to compensate even in the short term, and therefore it still pays to expand production unilaterally.[5] If the copper exporting countries agree through CIPEC on joint action to restrict output, Zambia's bargaining position in seeking a large quota undoubtedly would be strengthened if production increases were already under way. The impact of lower copper prices is further discussed in the next section in the context of import forecasts and growth.

One element that has been left out of the calculation of induced balance of payments changes is that of direct increases in imports caused by increased capital and current spending by the copper mines. This element is really part of the general increase in imports made possible by expanding exports, and therefore the economy, generally. In practice, significant changes because of this factor do not occur until 1973 and after, by which time the induced balance of payments changes are positive in any case (this statement is based on comparison of figures for current and capital expenditure in Tables 7.7 and 7.8). Therefore, it is unlikely that directly induced imports change the general picture significantly.

All the comparisons in this section have been made with the immediate pre-takeover situation. Yet the takeover announcement was made only 18 months after the 1968 Mulungushi speech, before which there was no restriction on remission of post-tax profits and no such immediate expectation of tax changes. If the 1968 Mulungushi reforms are considered part of the takeover package, it would be legitimate to compare the pre-Mulungushi situation with the post-Matero situation. This comparison would appear much more favorable to the Government since the item "decrease in remittable dividends" in Tables 7.2 and 7.3 could be increased by about K20 million per annum. (see Table 7.7 in the Statistical Appendix to this chapter). Furthermore, it might be reasonable to add rather more of the production increases announced since 1968 to the "credit" of the various reforms.

Certainly the 1968 reforms set up certain tensions—the expectation of tax reform, the piling up of unremittable dividends owned by shareholders but not usable as cash or needed for investment, and the expectation of some move to control or own the mines after the first set of takeovers—all of which had to be somehow resolved; from this standpoint, the Matero reforms can be reviewed as an inevitable continuation of what was begun at Mulungushi.

THE TAKEOVER AND GROWTH

During the period since independence, the balance of payments has not been much of a constraint on growth: in most years, there has been a substantial addition to the reserves. The real constraints have been in such areas as transport and skilled manpower, and the financial constraints have been the internal capacity of the economy and the amount of inflation considered tolerable.[6] However, it would be foolhardy to depend upon a rising copper price to continue to remove all balance of payments difficulties; if the copper price does rise sufficiently, then the same constraints as before will continue to operate. Meanwhile, to what extent have the takeover-induced investments increased the growth capacity of the economy, in the sense of allowing a continuation of growth without a reduction in reserves, at a fixed copper price?

If imports continue to grow, as in the past, at the same slightly slower rate than domestic expenditure, then a 5 percent growth rate of national income implies a 4.7 percent growth rate of imports. Supposing for the sake of argument that this is the target growth rate, it is possible to see what difference the takeover has made, using figures from the previous section (see Table 7.4). The figure for imports in 1970 is based on a fairly accurate guess for visible imports and on the assumption that all other current account transactions except those caused by the takeover increased pro rata. The 1970 figure represents a 12 percent growth over 1969, but was inflated by some exceptional items—notably construction for the Lusaka Conference of Non-Aligned Nations and exceptionally heavy maize imports—that one hopes will not recur. For the following years, we have postulated a 5 percent growth rate for the economy, which would involve a 4.7 percent per annum growth in imports if the relationship between the two growth rates stays the same as in the past.

The cost of imported services (net of exported services) has been assumed to increase pro rata with visible imports; other current account costs (mainly personal remittances by expatriates and the profits sent abroad by companies other than the mines) have been assumed constant in the perhaps pious hope that Zambianization will offset the effects of growth.

TABLE 7.4

Balance of Payments Projections to 1975
Based on 5 Percent Per Annum Growth in National Income
(millions of Kwacha)

	1970	1971	1972	1973	1974	1975
1. Copper exports (pre-takeover projection)	525	572	583	583	592	600
2. Other exports	40	42	44	46	48	50
3. Total exports (pre-takeover projection)	565	614	627	629	640	650
4. Imports, including net transfers and net income paid abroad	578	601	626	652	689	707
5. Balance of payments without takeover effects*	-13	+13	+1	-23	-49	-57
6. Effects of takeover (line 7 of Table 7.2)	-15	-39	-9	+41	+51	+55
7. Balance of payments including takeover effects	-28	-26	-8	+18	+2	-2

*Line 5 is the balance of payments surplus or deficit on current account.

Sources: Balance of payments figures for 1969 in Monthly Digest of Statistics (Lusaka: Central Office of Statistics, January 1971); Table 7.2 (same financing assumptions as those spelled out in text for Table 7.2).

165

The viewpoint is once again that of January 1970, and thus takes no account of events since then (except that it uses a better estimate for 1970 imports than would have been available at that time). To pre-takeover forecasts are added the estimated effects of the takeover itself, taken from Table 7.2; Table 7.4 therefore incorporates all the assumptions underlying the calculations in Table 7.2.

From the growth point of view, Table 7.4 shows that the effect of the takeover is to postpone from 1972/73 to 1974/75 the time when the balance of payments goes into deficit, if imports grow at 4.7 percent per annum. This result is quite sensitive to import estimates. If, for example, one assumes imports the same in 1971 as in 1970 (on the grounds that the 1970's were artificially high or that in January 1970 the exceptional boost in 1970 imports could not have been forecast), and a 4.7 percent per annum growth rate thereafter, the period of balance of payments deficit is shifted from 1973/74 to 1975/76. This is again a two-year shift. But under this more optimistic assumption the surplus accumulated by 1975 is not used up until 1979 (discounting to allow for the investment of reserves), so that the takeover postpones a net deterioration in the reserves from 1976 to 1979, a gain of three years. This proposition assumes that, although there is a continuing growth in imports, exports are static. Naturally, if further copper deposits are developed after 1975 or if our forecast of 899,000 metric tons by 1975 proves too low, then more growth can take place—either more rapidly or at 5 percent per annum for a longer period of time.*

The effect on these projections of taking a higher copper price is both to increase the number of years before the balance of payments goes into deficit and to increase the amount of time "bought" by Matero-induced projects. Postponement of this nature is highly significant to Zambia. In 1964, the independent government inherited large flows of money that previously had left the country. Spending that money and the further amounts made available by rising copper prices has created an economy more than ever dependent on copper. For example, the new social infrastructure in education and health requires

_____

* There are many possible alternative assumptions about policy toward the foreign exchange reserves, for examples, that they be run down gradually, relying on IMF borrowing powers for emergencies, or that they be continuously increased to maintain a constant ratio to annual imports. Maintenance of a constant absolute level is the simplest assumption and gives the right order of magnitude as answer to the question we have asked.

heavy current expenditure by government. More than half this current expenditure is paid for directly by copper taxation, and virtually all the induced imports must be paid for by copper's foreign exchange earnings. All the policies for reducing dependence on copper are more or less long-term; therefore, what the economy needs is more time. That time must still be used efficiently, but it is a necessary if not a sufficient condition for further economic growth.

THE POSITION OF THE PUBLIC SECTOR

Since independence, Zambia has only once had an overall budget deficit (in 1968). Budget deficit is here defined to include capital as well as current spending, so that, except in 1968, the Zambian Government has had surpluses of tax revenue, even after paying for capital expenditure. This does not mean that revenue has never been a constraint on spending, since the surpluses have been created by high copper prices. The resulting high revenues do not increase the government's ability to spend, since all of its spending has some local content and is thus constrained by its ability to secure internal resources: that is, by its ability to borrow internally from nonbank sources and to secure tax revenue other than from copper. Therefore, it may appear that any effects of the takeover on the government's budget are irrelevant because they are merely adjustments of the flow of copper revenues and do not affect the government's spending power. This is true in the short term, but in the longer term it makes a considerable difference whether additional profits earned in copper accrue to government or to private shareholders. In addition, one imagines that, as with most government agencies that earn income, there will be some difference in the allocation of public sector revenues if they accrue to Zimco rather than directly to government. The position of Zimco and of government and the build-up of foreign debt are shown in Table 7.5.

The large decrease in tax receipts by government to 1973 is mainly caused by the heavy capital expenditure projected for those years and the new provision that it can be written off against tax in the year in which it is spent. The position is little changed by different financing assumptions.

The apparent cost to government in terms of lost revenue will be at least partially offset by gains in other forms of taxation receipts caused by economic growth. For example, in 1971 the budget projected an increase in noncopper tax revenues of some K22 million. Not all of this can be attributed to the expansion in copper mining—for

TABLE 7.5

Change in Public Sector's Revenue and
Asset Position as a Result of the Takeover
(millions of Kwacha)

	1970	1971	1972	1973	1974	1975
Zimco Revenue	+13	-1	-1	+7	+9	+7
Increase in lending to RCM and NCCM	+9	+15	+17	+1	-5	-6
Total Zimco	+22	+14	+16	+8	+4	+1
Government increase in taxation	-19	-32	-36	-3	+9	+14
Net foreign borrowing by RCM and NCCM	-9	-14	-16	-1	+4	+6

Note: Foreign borrowing by RCM and NCCM is only indirectly, and to the extent of 51 percent an increase in public sector indebtedness. Similarly, Zimco's lending to RCM and NCCM is in part (51 percent again) lending by one Government body to two others.

Source: Table 7.2 (same financing assumptions as those spelled out in text for Table 7.2).

example, some of it must be caused by inflation. But to the extent that the Government is able to trade off copper tax revenues for growth, which causes increases in noncopper tax revenues, it is reducing its dependence on copper taxation and replacing a form of tax that has little or no deflationary effect with forms of tax that directly reduce internal purchasing power.

Zimco's net revenue position improves quite sharply if RCM and NCCM borrow more from abroad and less from Mindeco, although the overall asset position is little changed. If only a small part of profit is retained for capital spending, dividends are so large that accelerated compensation takes place, leaving Zimco worse off in the short term although better off in due course when compensation payments finish early.

In 1970, Mindeco had a chance to build up reserves because of the provision that accelerated compensation payments were not to begin until 1971 (RCM) and 1972 (NCCM) and because only one half-yearly payment was due in 1970 (in October). High copper prices during much of 1970 meant that Mindeco did in fact have revenue of over K20 million after payment of K14 million compensation.

In general, there is still a certain amount of slack in the government's cash position that has not been utilized. Its revenue surpluses, even after paying for budget capital expenditure, have meant that local borrowing has been negligible, maintained merely in order to keep the local capital market in existence. As a result, the large losses of revenue in the years to 1973 should not act as a constraint on government spending.

Taking a longer-term view, the government is acquiring a very large asset and paying for it out of revenue that previously accrued to private shareholders, although in the period immediately prior to the takeover that revenue was forcibly prevented by exchange control rules from leaving Zambia.

THE POSITION OF THE PRIVATE SHAREHOLDERS

In very broad terms, the residual 49 percent shareholders * will be receiving a rather larger cash flow until 1978 or 1982, while

---

* We have assumed throughout that all the private shareholders

their assets in Zambia decline. This is the natural consequence of
any takeover. However, it is only true if one compares their post-
takeover situation with their position immediately before the takeover.
Before April 1968, all dividends were freely remittable out of Zambia.
At Mulungushi in April 1968, President Kaunda announced that only
50 percent of post-tax profits (or 30 percent of equity, if that were
less) could be remitted abroad, the remainder being forcibly retained
in Zambia.

The immediate effect of this Mulungushi ruling was to cause a
large increase in foreign-held liquid assets, of which the greater
part was accounted for by the mines. Whether without reform of
taxation and ownership these assets would eventually have been invested in mining development or some other productive activity is
now an academic point of no importance. However, it is certain that,
whatever investment was chosen for forcibly retained profits, the
whole process would have resulted in an increase in foreign ownership
of domestic assets (see Chapter 1), a dilemma that one suspects the
government may not at first have faced up to fully, if at all.

The interesting point is that of the subjective valuation put on
profits retained in Zambia by the overseas shareholders who were
the legal owners of these profits. Given the long gestation period of
investment in mining and the high-risk rating of Zambia among foreign
investors, it seems likely that any contribution of the retained profits
to a future increase in profits via reinvestment was being pretty
heavily discounted. However, this conclusion depends on the assumption
that shareholders believed the restriction on remittances would
continue; since Government was under some pressure to remove this
restriction, some shareholders must have believed it to be temporary.
Nevertheless, the uncertainty in itself must have reduced shareholders'
subjective valuation of the profits retained but not invested.

From the point of view of Zambia's desire to retain overseas
investors' goodwill, this is just as well. Table 7.6 shows that Zimco
will be making compensation payments basically out of the 50 percent
of post-tax profits previously retained in Zambia, since these profits
now accrue to Zimco as 51 percent shareholder. This is the reason

---

were and are resident outside Zambia. This is not strictly true. The
most significant exception arises from the RST employee share
purchase plan, which by 1969 had an accumulated shareholding of
K 4.5 million. However, this makes little difference to our arguments.

that government has been described as buying the mines for nothing—
or, in more emotional terms, as having expropriated the shareholders
of 51 percent of their assets.

In formal terms, there is no question of expropriation since the
shareholders have been issued Zimco bonds to replace their taken-over
shares; furthermore, the takeover deal was agreed to by the mining
company directors and approved in due course by the various shareholders involved.* Although the mines negotiated under some threat
of worse to come if they could agree on a package, the threats were
not all on one side. As we have argued before, both parties to the
negotiations had bargaining strength in different ways.

The 6 percent interest rate on the Zimco bonds is much lower
than the rate of return on equity was. The interest payments are
free of Zambian taxes (and exchange control regulations) but are not
treated as "tax paid." That is, a shareholder in a country with a
double taxation agreement with Zambia will not be able to claim that
Zambian tax already has been paid and so will have to pay any local
taxes in full.[7]

Institutional shareholders in tax havens, for example Zambia
Copper Investments (ZCI) in Bermuda, will receive the dividends tax
free and thus will be able to use them for reinvestment elsewhere in
the world without paying tax; however, if they distribute to their
shareholders, tax will again become payable. Thus, it is probable
that the Zambian Government has made a concession that will benefit
foreign governments more than foreign shareholders and therefore
was an unnecessary concession as far as the takeover bargaining was
concerned. It would have been better to give the Zimco bonds a 12
percent coupon subject to a 50 percent withholding tax in Zambia,
thus giving shareholders the same gross income and a chance of
paying less tax to their home governments.

The combination of interest and redemption payments on the
Zimco bonds, and the fully remittable dividends on their remaining
49 percent shareholdings, gives overseas shareholders an increased

————————————

*The takeover of minority interests in RST by Amax is being
challenged in the courts in the United States, although it already has
been approved in the Zambian High Court. This challenge does not
affect the Zambian Government's takeover.

TABLE 7.6

Changes in Position of Private Shareholders
as a Result of the Takeover
(millions of Kwacha)

	1970	1971	1972	1973	1974	1975
Pre-takeover projections						
Cash flow (dividends)	38	41	42	42	43	43
Reinvestment of profits (including replacement capital)	38	41	42	42	43	43
Total	76	81	83	83	85	85
Post-takeover projections						
Cash flow (dividends)	35	40	41	31	27	25
Cash flow (compensation)	14	28	29	28	28	28
Total cash flow	(49)	(68)	(70)	(59)	(55)	(53)
Reinvestment of profits (including replacement capital)	10	11	11	11	11	11
Total	59	79	81	70	66	64

Source: Tables 7.7 and 7.8 in the Statistical Appendix to this chapter (same financing assumptions as those spelled out in text for Table 7.2.)

cash flow in the years following the takeover and at the same time a reduced financial commitment to Zambia. These factors can be regarded as compensating for the lower yield of the Zimco bonds and for any element of forced lending or expropriation that may be thought to have existed in the takeover arrangements.

Table 7.6 shows the increased cash flow to private shareholders, accompanied by a reduction in their accumulation of Zambian assets. Because of the expansion of production and the more generous depreciation allowances after the takeover, this improved cash flow is more marked in the early years when projections of capital spending are heavy and less marked later when there are no continuing capital allowances from earlier spending and loans must be repaid. The figures would be different under different financing assumptions, but the general picture would be the same. The table does not show the years after 1975 when (1) increased production and profit will no longer be offset by loan repayments and (2) compensation payments will cease.

The private shareholders are in one important respect much better off than appears from Table 7.6. Although dividend payments will fluctuate with the copper price and are vulnerable to such events as strikes and disasters like that at Mufulira, compensation payments will not vary, being guaranteed by the Zambian Government in the event that Zimco dividends are not sufficiently large. Zimco could even find itself obliged to make accelerated compensation payments to one set of shareholders at a time when it has not enough money to meet even minimum payments to the other.

It is likely that in the years after 1970 some shareholders will be as much influenced in their opinion of the takeover arrangements by their actual cash flow as by changes in their cash flow from what it would have been without the takeover. In short, a high copper price will have more influence than fine calculations of hypothetical gains and losses from the takeover. This was an additional reason for including in Table 7.6 the effects of post-takeover planned production increases, since these are presumed to be part of the reality that shareholders will face. From this point of view, the shareholders got off to a good start in 1970 when the price of copper was very high; however, RCM shareholders will suffer somewhat from the loss of production (and profit) at Mufulira, with compensation payments being, of course, maintained.

ACCELERATION OF COMPENSATION

The financial arrangements contain a provision that, if in any year two-thirds of either RCM's or NCCM's dividend exceeds the minimum annual guaranteed payment, then the difference must be applied to additional bond redemptions. (The details of accelerated payments are slightly different for RCM and NCCM; see Appendix A.) If Zimco has a shortage of funds in a subsequent year, it must still make the minimum guaranteed payments, even though it has made accelerated payments in the past. Acceleration merely brings forward the time when compensation payments are completed.

Thus, the bondholders can receive accelerated compensation but never less than their guaranteed annual totals of K13.5 million (RCM) and K14.8 million (NCCM); in short, there is a sort of ratchet effect working in the bondholders' favor.

There were several possibilities open to government to reduce the burden of these provisions, which could become impossibly onerous if the copper price fell sufficiently or if a further mining disaster occurred.

As a minimum, it seems that the government should have tied compensation to a proportion of the Zimco dividend—even 100 percent if necessary—rather than have guaranteed minimum annual payments. In the event that copper price fell below the critical levels, compensation would have been delayed, completion of payment being extended beyond 1978 and 1982. If the bondholders had a subjective rate of discount greater than the effective rates of return on the Zimco bonds, then such a "deceleration" provision would have caused a reduction in the discounted present value of the bonds and thus in the price paid for the takeover.

The second possibility open to the government was to make it even more explicit that in effect the takeover price would vary over the period of compensation, with the price of copper and thus with the real value of the assets taken over. There are various ways in which this could have been done; [8] the method is not important now, since the opportunity has been missed. But the principle of forcing some of the risk onto the shareholders seems reasonable. After all, the government might have agreed to pay K208 million in compensation, only to find the assets, whose book value has been so carefully assessed, worth much less the following year because of a collapse

in the copper price.* A similar principle is used when a second-
hand car is guaranteed for a period by the seller: with such a high-
risk asset, whose price is large in relation to the buyer's assets and
income, the risk of breakdown is too great to be carried by the buyer
alone.

A third possibility was to negotiate reduced or zero compensation
payments in a specified number of "bad years" between the time of
the takeover and completion of payment. This idea was used in the
repayment provisions of the large U.S. loan to Britain negotiated after
World War II. Britain can choose not to make the annual repayment
(of about £60 million) in a given number of years before repayment is
complete at the beginning of the twenty-first century. A similar
principle could have been used by Zambia, perhaps with nonpayment
only claimable in such specified circumstances as when reserves
fell below a given level or when a declaration of force majeure was
made on copper sales contracts.

These possibilities discussed above were not remote at the time
of the takeover. Indeed, the chances of difficulty in meeting compensation payments on one or more occasions in a period of eight to
twelve years must be extremely high. The high-risk nature of mining
itself, Zambia's landlocked position and dependence on imported inputs, and the volatile copper price add up to a fair probability of mis-
fortune in any one year; over the number of years involved, the probability becomes high. The loss of production at Mufulira has simply
demonstrated what should have been anticipated in the agreement.

Clearly, once compensation payments are completed the government has paid, for better or for worse, for its assets, but the very
act of payment for those assets over an extended period of years
gave the government an opportunity to spread its risks, an opportunity
that was not taken.

---

*The choice of book value is especially arbitrary in mining in any
case because of different depreciation practices; as it turned out,
the "book value" of Luanshya had to be adjusted to the agreed price.
This method of valuation was probably chosen because of its supposed
simplicity and its successful use in earlier takeovers in Zambia
following the President's 1968 Mulungushi speech.

ZAMBIANIZATION

There is little one can say on the subject of Zambianization. Apart from the provision that RST and Anglo-American shall provide to people nominated by RCM and NCCM suitable experience in sales, marketing, purchasing, and other services provided by the management contractors, there is no specific mention of Zambianization in the takeover agreements.

In part, this lack of mention of Zambianization must be because the companies already had large training programs. The economic incentive to Zambianize was certainly there, and in fact was present even before Zambian independence, and the mining companies were an extreme example of institutions so large that in the short term top management's position was not threatened. In the long term, both groups had world-wide operations into which to absorb displaced senior management. The translation of these incentives to the shop floor, so to speak, is a question of management communication and has already been discussed (see Chapter 1). Certainly, there is no inherent reason for thinking that the takeover will make any difference in this regard. At best, it may improve understanding of the problems at board level, but the communication problem on this subject can only really improve when Zambianization itself has advanced.

Another reason for the failure to mention Zambianization must be that it depends to a great extent on the supply of suitably educated manpower. Government is by far the main supplier of basic education, and government therefore determines to a considerable extent the proportion of different skills produced, for example by applying a quota to the different specializations at the University of Zambia. Thus far, priority has been given to producing secondary school teachers, over 90 percent of whom were expatriates in 1970. The government also has some control over the employment of graduates and has shown a marked tendency to take students graduating in such fields as economics and politics directly into the civil service. Thus, it may be that Zambianization of the mines is not a particularly high priority.

Nevertheless, the moment of takeover was certainly an opportunity to negotiate an arrangement on Zambianization, perhaps with a timetable and agreed provisions for slowing it down or speeding it up according to circumstances. This opportunity was not taken, at least not publicly.

CONCLUSION

This chapter has shown how the various components of the take-over interact to form a quite complicated picture. It is not really possible to add up the gains and losses of each party to the deal; one must simply list them and come to some sort of subjective judgment. Nor is it really fruitful to try to identify the aspects of the deal that have had the most relevance. For example, a strong case could be made for saying that the tax changes alone would have given rise to the plans for the expansion of production that have been announced since the takeover. But, if tax reform had taken place on its own, the problems of "excessive" build-up in Zambia of retained profits or "excessive" expatriation of profits would have remained and created new political tensions. Nor is it certain that expansion would have taken place without some resolution of the takeover question itself.

Since, as a matter of history, the changes were all announced simultaneously, we have preferred to examine them as an entity and also to look at the results together rather than separately.

To give a subjective summary, then, the government has come out of an action that was initiated mainly for political and long-term reasons with quite good short-term economic results. Only in the area of tax receipts from mining are the discounted results negative to 1975; we have argued that this is an area where government can afford the losses and that in any case there will be some offsetting factors even in the field of taxation.

Although government has signed away a number of rights that sound important, we have argued that these were no more than was necessary to guarantee the rights of the minority shareholders. Having agreed on a price, it was necessary to grant the management, as the shareholders' agents, the right to ensure that the means to pay that price would be forthcoming. And after government had secured the existing management, which was essential to run the mines, management had to be guaranteed the right to run the mines as it thought best, within the normal framework of Government rules.

In other words, anyone who thought that a 51 percent takeover, or a 100 percent takeover for that matter, would lead to full government control of the management of the mines was certain to be disappointed, since the government never had the personnel to do this.

Given its bargaining and negotiating strength, the government achieved a great deal of what it could have achieved. The main weaknesses are in the lack of a deceleration provision for compensation payments and the lack of a negotiated program for Zambianization.

For government, the takeover has meant an opportunity to rationalize and reform several of government's indirect controls such as tax (but see the arguments in Chapter 9 concerning further tax reform), exchange control, and issue of exploration, prospecting, and mining licences (discussed more fully in Chapter 3); a significant increase in investment; a major step toward a rational structure of ownership; and a major step toward economic independence in the long term.

The private shareholders also have done quite well. As one might expect, their representatives appear to have missed fewer tricks at the negotiating table. Nevertheless, they are being bought out with profits that were once theirs; viewed in another way, they are losing 51 percent of their assets for a finite increase in their cash flow, so that one could argue that government has used the shareholder's shorter-term perspective to pay quite cheaply for its own longer-term objectives. Certainly, the result of the negotiating falls within the area of common interest that existed between the two parties.

NOTES

1. Roan Selection Trust Limited, "Explanatory Statement for Meetings of Shareholders to be held on 6th August, 1970,"Appendix L, p. 1-3.

2. President Kaunda, "Towards Complete Independence," the Matero speech on August 11, 1969 (Lusaka: Zambia Information Services, 1969), p. 28.

3. President Kaunda, "Take Up the Challenge," opening address to the UNIP National Council held in Mulungushi Hall, Lusaka, on November 7, 1970 (Lusaka: Government Printer, 1970).

4. See Roan Selection Trust Limited, op. cit., pp. C-14, C-15, which include an item "New management and consultancy, and sales and marketing, contracts—additional charge" that works out at K 5 per metric ton. Zamanglo additional costs have been assumed to be the same.

5. The short-term price elasticity of demand for copper is only about 0.2; that is, a 5 percent rise in the copper price causes a 1 percent fall in demand by the end of one year; eventually, demand falls by 14 percent, of which 4.5 percent occurs within 5 years. (Unpublished source.)

6. See C. M. Elliott, ed., Constraints on the Economic Development of Zambia (Nairobi: Oxford University Press, 1971); Charles Harvey, "Inflation in a Very Open Economy: Zambia 1964-69," Eastern African Economic Review, Vol. III, No. 1 (June 1971).

7. For information concerning the United States, Britain, France, and South Africa, see Roan Selection Trust Limited, op. cit., Appendix M.

8. One possible method was suggested by M. L. O. Farber and J. G. Potter in "A Future for Zambia's Copper Industry?" in Towards Economic Independence (Cambridge: Cambridge University Press, 1971).

TABLE 7.7

Copper Company Aggregated Accounts on the Basis
of Pre-Takeover Planned Expansion to 800,000 Metric Tons,
With Pre-takeover Rules
(millions of Kwacha)

	1970	1971	1972	1973	1974	1975
1. Production (thousands of metric tons)	701	762	777	777	789	800
2. Revenue (at K750 per metric ton)	526	572	583	583	592	600
3. Costs (at K431 per metric ton)	302	328	335	335	340	345
4. Gross profit	224	244	248	248	252	255
5. Royalty	60	65	66	66	67	68
6. Export tax	42	46	47	47	47	48
7. Capital spending	42	17	28	28	26	19
8. Capital allowances	20	17	20	20	20	18
9. Profits liable to income tax	102	116	115	115	118	121
10. Income Tax (at 45%)	46	52	52	52	53	54
11. Total taxation	148	163	165	165	167	170
12. Gross profit less tax	76	81	83	83	85	85
13. Dividends remittable abroad	38	41	42	42	43	43
14. Retained profits in excess of capital spending	-4	24	14	14	17	24
15. Tax as % of gross profit	66	67	67	67	66	67

NOTES TO TABLE 7.7

Explanation of Lines in Table:

1. Known expansion plans less those thought to have been induced by the takeover (see also Table 7.1).

2. (1) x K750.

3. (1) x K431.

4. (2) – (3).

5. (13.5 % of K750 – K16) x (1).

6. 40% of (K750 – K600) x (1).

7. Estimated from (1) plus estimates of the cost of capital replacement.

8. Calculated from (7) assuming 25% spent on prime moving machinery, 25% on other machinery, 50% on construction, plus estimated carry-over of capital allowances from earlier years.

9. (4) – (5) – (6) – (8).

10. 45% of (9).

11. (5) + (6) + (10).

12. (4) – (11).

13. 50% of (12).

14. (13) – (7).

15. (11) as % of (4).

Note: The figures in (8) are not sensitive to the assumptions about the breakdown of capital spending.

181

TABLE 7.8

Copper Company Aggregated Accounts on the Basis of Expansion to 899,000 Metric Tons Per Annum by 1975, With Post-takeover Rules
(millions of Kwacha)

	1970	1971	1972	1973	1974	1975
1. Production (thousands of metric tons)	701	763	793	858	887	899
2. Revenue (at K 750 per metric ton)	526	572	595	644	665	674
3. Operating costs (at K 436 per metric ton)	306	333	346	374	387	392
4. Gross profit	220	239	249	270	278	282
5. Capital spending	43	58	67	40	29	23
6. Capital spending financed by profit retention	20	22	23	23	23	22
7. Capital spending financed by borrowing						
From local sources	5	5	5	5	5	1
From Mindeco	9	16	20	6	1	-
From abroad	9	15	19	6	-	-
8. Loans at end-year						
Local	5	9	12	14	15	11
Mindeco	9	24	41	47	37	31
abroad	9	23	39	40	34	28
9. Interest payments						
Local	--	--	1	1	1	1
Mindeco	--	1	2	3	3	3
abroad	--	1	2	4	4	3
10. Capital repayments						
Local	--	1	2	3	4	5
Mindeco	--	1	3	5	6	6
abroad	--	1	3	5	6	6
11. Profit liable to tax	177	179	177	222	241	252
12. Tax (at 73.05%)	129	131	129	162	176	184
13. Profit available for distribution	71	81	84	64	55	52
14. Dividends remittable abroad	35	40	41	31	27	25
15. Mindeco dividends	36	41	43	33	28	27
16. Compensation payments	14	28	29	28	28	28
17. Mindeco revenue after compensation	22	15	19	13	9	8
18. Mindeco's share of capital costs	9	16	20	6	1	--
19. Mindeco revenue after all charges	13	-1	-1	7	8	8
20. Tax as % of gross profit	59	55	52	60	63	65

Financing Assumptions:

1. Gross borrowing from local financial institutions is K5 million per annum, repayable in equal annual installments over 5 years, at 8 percent.

2. Profit retention as in line 6.

3. Mindeco lends 51 percent of the remaining financing requirement (if any) at 8 percent, repayable in equal annual installments over ten years.

4. Foreign sources supply 49 percent of the remaining financing requirements (if any) after (1) and (2), at 10 percent, repayable in equal annual installments over 8 years.

Explanation of Lines in Table:

1. Known expansion plans, from company reports.

2. (1) x K750.

3. As in Table 7.7, plus K5 per ton to allow for the additional cost of the new management contract.

4. (2) - (3).

5. Estimated from company reports.

6. Estimated on a rough guess at requirements for replacement capital.

7. Derived from financing assumptions.

8. (7) the previous year, plus (7) the same year, less (10) the same year.

9. Derived from financing assumptions.

10. As for (9).

11. (4) - (5) -(9).

12. 73.05% of (11).

13. (4) - (6) - (9) - (10) - (12).

14. 49% of (13).

15. 51% of (13)

16. The greater of K28 million and two-thirds of (15), except in 1970 when only K14 million was due.

17. (15) - (16) + (9b) + (10b).

18. As 7(b).

19. (17) - (18).

20. (12) as a percentage of (4).

Note: No account has been taken of the fact that income tax is paid and dividends are distributed in the year after the relevant profits are earned, on the assumption that appropriations are made at the time. To this extent, the figures may partially represent accounting rather than cash flows.

TABLE 7.9

Copper Company Aggregated Accounts on
the Basis of Expansion to 899,000 Metric Tons Per Annum
by 1975, With Post-Takeover Rules: Financing Variation A
(millions of Kwacha)

	1970	1971	1972	1973	1974	1975
1. Production (thousands of metric tons)	701	763	793	858	887	899
2. Revenue (at K750 per metric ton)	526	572	595	644	665	674
3. Operating costs (at K436 per metric ton)	306	333	346	374	387	392
4. Gross profit	220	239	249	270	278	282
5. Capital spending	43	58	67	40	29	23
6. Profits liable to tax	177	181	182	230	249	259
7. Tax (at 73.05%)	129	132	133	168	182	189
8. Profit available for distribution	48	49	49	62	67	70
9. Dividends remittable abroad	24	24	24	30	33	34
10. Mindeco dividends	24	25	25	32	34	36
11. Compensation payments	14	28	28	28	28	28
12. Mindeco revenue after all charges	10	-3	-3	4	6	8
13. Tax as % of gross profit	59	55	53	62	65	67

NOTES TO TABLE 7.9

Explanation of Lines in Table:

1. Known expansion plans, from company reports.

2. (1) x K750.

3. As in Table 7.7, plus K5 per ton to allow for the additional cost of the new management contract.

4. (2) – (3).

5. Estimated from company reports.

6. (4) – (5).

7. 73.05% of (6).

8. (4) – (5) –(7).

9. 49% of (8).

10. 51% of (8)

11. The greater of K28 million and two-thirds of (10), except in 1970 when only K14 million was due.

12. (10) – (11).

13. (7) as % of (4).

Note: No account has been taken of the fact that income tax is paid and dividends are distributed in the year after the relevant profits are earned, on the assumption that appropriations are made at the time. To this extent, the figures may partially represent accounting rather than cash flows.

185

TABLE 7.10

Copper Company Aggregated Accounts on the
Basis of Expansion to 899,000 Metric Tons Per Annum by 1975,
With Post-Takeover Rules: Financing Variation B
(millions of Kwacha)

	1970	1971	1972	1973	1974	1975
1. Production (thousands of metric tons)	701	763	793	858	887	899
2. Revenue (at K 750 per metric ton)	526	572	595	644	665	674
3. Operating costs (at K 436 per metric ton)	306	333	346	374	387	392
4. Gross profit	220	239	249	270	278	282
5. Capital spending	43	58	67	40	29	23
6. Capital spending financed by profit retention	20	22	23	23	23	22
7. Capital spending financed by borrowed						
From local sources	5	5	5	5	5	1
From Mindeco	11	7	8	4	1	--
From abroad	7	24	31	8	--	--
8. Loans at end-year						
Local	5	9	12	14	15	11
Mindeco	11	17	23	25	22	19
abroad	7	30	57	57	49	40
9. Interest payments						
Local	--	--	1	1	1	1
Mindeco	--	1	1	2	2	2
abroad	--	1	3	6	6	5
10. Capital repayments						
Local	--	1	2	3	4	5
Mindeco	--	1	2	2	3	3
abroad	--	1	4	8	9	9
11. Profit liable to tax	177	179	177	221	240	251
12. Tax (at 73.05%)	129	131	129	161	175	183
13. Profit available for distribution	71	81	84	64	55	52
14. Dividends remittable abroad	35	40	41	31	27	25
15. Mindeco dividends	36	41	43	33	28	27
16. Compensation payments	14	28	29	28	28	28
17. Mindeco revenue after compensation	22	15	17	9	5	4
18. Mindeco retentions	11	8	9	5	4	4
19. Tax as % of gross profit	59	55	52	60	63	65

186

NOTES TO TABLE 7.10

Financing assumptions: Local borrowing and profit retention as in Table 7.8, Mindeco to retain half its revenue after paying compensation, the remainder borrowed abroad. Terms for each category as for Table 7.8.

Explanation of Lines in Table:

1. Known expansion plans, from company reports.

2. (1) x K750.

3. As in Table 7.7, plus K5 per ton to allow for the additional cost of the new management contract.

4. (2) - (3).

5. Estimated from company reports.

6. Estimated on a rough guess at requirements for replacement capital.

7. Derived from financing assumptions.

8. (7) the previous year, plus (7) the same year, less (10) the same year.

9. Derived from financing assumptions.

10. As for (9).

11. (4) - (5) - (9).

12. 73.05% of (11).

13. (4) - (6) - (9) - (10) - (12).

14. 49% of (13).

15. 51% of (13).

16. The greater of K28 million and two-thirds of (15), except in 1970 when only K14 million was due.

17. (15) - (16) + (9b) + (10b).

18. (17) - 7(b).

19. (12) as % of (4).

Note: No account has been taken of the fact that income tax is paid and dividends are distributed in the year after the relevent profits are earned, on the assumption that appropriations are made at the time. To this extent, the figures may partially represent accounting rather than cash flows.

8

THE PROSPECTS
FOR
NEW
MINE INVESTMENT

Andrew Gordon

THE NEW SITUATION

The changes accompanying the nationalization of the copper mines have transformed the Zambian scene as far as prospectors and potential mining investors are concerned. The burdensome taxes on production have been abolished and the transfer of all mineral rights to the state has led to the release of large areas for prospecting that previously were not generally available. It evidently is expected that future prospecting and development will come in large measure through private initiative, and indeed the international mining community has been quick to take fresh stock of the opportunities in Zambia. It is with this point of view in mind that we now examine the prospects for new mine investment.

The search for new mineral deposits is now carried out under a regime of prospecting, exploration, and mining licences. The lives of prospecting and exploration licences are strictly limited and expenditure obligations rise with time, but these provisions are not such as to embarrass any prospector with serious intentions. The detailed programs, which must be accepted by government before licences are granted and are the basis on which the period of the mining licence is determined, are a much more serious control whose effect will depend largely on the attitude of the government department administering the new law. Prospectors will hope that the present exemplary spirit of reasonableness will be long-lived, although many of them will know from first-hand experience that such attitudes are not universal among countries actively trying to stimulate mining development. The government's decision as to whether or not to participate in a new mine must precede the issue of a mining licence, and if government does decide to participate its share of prospecting expenditure in the whole of the original prospecting licence area (plus a reasonable contribution to overheads in the case of holders with licences for more than one area) will be paid out in cash (see Appendix D). Government also will put up additional capital for mine development on the same terms as the other shareholders.

The tax conditions for new mines have been made as uniform as possible with the new conditions for the existing mines. Thus, the rate of mineral tax will depend on the metal or mineral produced, the overall rate of profits tax being 73.05 percent for a new copper mine, 56 percent for a lead or zinc mine, and so on. Capital expenditure may be offset against operating profit for tax purposes in the year in which it is incurred or in the first year of operation, and tax losses may be carried forward indefinitely. Thus, no direct tax of any kind will be payable until all the capital laid out by the investors in a new mine has been recouped. There is also a provision whereby a mine that has reached the tax-paying stage may at intervals of three years claim a refund of mineral tax (but not income tax) to the extent that net income (after both mineral and income tax) has fallen short of 12 percent of equity.

Prospecting expenditure is given favorable tax treatment in that the person or company incurring the expenditure may either retain it as a deduction or a company may renounce the deduction in favor of its shareholders. Thus, any person who contributes money to a prospecting enterprise can offset the expenditure against his current taxable income in Zambia instead of waiting for the chance to offset it against ultimate mining profits. If the contributor is a nonmining company, then the value of the immediate deduction in terms of tax saved will be only 45 percent of the expenditure compared with as much as 73.05 percent if a copper mine is subsequently opened and makes taxable profits. The facility presumably depends on all shareholders being of one mind, but the time-value of money in Zambia is probably such that the option will be attractive to most investors.

Expenditure that is retained for tax purposes in a prospecting company also may be renounced in favor of a subsequently formed mining company of which it is a shareholder. Thus, all the expenditure of a prospecting company that finds a workable deposit (including expenditure in areas outside the location of the ultimate mine) can be

offset against the profits of the mine. This may be attractive for a
group of investors who prospect through a prospecting company in
several areas at once, decide to form a mining company (possibly
with other investors) to exploit a mine in one of the areas, and continue
prospecting in other areas through the prospecting company. If other
investors are brought into the mining company, this option will only
be attractive if the new investors compensate the prospecting investors
for the tax advantage so conferred on the new mine. Although this
may be expected from new private investors, it is unlikely that any
such compensation would come from government if it decides to
participate. Hence if, as now seems likely, government normally
exercises its option to acquire 51 percent of any new mine, the prospecting company's option to confer deductible expenditure on a new
mining company in respect of expenditure outside the area of the new
mine will be of little use.

What is the object of the legislation as far as new mining investment is concerned, and how far will the achievement of that object be
promoted by the package described above? It will be clear from
earlier chapters that Zambia's principal needs in the medium-term
future are the growth of industries that are less dependent on the
copper market and the development of local food production and of the
rural areas generally. The need for additional State revenue is much
less important than the need to diversify the sources of revenue away
from copper mining. In this context, the role of new mines would be
principally to generate new opportunities for employment and especially to develop new centers of economic activity away from existing
urban areas and the rail line. There is no doubt that in Zambia at
present any new mine approaching commercial viability would be of
positive economic benefit, even if its direct taxable capacity were nil.
In these circumstances, although government would not want to forego
possible revenue from new mines unnecessarily, it would be a serious
fault in the system if the tax conditions ever prevented the development
of a mineral deposit that was "economically" viable. How susceptible
are the Zambian conditions to this possibility?

For a private investor to make the decision to go ahead with a
mining proposition, he must be in a position to envisage a mining
plan that will, assuming a reasonably "safe" price for the product,
return his capital outlay together with a commercial rate of interest
within a limited period. This is a perfectly normal commercial
attitude and does not imply that the investor will thereupon pack up
and leave; all the large mining companies certainly expect to continue
to develop their mines at a profit long after their initial investment
criteria have been met. Although the new Zambian tax system ensures

that tax will not frustrate the recovery of the capital outlay, the very
high rate of tax applicable as soon as the capital is recovered makes
it a comparatively lengthy process to achieve both the return of the
capital and a minimum profit. For example, if a copper mine takes
three years to construct with capital expenditure spread evenly
over the three years and subsequent annual gross profits are equal to
35 percent of the total capital expenditure, the capital is entirely
recouped in 2.86 years of operation. If the investor requires the
return of his capital together with interest at 12 percent on the unrecouped balance, the 73.05 percent tax rate for copper will ensure
that this is not achieved until the end of 10 years of operation. If the
investor seeks a 15 percent return, the time needed will be over 20
years.

If we assume for any project a particular pattern of initial
capital expenditure and a constant rate of profit before taxation, then
the gross profit necessary for a particular discounted yield on the
investment within a particular period can be expressed as a fraction
of the original investment. For example, whatever the scale of the
investment, if expenditure on construction of a copper mine is spread
evenly over three years the annual gross profit over the following 20
years necessary to recover a DCF yield of 20 percent is exactly half
the total initial capital outlay. If the initial expenditure is 100, the
project starts with three years expenditure of 33.3 followed by two
years of cash flows of 50 (untaxed) and 18 years of cash flows of
13.475. This is just sufficient to repay the original outlay of 100 plus
20 percent interest annually on the amount not repaid. In Chart 8.1,
the curve Z plots the DCF yields for annual gross profits between 10
and 70 percent of the original capital invested, assuming that the
initial investment is spread evenly over three years and considering
an operating life of ten years. The curve also assumes that the mine
will be entirely financed by equity and the most generous possible
interpretation of the 12 percent mineral tax refund concession (see
below). The dotted line trailing from curve Z shows what the yields
would have been without the mineral tax refund concession. Curve
A shows the yields assuming no tax were payable at all.

Let us suppose that the investor's criterion for deciding to go
ahead with a mine is the prospect of a 15 percent discounted yield
over a maximum of 10 years of operation on the basis of 100 percent
equity finance. (If the project meets this condition, he may subsequently try to increase the yield—and the risk—by raising some of
the capital in the form of loans.) We can read from the graph that
the minimum gross profit that any projected copper mine must show
is 42 percent of the capital invested, whereas if there were no

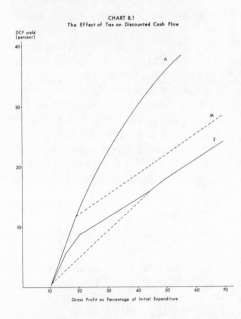

CHART 8.1
The Effect of Tax on Discounted Cash Flow

DCF yield
(percent)

Gross Profit as Percentage of Initial Expenditure

taxation a mine would be viable if the gross profit were only 23 percent of capital expenditure. Thus, if this is indeed the private investor's criterion, any mining project that showed a rate of gross profit between 23 percent and 42 percent of the initial expenditure, although patently viable "economically," would be turned down because of the tax conditions. This can be translated into physical terms with a few assumptions based on typical Zambian conditions. The capital cost of a small to medium-sized underground copper mine with concentrator and infrastructure and without exceptional complications is now about K30 per annual metric ton of ore mined (it has been rising rapidly in recent years). Operating costs to produce concentrate are about K6 per metric ton of ore milled. Assuming that the mine produces and uses existing Zambian facilities for further processing, the costs of smelting, refining, freight, and marketing would come to about K150 per metric ton of metal. If a "safe" price of K800 (467) per metric ton and overall recovery of 70 percent are assumed, then the minimum workable grade would be 4.09 percent with existing taxation and 2.83 percent without tax. Hence, if all our assumptions (the investor's minimum financial requirements and the various cost estimates) are correct, then at a price of K800 per metric ton of copper underground mines with grades between 2.83 percent and 4.09 percent are rendered unviable by the existing tax system. (It may be noted that none of the mines on the Zambian Copperbelt regularly show average grades over 4.09 percent.)

The range of grades rendered unviable by taxation increases as
the capital cost increases as the assumed price falls. Thus, with a copper price of K800 per metric ton grades over a range of 1 percent are
made unviable when the capital cost per metric ton ore is K24 (i.e., minimum grade is 3.53 percent with tax and 2.53 percent without) and a range
of 1.5 percent is made unviable when the capital cost is K36. At a price
of K700 per metric ton, a range of 1 percent is made unviable at a
capital cost of K24 and a range of 1.5 percent at a capital cost of K30.
In a "zone of interest" between a highest likely grade of about 5
percent and a minimum economically viable grade of about 1.5 percent, a loss of this order has a very important effect on national
reserves of ore. If due to natural causes, it would be considered a
disaster.

THE MINERAL TAX REFUND

The provision that mineral tax may be reclaimed to the extent
that the return on equity falls short of 12 percent suggests that this
effect of the high tax rate was to some extent recognized by government. Since the refund itself is not taxable, the theoretical minimum
rate of tax for a copper mine making taxable profits is 22.05 percent.
Paradoxically, the theoretical minimum for a mine paying a lower
rate of mineral tax would be higher: e.g., a lead/zinc mine paying
mineral tax of 20 percent could only reduce its overall tax rate to
36 percent by claiming maximum refunds. The minister also has
the power to exempt a mine from all or part of mineral tax but, since
this is an exemption rather than a repayment, the taxable profit
would bear income tax at 45 percent where the whole of mineral tax
is exempt. A mine with this exemption would thus be at a disadvantage
compared with a mine without it if the mine were earning net profits
less than 12 percent of equity.

The mineral tax refund system is evidently designed to "protect"
a level of profit equivalent to 12 percent of equity. The procedure
is that, after three years in which the company has been paying tax
(i.e., after cumulative operating profits have surpassed capital
expenditure), the average of net profits for each of the three years
is compared with 12 percent of the average of the level of equity
funds at the beginning of each of the three years. If the former is
less than the latter, an amount of mineral tax equal to the difference
can be reclaimed for each of the three years (provided that such
amount has been paid). (The Mineral Tax Act, 1970, appears to
provide for only one-third of this amount, but potential investors

have been assured that the intention is as described.) The same procedure may be carried out at subsequent intervals of three years. Equity for the purposes of this concession includes paid-up capital and deferred and preferred stock (provided that it carries no rights of early repayment on demand) but excludes all forms of debt capital (including convertible stock). It includes capital reserves insofar as they are not capable of distribution (other than by a change in capital) and revenue reserves insofar as they have remained constant throughout the previous 12 months. The size of reserves depends to an important extent on the rate at which fixed assets are depreciated. It obviously would not be very satisfactory as far as this concession is concerned if balance sheet assets were depreciated on the same basis as they are allowed for tax. The problem is discussed later in this chapter, but in the discussion which follows the most generous possible inter- pretation of reserves is assumed—i.e., that which follows from not depreciating balance sheet assets at all. Hence, in the absence of any official guidance on this point, it should be remembered that the concession might turn out to be worth even less to the investor than appears here.

The exact value of this concession to a project depends, of course, on the proportions of the initial investment financed by loans and equity. As loan replaces equity, the threshold of net profit below which refunds may be claimed is reduced. The effect of the concession under three different financing conditions (50 percent, 33.33 percent, and zero loans) is shown in Chart 8.2, where the loans are at 8 percent interest repayable over the first 8 years of operation, the axes and project parameters being otherwise the same as in Chart 8.1. The dotted lines trailing from the solid lines show what the situation would have been without the mineral tax refund concession. Although the concession can undoubtedly help mines if they get into unexpected difficulties, its effectiveness in promoting investment in new mines can only be seen in terms of the extent to which it makes investors accept projects that they would otherwise have turned down. We can now read from the graph that, if 100 percent equity financing is con- templated and 15 percent over 10 years is the minimum acceptable return, the minimum gross profit is reduced by the concession from 43 percent of the capital invested to just under 42 percent—i.e., as far as this investor is concerned, the concession is of negligible value. If a 12 percent return is all that is required, the gain is more significant—minimum gross profitability is reduced from 37 percent to 32 percent—but investors in this field seeking such modest rewards would be hard to find. If 15 percent is the investor's criterion, then loan finance considerably reduces the minimum gross profit,—e.g.,

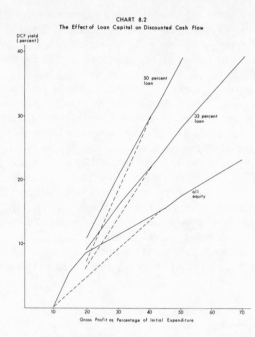

CHART 8.2
The Effect of Loan Capital on Discounted Cash Flow

to 29 percent with one-third loans and to 24 percent with 50 percent loans—but even here the benefit due to the mineral tax concession (the horizontal space between the points where the 15 percent DCF line is intersected by the solid and dotted lines) still is not very significant. However, it should be remembered that, the greater the proportion of loan finance, the greater the risk borne by the equity holder and hence the greater his minimum profit requirement. Thus, with a Zambian mining project financed as to 50 percent by loan capital, an investor may well refuse to go ahead unless a 25 percent return to equity is foreseen. In this case, the minimum gross profit will be 34.5 percent of the initial expenditure with the concession and 35.5 percent without it.

It is clear that, for any given debt/equity ratio and any corresponding realistic minimum rate of return, the advantage conferred on a project by the 12 percent mineral tax concession is very small. Moreover, the minimum gross profit under any likely financing hypothesis remains far above the hypothetical minimum without taxation. In consequence, the number of projects that are viable with the concession and unviable without it is likely to be very small, and there remains a considerable likelihood of the discovery of deposits that, although viable economically, will be turned down by investors subject to ordinary taxation.

"SPECIAL" CONDITIONS

Potential prospectors in Zambia who have in various ways pointed out to government the consequences of the high rates of tax have been met with the reply that in the event of discovery of a mineral deposit government will be prepared to negotiate lower rates of tax if these appear to be justified. But this attitude ignores the need of those financing a prospecting program to have a clear idea of the sort of profit the discoverer of a mineral deposit will be allowed to make, since this will have an important bearing on prospecting strategy. Gone are the romantic days when prospecting was carried out by adventurers who roamed the bush with no more equipment than hammer, shovel, and pan and who came up with a bonanza on the average somewhat less than once in a lifetime. Prospecting now involves much more sophisticated equipment, is normally very expensive, and is carried out by companies that deploy their expenditure on prospecting after careful calculation of the probability of success and the likely returns. Risks are reduced by participating in prospecting ventures through consortia and by spreading expenditure geographically. The amount of funds placed in any one area will be closely related to the scale of possible returns, which in turn are a function of the probability of discovery and the likely profit to be made in the event of success. The basic equation is that the cost of a prospecting campaign in any area should not be greater than the product of the net present value of a possible discovery and the probability of making such a discovery.

In practice, there are considerable problems in rigorously applying the formula described above, but the interrelationships described would underlie the approach of any modern business to a prospecting venture. Thus, if two areas showed equal promise from a geological point of view, more funds would go to the area where a given discovery would yield more profit. An area that imposed a very high tax rate, thus limiting profitability potential for private investors, might still be able to retain the flow of prospecting expenditure if the probability of discovery were unusually high. The important point is that it is to the advantage of both prospector and host country if the prospector knows in advance as precisely as possible the conditions under which he will be able to operate a mine if a viable deposit is found. If the conditions are not clear, the prospector will tend to take an unnecessarily prudent view and potential prospecting effort will be lost to the country concerned.

Seen against this background, the Zambian Government's offer to negotiate special tax conditions where it thinks these are warranted is not very satisfactory, since there is no clear indication of what circumstances would be held to warrant special conditions or what kind of profit would be regarded as reasonable. Under the present arrangements, potential investors might draw inferences from the "protected" 12 percent annual return on equity, in which case they would probably be underestimating the State's sympathy with private enterprise and allocating less expenditure to Zambia than they might have done.

Considering the equation given above, the Zambian tax conditions not only reduce the net present value of possible discoveries but also, by increasing the minimum viable grade, greatly reduce the probability of a successful find. Although a reduction in NPV through taxation is, of course, inevitable up to a point, the shrinking of the probability factor in the equation through the effect on minimum grades is avoidable. Not only will the flow of prospecting expenditure to Zambia be reduced by these factors, but even funds that are committed to Zambia may be inefficiently used as a result of harsh tax conditions or uncertainty about possible concessions. A prospector might refuse to search more than a short distance from the line of rail, beyond a certain depth, or in rock formations where it is highly unlikely that mineralization will be higher than 3 percent although 1.5 percent would have been viable with suitable concessions.

It is true that a number of prospectors seized the opportunity of the new legislation to acquire prospecting licences in Zambia, and this may be held to demonstrate the reasonableness of the new tax provisions. However, it should be remembered that promising areas are in limited supply and prospectors would be acting quite rationally if they acquired the licences first and argued about taxation afterward. The initial stage of prospecting need not be particularly onerous. The success of the legislation should rather be judged by the amount of money committed to Zambia on a commercial basis in the early 1970's. And, even supposing that Zambia became a relatively popular place in which to look for minerals, there is a risk that much of the nation's mineral endowment will not even be discovered if there is a significant gap between what is commercially exploitable and what is economically exploitable.

PROPOSALS FOR A TAX ALLOWANCES SYSTEM

If the extent of tax concessions (beyond the mineral tax refund provision discussed above) is so crucial for the minimum viable

grade, then, given that private investors tend toward prudence, maximum expenditure on prospecting would only be attracted to Zambia
if the terms of such concessions were made absolutely clear. Ideally,
concessions would become available automatically. The advantages
of automatic tax concessions for industrial investment apparently
have been recognized, since the discretionary Pioneer Industry facilities (which confer a tax holiday for three to five years) appear to have
been replaced, at least in part, by automatic investment allowances.

The case for automatic concessions is probably even stronger
for mining than for secondary industry, since the industrial investor
at least knows the approximate cost of his project and the marketing
conditions for his product before he decides to proceed, while the
prospector invests with no knowledge of his eventual production costs
or even of what his product will be and with a market completely
outside his control. As was shown above, the 12 percent of equity
mineral tax refund concession does not significantly reduce the minimum "gross profitability" of a mine or, therefore, the minimum
viable grade. This concession appears to protect an annual return of
12 percent on the equity capital. Its practical value is so small in
part because the refund is paid up to three years in arrears and in
part because income tax remains payable, but principally because
the profits during the tax-free phase are regarded wholly as capital
recoupment, whereas in the investor's view they are partly interest
on the unrecouped balance. The logical way to protect an annual
return of 12 percent on equity from taxation would be to add 12 percent
of the equity to tax allowances each year. Then, provided that mining
companies were willing to invest in mines in Zambia for a return of
12 percent on equity, prospectors could calculate their minimum
viable grades without taking any account of the effects of taxation.

Both this concession and the mineral tax refund concession now
in force involve the tax authority in considering the company's balance
sheet. One may ask whether this innovation is really necessary. In
the past, it appears to have been accepted that the companies' pres-
entations of profit and loss accounts to the tax authority and to shareholders would be different, the main difference being in the provision
for depreciation. For example, in industries with a rapidly evolving
technology companies frequently think it prudent to depreciate sophisticated items of plant more rapidly than is allowed for tax purposes.
In Zambian mines, very rapid depreciation is allowed by the tax
authority and if this were carried into the balance sheet the value of
assets, and hence also of reserves, would be seriously understated.
Not only would this not be "a true and fair statement" of the company's

position but also, insofar as equity funds would be understated, the value of the 12 percent concession would be much reduced. There are fundamental problems in depreciating mining assets, stemming principally from the nonrealizability of such assets as shafts and from the fact that a company established to operate a mine with limited life does not normally set aside funds for maintaining its earning power. The simplest solution would be for shareholders and the tax authority to accept the convention that assets should not be depreciated at all for balance sheet purposes. This approach would be the most favorable for the mining company with regard to the mineral tax refund concession, but it may be at variance with the State's philosophy of valuing mines at net asset value for the purpose of compulsory purchase.

It would appear that a concession that did not involve the tax authority directly with the company's balance sheet would be preferable. One system that has been suggested involves the suspension of all tax not only until the original expenditure has been recovered but also until a reasonable rate of interest has been achieved on the whole of the unrecouped balance calculated annually. Thus, if 12 percent were the accepted rate of interest, the tax loss at the end of each year would be carried forward to the following year with an increase of 12 percent. When the tax loss treated in this way had been wiped out by operating profits, tax would be applicable at the full rate and the concession would be of no further benefit. This system does not involve the tax authority with defining equity and is very easily grafted onto the existing tax system. It also has the advantage that it is couched in the same terms that the mining investor is most likely to use in assessing a project, with the result that it is potentially most efficient in terms of maximizing prospecting expenditure attracted and minimizing revenue sacrificed. Under this system, tax becomes payable at the full rate as soon as the specified yield (in the above case 12 percent) has been earned on the total sum invested on a DCF basis. If this is indeed the investor's minimum requirement on an all-equity basis, government could be sure that no mineral deposit would remain unworked because of taxation. From the prospector's point of view, the range of interest and therefore the probability of success would be maximized. From government's point of view, there would be a sacrifice of revenue from new mines that would have been opened without the concession, but this would be small and would diminish if profits were higher than expected since this would bring forward the tax-paying stage and reduce overall allowances. Any such sacrifice should, of course, be negligible compared with the revenue and economic benefits accruing from mines that would not have been worked and possibly not even discovered without the concession.

It should be remembered that mines are opened on the basis of an adequate rate of return at a "safe" price for the product and, because investors usually err on the side of prudence, the price envisaged usually is exceeded in practice. Thus, it could easily happen that a mine could have been worked at the metal price as it turned out but was not in fact opened because the threshold of viability was so high. The allowance system here proposed reduces the threshold of viability to the minimum at what is probably the minimum conceivable cost to Government in terms of sacrificed revenue. The relationship under this system of allowances between DCF yield and gross profit as a proportion of initial investment and an "allowed" return of 12 percent is shown by the dotted curve M in Chart 8.1 above. It will be seen that, as gross profitability rises, the new curve follows the "no tax" curve until a 12 percent yield is achieved and then follows a course almost parallel and slightly convergent with the curve for the existing system. The lower range of gross profitability is thus brought into the zone of viability in the most economical way.

There is a further incidental advantage to this system of allowances. Under the present system, an established mining company that incurs expenditure on new production, whether from an expansion of its existing workings or from a noncontiguous area, can offset the expenditure against its current profit for tax. A newly established company, on the other hand, can only offset mine development expenditure against profits generated by the expenditure, which will not occur until some years later. Therefore, any particular mining project will look much more attractive on a discounted yield basis in the hands of an established mining company than it would if operated by a newcomer. The difference may not be marked with tax rates at conventional levels, but with tax at 73 percent the bias in favor of the established operator creates an important incentive for the newcomer to sell out to or merge with one of the existing groups. However, if the newcomer is able to increase his unrecouped expenditure annually by the "allowed" rate of return, as recommended above, then the net present value of his project discounted at the same rate will be the same as the net present value of the project in the hands of an established mining company. Thus, the disadvantage to the newcomer is redressed. For example, let us suppose that a copper project was developed in one year at a cost of 200 and produced gross profits of 100 each year thereafter. Cash flows for an established copper-mining company, for an independent newcomer, and for a newcomer, with a 15 percent return "allowed" tax-free may be compared in Table 8.1.

Thus, if 15 percent is regarded as the minimum profit requirement for money invested in a Zambian copper mine, the 15 percent

TABLE 8.1

Cash Flows for Established and Independent Copper-Mining
Companies, First Five Years of Operation

Year	Gross	Established Company	Independent Company	Independent Company with 15 percent Allowance
1	(200)	(53.9)	(200)	(200)
2	100	26.95	100	100
3	100	26.95	100	100
4	100	26.95	26.95	68.53
5	100	26.95	26.95	26.95
NPV at 15 Percent		23.1	(4.3)	23.1

Note: From year 5 onward, cash flows are the same in each case.

Source: Compiled by author.

"allowance" brings the value of a project to a newcomer up to exactly
the same as its value to an established company. By contrast, an
independent without the allowance would consider himself still out-of-
pocket at the end of five years and after paying mineral and income
tax for two full years. There may well be other forces at work tending
to push newcomers into close association with the established groups,
for example, the possible need to use their smelting and refining
services. If it were government policy to encourage the establishment
of new mining companies in Zambia, the adoption of this system of
allowances would assist by removing one of the main centripetal
forces.

THE PARTICIPATION REQUIREMENT

How will potential prospectors and mining investors view the
State's option to participate in any new mine up to 51 percent and, in
particular, is any potential expenditure likely to be deterred by the
existence of the option? Accepting the fact of economic nationalism,
it is likely that investors will regard government participation as an
advantage rather than a disadvantage. Indeed, after three rounds of
nationalizations it is evident that in Zambia private investment without
government participation will be negligible for at least some years.
The disappearance of the Foreign Investment Protection Act, which
was promised in the Mulungushi speech of April 1968 and is known to
have reached draft form, suggests that government has accepted this
situation. However, although in the present Zambian context foreign
investors may regard some government participation as indispensable,
they may consider a 51 percent interest by the State somewhat less
favorably than a smaller holding. Many investors, and in some cases
their governments, will hesitate to commit large sums to projects as
complex and unpredictable as mines if they feel they will have to
surrender control of policy and day-to-day management to individuals
with whom they may not always agree on commercial policy. Although
government's option is to acquire not more than 51 percent, there is
at present no indication that government will exercise its option
in a mining venture for any share less than 51 percent. Therefore,
there is a definite possibility that, even accepting all the implications
of economic nationalism, potential prospecting effort will be wasted
because of the State's insistence on formal control. The amount
sacrificed is, of course, unquantifiable, but the economic advantage
to the State in obtaining control of new mines is probably fairly small.

Financially, the terms of State participation are not unreasonable.
Participation on the same terms as with the established mines would

have been impossible since very few investors would have been willing to accept terms that obliged them not only to finance their 49 percent of the equity but also to lend funds for government to finance its 51 percent at a fraction of their normal minimum rate of return. As it is, government has agreed to pay for its share of prospecting and development carried out in the whole of the original prospecting area in which the new mine concerned is found and to pay for mine construction expenditure on the same terms as other shareholders. Thus, for his outlay on prospecting the prospector gets only half a mine instead of a whole mine, and the only "unreasonable" loss he incurs is the interest and reward for risk on the prospecting expenditure eventually reimbursed by the State. The fact that prospecting expenditure is only being employed at half its normal efficiency (as far as the prospector is concerned) may cause the investor to compensate by slightly raising his minimum rate of return (to the detriment of national ore reserves and potential prospecting effort).

Government participation in new mines also may lead to a tax disadvantage that would be felt especially by those who do not already have taxable income in Zambia. If a company prospects in various areas of Zambia, finds a mineral deposit, and opens a mine, for the purposes of both mineral and income tax all its prospecting expenditure can be offset against the profits of the mine. If the mine produces copper and makes sufficient taxable profits, the net undiscounted cost to the prospector of all his prospecting expenditure will be 26.95 percent of the gross cost. If Government decides to participate, there will be an inequity since Government benefits from the reduction in taxation accruing from all the prospecting expenditure but only pays its share of the expenditure in the area in which the mine is found. As noted earlier, for tax purposes the prospecting company may renounce its expenditure in favor of its shareholders. If the shareholders have taxable income in Zambia, they may offset the expenditure against their profit for income tax. In this case, the value of the expenditure in terms of reduced tax is only 45 percent of the gross amount spent instead of 73.05 percent if offset against the ultimate profits of a copper mine, but the earlier availability of the tax saving may easily make this option preferable. If, for example, the shareholder discounts future profits at 15 percent, an immediate allowance for income tax is equivalent to an allowance of the same amount for both income tax and copper mineral tax in 4 years' time.

However, the option described above would not be available to a newcomer to Zambia with no immediate Zambian income. He would have to accumulate his tax losses (forming a company to receive them if necessary) until he started receiving dividends from the mine

opened with Government as a result of his successful prospecting.
In Zambia, dividends paid by companies are declared gross and net,
net being the amount actually distributed and gross being the amount
from which the deduction of 45 percent leaves the net amount. Thus,
if the amount distributed is 55, the gross amount is 100, whether or
not the company was liable to income tax, and the recipient of such a
dividend is considered to have received 100 on which tax of 45 percent
has been paid. A newcomer prospector will be able to deduct his
prospecting expenditure from his gross dividends received, calculate
the income tax due on the remainder, and reclaim from the tax authority the difference between this and the tax shown as "paid" on his
dividend certificates.

In this way, the newcomer is able to use his expenditure to
reduce income tax and, provided the mine pays sufficient dividends,
the net cost of his prospecting expenditure will be 55 percent of the
gross cost. However, he is in a less advantageous position than if
Government had not participated, since the expenditure would then
have been allowed for mineral tax as well and would thus have cost
him only 26.95 percent of the gross amount if the mine was for copper.
This disadvantage does not appear to have been intended by the legislation. Moreover, the newcomer does not have the recourse available
to the established company of the early reduction of income tax, which,
as noted above, may in the investor's view be reasonable compensation
for the loss of reduced mineral tax at a later date.

This anomaly can be corrected either by State agreement to pay
to the prospector in whose mine it wishes to participate 51 percent of
the tax benefit accruing to the mine resulting from the endowment of
outside expenditure by the prospector or by making the dividends
paid by the mine to the prospector gross of both mineral and income
tax, instead of just income tax as at present. In the former case,
expenditure of 100 endowed to the mine would, if a copper mine,
reduce its total tax bill (and increase dividends) by 73.05 and Government would pay the prospector 51 percent of this sum (or 37.26) on
taking up its participation; the prospector receives the remaining
35.79 through its 49 percent share of dividends. Under the grossing
up procedure, the prospector sets his 100 of expenditure against his
gross dividends received. If the net dividend is 26.95, the gross dividend will be 100 with mineral tax of 51 "paid"and income tax of 22.05
"paid." The 100 of expenditure is deducted from the 100 gross dividend,
reducing tax liability to nil and allowing all tax "paid"to be reclaimed.

For the State, payment for a future tax benefit conferred by a private shareholder would appear to breach the "book value" principle and would look suspiciously like a "future profits" valuation, which would be anathema. On the other hand, the grossing up procedure would be rather complex administratively. Mines would pay special gross dividends to shareholders who were prospectors and ordinary gross dividends to other shareholders, while prospectors could offset only prospecting expenditure against their special gross dividends. The possibilities of mines producing more than one mineral, prospectors with additional discoveries of different metal, and prospectors with nonprospecting income or expenditure would need careful study. Apart from differences of timing, both these courses put the prospector on the same footing fiscally as if there were no State participation, and the financial consequences of each course for the State are the same if no distinction is made between the State as shareholder and the State as tax collector.

CONCLUSION

We have seen that, despite the allowances, the high rates of tax adopted for new mines will deter investment in many cases where investment taxed at lower rates or even not taxed at all would have been in the public interest. This leads not only to a reduction in the nation's ore reserves but also to reduced interest on the part of prospectors, making it less likely that mineral deposits will be found. These effects can be corrected by suitable incentives, but of those now in force the automatic one is inadequate and the discretionary one insufficiently firm. The rates of tax are simply the rates that yield approximately the same amount of revenue from the existing mines taken together as Government was receiving under the former system, and therefore they have no relevance to new mines at all.

The costs of producing any mineral are infinitely variable, and there is no economic reason why the rate of tax should vary with the metal produced. It was contingently true at the time of the takeover that the Zambian copper mines were collectively more profitable than the Zambian lead/zinc mine, but this need not apply to newly discovered copper or lead/zinc mines and may not even remain true of the mines originally in question. If mines are to be taxed at different rates, in determining the rate the mining conditions of the individual mine should receive at least as much consideration as the mineral mined. Thus, the Zambian package for new mines appears to have been made unnecessarily dependent on the package for existing mines,

which was designed with very different objects in mind. A simpler
and more effective system would be to tax all new mines at a single
rate and use the "minimum yield" allowance described above to make
concessions appropriate to the profitability of each particular mine.

We have also seen that State participation, although not in itself
a serious deterrent to investors, could become one if 51 percent
participation were insisted on. It is almost certainly true that any
project with which a private investor decided to proceed would become
a mine, whether or not the State decided to participate. Therefore,
one may ask precisely what the State receives for the 51 percent of
the development cost that it subscribes and whether, since the funds
would readily have been provided by others, the State's money was
optimally allocated.

A mine produces revenue, profits, and employment. From the
purely financial point of view, the State should be indifferent as to
whether it receives taxes or dividends. Since by taxation it could
achieve a financial result equivalent to its cash flows as an equity
holder but without risking funds at the initial stage of the project,
one may infer that its motive in participating is not commercial. As
for employment, the initiative to open the mines does not come from
the State but from the private investor; hence, the existence of jobs
owes nothing to State participation. The State may use its influence
to secure jobs for its own nationals in a marginal area, but the difference between what it can achieve in this area with participation and
what it can achieve without is negligible. Participation does give the
State the right of access to information and control over company
policy and day-to-day management (although the latter may be surrendered by a management contract), but even here the State usually
has de facto power to obtain any information it wants and it is difficult
for a company to pursue policies that are far from the wishes of the
State. The method of reconciling social and commercial goals (when
they diverge) must in any case be decided at the outset, regardless
of whether the State participates.

The social parameters within which a commercial company
operates usually are fairly well defined at any one time, and private
companies accept the more or less steady adjustment of these as a
country develops. To the extent that State participation implies the
imposition on the company of noncommercial decisions (e.g., in
enforcing social policies that are excessively "avant-garde"), investors
will be deterred unnecessarily. It should be emphasized that it has
always been the assumption in Zambia, for new mines as for the

agreements with Anglo-American and RST, that the agency through which the State participates will operate on strict commercial lines. Any breach of this principle would, of course, change the attitude of the private investor fundamentally.

Although Government appears to make little tangible gain from the acquisition of control of new mines, there may be political benefits in the formalization of its de facto control and it may be true that ownership is indeed the platform from which the campaign to achieve real economic independence must be launched (it is hard for the businessman to take a position on this point). It might be possible to accommodate the susceptibilities of both private investors and Government by allowing new mines to be developed wholly by private investors, exempting them from all tax until the achievement of the "minimum yield" as described above and providing that on arrival at the tax-paying stage they automatically become 51 percent owned by Government and liable to income tax but not mineral tax. Government would thus put up no risk money, and its share in profits in the taxable stage would be 73.05 percent. At the same time, provided that the minimum yield allowed did indeed reflect the investor's minimum profit requirement, all the objections raised in this chapter to the existing system would be removed.

STATISTICAL APPENDIX: METHOD OF CALCULATING MINIMUM GRADE

Minimum grade $\bar{g}$

Capital cost to concentrate per metric ton of ore $\quad$ K

Capital cost per metric ton of copper $\quad$ K/g

Minimum profit required
  (as percentage of initial investment)
  e.g., 42 percent with tax, 23 percent without $\quad$ P

Profit required per metric ton $\quad$ PK/g

Realized price per metric ton of copper $\quad$ R

Costs other than mining and concentrating $\quad$ C

Maximum cost of mining and concentrating
  (per metric ton of copper) $\quad$ R - C - PK/g

Mining and concentrating cost per metric ton ore $\quad$ M

Then:
$$g = \frac{M}{R - C - PK/g}$$

From which we get:
$$g = \frac{M + PK}{R - C}$$

This gives recoverable grade; for grade in situ, (g)
apply overall recovery factor (V) thus:
$$g = \frac{M + PK}{V(R-C)}$$

Some examples are shown below (M = K6; C = K150; V = 0.7):

		K800/Metric Ton		K700/Metric Ton	
		With Tax	Without Tax	With Tax	Without Tax
Capital cost per					
metric ton ore –	K25	3.63	2.58	4.35	3.05
	K30	4.09	2.83	4.83	3.36
	K35	4.54	3.09	5.37	3.64
	K40	5.01	3.34	5.93	3.94

THE CONTINUING SEARCH FOR INDEPENDENCE

Although it is dangerous to look too closely for historical paral-
lels, there are interesting similarities between the efforts of the
British South Africa Company to exploit its mineral rights and the
recent moves of the Zambian Government to secure control of the
mining industry. Both sought to find means of granting exploration
and prospecting rights in such a way as to ensure the maximum possibility of mineral discoveries, and both insisted on an option to participate in subsequent mining development.

The question of the legality of the British South Africa Company's
mineral rights was raised soon after substantial and profitable copper
production began in the 1930's. After World War II, attempts to buy
out the mineral rights foundered on a steep rise in the copper price.
This increased the official assessment of a reasonable purchase price
to the extent that it appeared too great a gamble to agree to pay from
the highly variable future royalties. Instead, in 1950 the Northern
Rhodesian Government obtained a 20 percent share of the royalty
income, and in return the company was to enjoy the balance for another 36 years. In 1969, the Zambian Government, having agreed to
guarantee minimum annual compensation payments for the mining
companies, had to face a similar risk in that a fall in copper revenues
would create financial problems. But in 1969 the opportunity was
missed to make a purchase through payments that varied (down as
well as up) with the value of copper production.

211

Although all mineral rights in Zambia have now finally reverted to the Government and 51 percent State participation in the copper production companies has been established, it is probable that the question of Government control of the industry has not yet been fully settled. As has been argued here, the 1969 arrangements fall within the area of common interest of the companies and the Zambian Government, and it provides a stable basis for development in the early 1970's.

However, in negotiating the new arrangements the Government was faced with a dilemma. Its first priority was to gain control, but the mines had to be kept in operation as going concerns and that meant that an amicable arrangement with the former management was absolutely necessary. This one basic factor in the situation was responsible for many provisions in the takeover agreements, including the specific commitments to allow the management contractors to run the mines their way, that is, "to optimise production and profit." This commitment also was necessary to secure the interests of the minority shareholders, and of Government insofar as it wished to meet compensation payments out of dividends to the greatest extent possible. In giving management free rein to maximize profits, certain other objectives—most notably the localization of management itself—apparently were neglected. Insofar as the management contractors see accelerated localization as a threat to profitability, even if only in the short term, they have a direct disincentive to promote localization, although politically this is a most sensitive question. The other big weakness of the takeover arrangements, highlighted in the second half of 1970 by the disaster at Mufulira and a falling copper price, is the lack of any way of reducing or postponing payment of annual compensation installments. Guaranteeing minimum compensation may or may not have been necessary to satisfy management in its capacity as representatives of minority shareholders, but the whole takeover arrangement might be challenged politically if Government has to contribute large sums from general taxation to meet compensation payments, thus negating the declared aim that the mines would be bought entirely out of future profits. In short, the weaknesses in the bargain from the Government point of view are the biggest threat to the future stability of the industry in its present institutional form.

FUTURE SOURCES OF TECHNOLOGY

Although the Zambian mining industry will continue to need foreign technology, and thus foreign partners in one form or another, this does not mean that the foreigners must always come from the same countries. Indeed, prospecting companies from several countries are already at work (even if they have not as yet committed very significant sums of money). This diversification, hopefully leading to the establishment of at least one more substantial mining group in the country, was probably one of Government's objectives in 1969. But it raises some fundamental questions concerning the relationship between economic and political independence.

Since by now Zambia must rank rather far down on the list of countries in which new private foreign investors would like to be committed, it is likely that such commitment must be purchased at a high price, higher perhaps than the price paid for continued partnership with the former mining companies. With the centrally planned economies, on the other hand, Zambia must rank rather higher, simply because relatively few countries are prepared even to consider playing host in partnership arrangements with the socialist states. On the face of it, then, the price for attracting technology and capital from the socialist states should be rather lower. The difficulty arises in trying to identify the price. Because of the shortage of foreign exchange, many socialist countries are unwilling to purchase, for example, copper with convertible western currency, and the true value of barter deals is very difficult to assess. In addition, the strength that lies behind the bargaining positions of noncapitalist countries is also different, being more political than economic. Of course, political sanctions are none the less real for being more difficult to translate into economic terms.

PRICE

This study has considered the mining takeover almost entirely from the point of view of the Zambian economy. It has thus neglected the shareholders' point of view and distinctions between the individual mines and mining groups. These last few remarks about the price paid for the mines are also presented from the viewpoint of the Zambian economy.

It has been argued that, in dealing with multinational companies, governments should only pay for what they want. Zambia sought to gain control of the local mining industry, to keep the present mining management, to expand output and prospecting activity, to retain investor confidence, and to acquire control of new mining development. All these objectives have been achieved; only on the question of expansion of output, where a general but not a quantified objective was

specified, is it unclear whether the Government achieved its goal as
a direct result of the takeover.

The question remains as to whether Government paid too much.
This question can only be answered if it is clearly understood that
there is no such thing in this case as a static concept of price. The
financial consequences of the takeover must be examined in terms of
a series of flows of money over time. These flows are dependent not
only on the actual terms of the takeover—taxation, exchange control,
compensation—but also on its consequences: notably, in the short
term, the amount of additional expansion of existing mines that actually
takes place and the way it is financed and, in the long term, the extent
of exploration and new mine development. Thus, a whole series of
questions must be asked concerning the financial value to Government
of the takeover; these questions relate to several objectives, some
of which we may have made more explicit than Government itself did.

It would appear that in general the short-term rate of return
to Government on its various financial commitments is positive and
probably greater than 10 percent—except that Government must bear
an immediate fall in tax revenue as a direct result of expansion—if
the price of copper does not fall substantially below K750 (£437) per
metric ton, if present cost levels remain more or less static, and if assumptions about the amount of expansion induced by the takeover are
approximately correct. As the price of copper falls or costs increase,
the Government becomes increasingly committed to paying compensation out of taxation rather than future dividends and the balance of
payments burden becomes increasingly severe. Thus, one's view of
the takeover arrangements depends very much on one's view of the
price of copper, as do so many things in copper-dependent Zambia.

It is perhaps appropriate to conclude by pointing out yet another
dilemma: short-term growth depends on increasing copper earnings,
yet if this happens the economy grows even more dependent on copper.
Even if noncopper exports doubled in two years, the increase in foreign
exchange earnings would not pay for a 5 percent annual increase in
imports. As yet, Zambia has done little to tackle this aspect of the
country's economic dependence.

INTRODUCTION

On December 24, 1969, Heads of Agreement were signed between the Zambian Government and Indeco (a wholly owned subsidiary of Zimco, a Government company) on the one hand and the Zambian Anglo-American group of mining companies (Zamanglo) on the other, and between Government and Indeco, on the one hand and Roan Selection Trust Limited (RST) on the other. These two separate Heads of Agreement set out the terms on which the Government of Zambia would acquire a 51 percent interest in the mining, smelting, and refining operations of the Zamanglo and RST subsidiaries in Zambia. The mining companies affected are shown in Appendix Table 1.

BASIC LEGAL DOCUMENTS

The basic legal documents or arrangements for implementing the Zambian takeover were a main Heads of Agreement, signed December 24, 1969 (referred to as the "Master Agreement"), various subsidiary documents arising out of the Master Agreement (i.e., an indenture or trust deed, a management and consultancy contract, a sales and marketing contract, an arbitration agreement, and the respective Memorandums and Articles of Association of Roan Consolidated Mines Limited and of Nchanga Consolidated Copper Mines Limited, the two new Government mining companies), legislation enacted by the Zambian Parliament, and a Scheme of Arrangement pursuant to the Zambian Companies Ordinance. The Master Agreement was intended to set forth the general principles governing the takeover, leaving the details to be set forth in the subsidiary agreements, the legislation, and the Scheme of Arrangement. Similar documents were drawn up for both the RST and Zamanglo arrangements; this appendix has been drawn from those documents made public, in particular:

> Zamanglo: Scheme of Arrangement (annexed to a letter to shareholders dated April 27, 1970), which includes proposals for the merger of Bancroft Mines Limited, Nchanga Consolidated Copper Mines Limited, Rhokana Corporation Limited, and Rhokana Copper Refineries Limited and for the acquisition of a 51 percent interest therein by Zambia Industrial and Mining Corporation Limited.
>
> RST: Explanatory Statement dated June 30, 1970 (for meetings of shareholders held on August 6, 1970), which

Mining Companies Affected by the Takeover

	Ore Reserves[a] (thousands of metric tons)		Finished Production 1969 (thousands of metric tons)			
		Percentage Copper	Blister	Wirebar	Cathode	Total
RST						
Mufulira Mines Ltd.						
Mufulira Mine	145,463	3.28	1.4	163.6	4.8	169.8
Chibuluma Mine	5,764	5.12	1.0	21.4	3.1	25.5
Chambishi Mine	29,690	3.08	0.2	22.0	0.3	22.5
Luanshya Mines Ltd.	69,586	2.87	0.8	94.7	7.6	103.1
Mwinilunga Mines Ltd.						
Kalengwa Mine	(592	17.25)	—	1.1	—	1.1
	(204	3.50)				
Baluba Mines Ltd.*[b]	59,694	2.71	—	-	—	-
Total	310,993	3.12	3.4	302.8	15.8	322.0
Zamanglo						
Nchanga Consolidated Mines Limited	223,806	4.00	64.8	169.0	8.5	242.3
Rhokana Corporation Limited	129,573	2.64	26.6	69.9	3.5	100.0
Bancroft Mines Ltd.	82,937	3.51	13.5	35.1	1.8	50.3
Total	436,316	3.50	104.9	274.0	13.8	392.6
Total Zambia	747,309	3.34	108.3	576.8	29.6	714.8
of which: Copperbelt	746,513	3.33	108.3	575.7	29.6	713.7

[a]As declared on June 30, 1969 (RST) or December 31, 1969 (Zamanglo).
*[b]Not included in the takeover arrangements as such, the company will be purchased by Mindeco when mining commences.

includes the Scheme of Arrangement between Mufulira
Copper Mines Limited, Mwinilunga Mines Limited, and
Luanshya Mines Limited.

EQUITY INTEREST ACQUIRED

The 51 percent interests acquired by Government are to be held
finally by Mindeco, although initially they were vested in Zimco, a
State-owned corporation holding a 100 percent interest in Mindeco.

PRICE

The price for the assets was based on the "book value" as at
December 31, 1969.

RST

Zimco acquired and subsequently transferred to Mindeco a 51
percent interest in the mining, smelting, and refining operations of
RST's subsidiaries. This was effected in two steps: (1) by the amalgamation of Luanshya Mines Limited and Mwinilunga Mines Limited
with Mufulira Mines Limited, which subsequently was renamed Roan
Consolidated Mines Limited (RCM), and (2) by the subsequent acquisition of 51 percent of RCM shares by Zimco. The share capital of
the three RST mining companies at December 31, 1969, was as
follows:

| Company | Shares | | Of Which | |
	Authorized	Issued	RST	Zamanglo Group
Mufulira (K2 each)	40,000,000	37,006,652	24,261,824	12,744,828
Mwinilunga (K2 each)	3,000,000	2,750,000	1,478,436	1,271,564
Luanshya (K2 each)	24,000,000	22,160,600	22,160,600	—

The Mufulira authorized capital became K160million ($224million),
consisting of 20.4million "A" ordinary shares at K4 (subsequently
acquired by Zimco) and 19.6million "B" ordinary shares at K4. The
issued capital was K121,260,264 ($169,764,370), of which the "B"
shareholding was fixed at 11,140,787 shares to RST and 3,713,595

shares to the Zamanglo group, now held by Zambia Copper Investments Limited (ZCI). As a result of the reorganization of RST, which was approved by its shareholders on July 6, 1970, 5,077,774 of their "B" shares have been distributed to the former non-Amax shareholders of RST, and the RST holding is now in the name of RST International, Inc. In summary, the shareholding of RCM was settled as follows: Mindeco, 51 percent; RST International, 20 percent; public, 16.75 percent; and ZCI, 12.25 percent.

The payment to the former shareholders of the RST mining companies was effected by a Mufulira dividend of K96,993,411 ($135, 790,775) to the new "B" shareholders of RCM. This amount consisted of the following:

	To RST		To Zamanglo Group		Total	
	$million	Kmillion	$million	Kmillion	$million	Kmillion
Excluded assets*	12.84	9.17	5.14	3.67	17.98	12.84
Included assets	90.20	64.43	27.60	19.72	117.80	84.15
Total	103.04	73.60	32.74	23.39	135.78	96.99

It is not possible to give a breakdown on the net asset value of each of the former RST mining companies as it is for the Zamanglo Group of companies, since the agreed figure of K84.15million ($117.80million) was the determined purchase value for the whole group and was not strictly based on the book value as shown by audited accounts at December 31, 1969. The difference in the treatment of the two mining groups was due largely to the problem of assessing the value of Luanshya Mine, which was not accurately reflected in the book value because of the accounting procedures adopted (Luanshya Mine had an estimated life of approximately ten years as at January 1, 1970).

So far as the RST group is concerned, the position was made more complex by the Scheme of Arrangement involving a reduction of capital of RST necessitated by the company becoming a wholly owned subsidiary of Amax Limited. The Scheme of Arrangement whereby Mindeco secured a 51 percent share in Mufulira (now RCM)

---

*Excluded from Scheme of Arrangement: K1.10 million ($1.54 million) from Luanshya and K11.74 million ($16.44 million) from Mufulira.

was conditional to the RST Scheme for a Reduction of Capital. The latter was sanctioned in the Zambian High Court by Court Order No. 1970/HP/719 on August 11, 1970, following the shareholders' meeting on August 6, 1970.

Zamanglo

In the case of the Anglo-American group of companies, the mining assets and liabilities of Nchanga Consolidated Copper Mines Limited, Rhokana Copper Mines Limited, and Rhokana Copper Refineries Limited were vested in Bancroft Mines Limited, which was subsequently renamed Nchanga Consolidated Copper Mines Limited (NCCM). After this change was completed, 51 percent of the NCCM shares were acquired by Zimco. The share capital of the Zamanglo companies at December 31, 1969, is shown in Appendix Table 2.

The Bancroft authorized capital was increased to 125million shares of K2 each, of which 51 percent were "A" ordinary shares and the balance "B" shares, 434,000 5 percent redeemable cumulative preference shares of K2 each, and 500,621 5 percent redeemable cumulative preference shares of K2 each. The issued ordinary shares were distributed as follows:

Mindeco	"A" shares (51 percent)	62,877,900
ZCI	"B" shares (49 percent)	60,412,100
Total		123,290,000

The value of the mining and excluded assets was based on the audited accounts at December 31, 1969, and was as shown in Appendix Table 3.

PAYMENT

Payment for the Zimco 51 percent interests in RCM and NCM was effected by the issue of Zimco Bonds in the case of RCM and Zimco loan stock in the case of NCCM.

For RST, Zimco created K84.15million ($117.8 million) principal amount of bonds, repayable with interest at 6 percent by sixteen semi-annual installments. The first such payment was made on October 1, 1970, and later installments will be payable each April 1 and October

APPENDIX TABLE 2

Share Capital of Zamanglo Companies at December 31, 1969

	Authorized Shares	Issued	Of Which: Zamanglo	Nchanga	Rhokana	Public
Bancroft						
Nondividend ranking redeemable preferred Shares of K2 each	7,500,000	7,500,000	–	–	–	7,500,000
Ordinary shares of K0.50 each	25,000,000	25,000,000	–	24,853,232	–	146,768
Nchanga						
Ordinary shares of K2 each	32,066,667	32,001,085	7,154,002	–	11,110,574	13,736,509
Rhokana						
5.5 percent redeemable cumulative preferred shares of K2 each	1,500,000	434,000	–	–	–	434,000
Ordinary shares of K2 each	24,950,342	24,950,342	13,418,415	–	–	11,581,605
"A" shares of K2 each	50,000	49,678				
Rhokana Copper Refineries						
5 percent redeemable cumulative preferred shares of K2 each	1,300,000	500,621	–	–	–	500,621
Ordinary shares of K2 each	2,200,000	1,700,000	–	850,000	850,000	–

Sources: Company annual reports.

APPENDIX TABLE 3

Mining Assets and Excluded Assets of Zamanglo
Companies at December 31, 1969

	Mining Assets		Excluded Assets		Total	
	$million	Kmillion	$million	Kmillion	$million	Kmillion
Bancroft	77.84	55.60	—	—	77.84	55.60
Nchanga	143.24	102.31	31.19	22.28	174.42	124.59
Rhokana	110.35	78.82	72.86	52.04*	183.21	130.86
Rhokana Copper Refineries	13.78	9.84	—	—	13.78	9.84
Total	345.21	246.58	104.04	74.32	449.25	320.90

*Includes Rhokana's RST interests amounting to K34million ($48million) which will be vested in ZCI as follows:

		Book Value Kmillion
Baluba	460,264 shares of K2 K331,653 loan	1.25
Chisangwa	366,900 shares of K2 K309,000 loan	0.08
Mwinilungwa (Prospecting)	K338,287 loan	0.12
Mufulira	9,848,657 shares of K2	15.04 of RCM "B" shares
Mwinilungwa	237,344 shares of K2	14.48 of U.S. $20.27 million Zimco bonds 1978
(Kalengwa)	K202,829 loan	3.10 excluded assets- Mufulira
Total		34.07

Sources: Company annual reports and statements to stockholders.

225

APPENDIX TABLE 4

Distribution of Zimco Bonds 1978
and RCM Private Shareholding

RST[a]	Distribution of Zimco Bonds 1978 to Former Shareholders in the RST Group (dollars)	(percentage)	Distribution of RCM Private Shareholding (percentage)
Amax	39,429,000	33.4	40.8
Public	50,777,800	43.1	34.2
Total	90,206,800	76.6	75.0
Zamanglo			
Zamanglo[b]	7,331,085	6.2	
Rhokana[b]	20,272,115	17.2	25.0
Total	27,603,200	23.4	25.0
Total	117,810,000	100.0	100.0

[a]After reorganization and "reduction in capital" (see Appendix D).

[b]To be vested in ZCI.

1 up to and including April 1, 1978, (Zimco bonds 1978) if no acceleration takes place. The distribution of Zimco bonds 1978 and RCM private shareholding is shown in Appendix Table 4.

For Zamanglo, the principal amount of loan stock is K125,766, 000 ($178,698,992) repayable with interest at 6 percent by twenty-four equal semiannual installments starting on October 1, 1970, and ending April 1, 1982 (Zimco loan stock 1982). The distribution of the loan stock was made to Zambia Copper Investments Limited, a subsidiary of Zambian Anglo-American Limited, both of which are registered in Bermuda. Just over 50 percent of ZCI is now owned by Zamanglo and 80,850,198 units of ZCI loan stock 1982 (45.24 percent of total) have been issued to Zamanglo together with 18,211,858 of the ZCI loan stock 1978 (65.98 percent of total ZCI).

The differences in the timing of payments to former RST and
Zamanglo shareholders of eight years and twelve years respectively
partly reflects the higher profitability of RCM. The annual payments
to be made by RCM and NCCM are:

	Kwacha	U.S.$
NCCM to former shareholders (Zamanglo)	15,073,770	21,103,278
RCM to former shareholders (RST)	13,599,481	19,039,276
Total	28,673,251	40,142,554

DOLLAR BONDS AND LOAN STOCK

Both the Zimco 1978 bonds and 1982 loan stock carry 6 percent
interest and are fully and unconditionally guaranteed by the Republic
of Zambia. The RST Explanatory Statement for shareholders (dated
June 30, 1970) states "the Bonds will enjoy the unconditional guarantee
of Zambia and the full faith and credit of Zambia will be pledged for
the due and punctual payment of the principal of and interest on the
Bonds and for the performance of all obligations of Zimco with respect thereto." Thus, the redemption of principal and interest payments on the Zimco Bonds and loan stock are in no sense dependent
on the future profits of RCM and NCCM respectively. The bonds and
loan stock will be freely negotiable, repayment will be in U.S. dollars,
and the 6 percent interest will be free of Zambian taxes. The bonds
and loan stock were issued pursuant to an indenture (in the case of
RST) and to a trust deed (in the case of Zamanglo), both in a form
commonly used in London and New York financial markets. They
both provided for the following events of default (inter alia):

1. Default for 30 days in the payment of principal or interest
due on the bonds and loan stock;

2. The sale by Zimco or RCM or NCCM of all or a substantial
part of assets;

3. Zimco or Mindeco or RCM or NCCM becoming bankrupt or
being wound up or amalgamated or subject to a compromise or arrangements prejudicial to bond or stock holders;

4. Unlawful cancellation or abrogation by RCM or NCCM of
the management and consultancy or sales and marketing contract;

5. Unlawful abrogation or breach by Government or Zimco of its obligations under the Master Agreement (e.g., undertakings in respect of taxation and exchange control);

6. Material failure by RCM or NCCM to abide by any of the provisions of their Articles of Association designed for the protection of the "B" shareholders (e.g., the "B" director "veto" provisions described below);

7. Failure by RCM or NCCM to pay net profits on dividends to the extent required by the Articles of Association;

8. Unlawful cancellation or abrogation by the Zambian Government, Zimco, RCM, or NCCM of obligations to arbitrate disputes in the manner described below.

ACCELERATION OF COMPENSATION PAYMENT

If two-thirds of the Mindeco dividends from either RCM or NCCM exceeds the guaranteed fixed annual payment of K13.6 million ($19.0 million) and K15.1 million ($21.1 million) respectively, the excess will be applied to additional bond redemptions. In the case of RCM, these provisions apply from the calendar year 1971 and in the case of NCCM from 1972. If accelerated payments take place, the period of repayment will be shortened. However, accelerated repayment will not reduce the obligation to make the same semiannual payments in future years until the bonds and loan stock are fully redeemed.

EXTERNALIZATION OF ASSETS

In terms of an agreement with the Zambian Government's Exchange Control Authority, both RST and Zamanglo are able to externalize nonmining assets.

RST

The Master Agreement permits RST assets other than those held by RCM to be freely transferred outside Zambia. In particular, agreement has been reached for the externalization of K17.9 million ($25 million) in equal monthly installments up to December 1971. At the same time, RST has undertaken to the Zambian Government that, to the extent it is called upon to do so, it will contribute from funds

not subject to Zambian exchange control a 36.75 percent share, up to
an aggregate amount of K15 million ($21 million) of the capital finance
required by RCM for the development of existing or new mining ventures in Zambia considered to be commercially viable by the RCM
Board (e.g., Baluba, Chambishi underground).

Zamanglo

Agreement was reached for the externalization of K11.7million
($16.4million), the liquid funds included in the nonmining assets vested
in ZCI, in equal monthly installments over the period ending June 30,
1972. At the same time, Zambian Anglo-American Limited (Bermuda)
reached agreement for the externalization of K16.8million ($23.6mil-
lion) during the period ending June 30, 1972. In return, Zamanglo
and ZCI have jointly undertaken to hold available K12million ($16.8
million for reinvestment in Zambia over the five-year period ending
December 31, 1974.

In addition, permission was granted for the externalization of
the RST and Zamanglo pension funds.

MANAGEMENT AND CONSULTANCY CONTRACT

RCM and NCCM agreed to enter into separate management and
consultancy contracts with RST and a company within the Anglo-American group. Details of the RST contract are given below. The Zamanglo contract is in similar terms, although the precise details have
not been disclosed.

Management and Consultancy Functions

"RST shall provide to RCM all managerial, financial, commercial, technical and other services which, prior to 1st January,
1970 were supplied or procured by the RST group to Mufulira, Luanshya
and Mwinilunga with the intention that the business affairs and operations of RCM shall be maintained in a manner no less efficient and
standard no less than those before 1st January, 1970, and which shall
be directed towards the optimization of production and profit of RCM
and any subsidiary companies." These services include:

1. Technical services such as "preparing progress reports,
short and long term plans and viability studies for maintaining,

expanding or improving operations and production, capital expenditure estimates, advice on operating problems in the mining, geological, metallurgical and engineering activities, advice on scheduling copper production, recommending policies on ore reserves, research and development, and the provision or procurement of further technical services if reasonably called upon to do so."

2. General services "in connection will all aspects of RCM's business and operations, including advice on the preparation of company reports and financial statements, production and marketing, financial matters, development and processing of minerals, operational research, work-study, computers and management information services, labor relations, public relations, purchasing services and all aspects of the administration of RCM's affairs."

3. Specialized services

a. Civil, metallurgical, mechanical, electrical, structural and mining engineering services; in other words, RST will act as engineering consultants to RCM.

b. Recruitment of expatriate staff required by RCM. Contracts relating to the terms and conditions of service of recruits will be determined by RCM.

c. Purchasing services on behalf of RCM outside Zambia on a cost reimbursable basis. These services are exclusive to RST until June 30, 1971, but may be terminated by RCM giving twelve months' notice to expire at any time after June 30, 1972. RCM will fulfill its own purchasing requirements within Zambia.

4. Provision of personnel: "RCM shall employ such personnel as may be necessary or desirable for the efficient operation of its business. RST shall procure the provision of staff either by recruitment for RCM, or by attachment or transfer of RST personnel. The cost of administration of and the emoluments of attached personnel will be borne by RCM. The terms and conditions of employment shall be attractive enough to ensure the recruitment and retention of suitable personnel."

Remuneration

Remuneration to RST under the contract will be as follows:

1. The amount of .75 percent of RCM's gross sales proceeds.

2. Two percent of RCM's consolidated profits after charging "all revenue expenditure and outgoings and after provision for replacements and mineral tax and after the deduction of all the fees payable by RCM to RST under their agreement, but before all other income tax and before deduction of reserves."

3. An engineering service fee of 3 percent of the constructed cost of projects undertaken by RCM "which involve expenditure on capital account or expenditure on such replacement items as involve improvement or modernization but excluding all items, whether capital or replacement, which RCM on the recommendation of the Managing Director may decide to undertake itself."

4. A recruiting fee of 15 percent of total emoluments (before taxes) payable in respect of each expatriate employee's first year.

Managing Director

RST will nominate one of the "B" directors of RCM as Managing Director and "shall afford such assistance as RCM shall, through its Managing Director, request of both an executive and as advisory nature towards effecting the policies and directions of the Board of RCM and towards the general management of RCM's business and specifically directed towards the optimization by RCM of production and profit."

Terms of Contract

The Contract shall be deemed to have commenced on 1st January, 1970 and shall continue in force until terminated as follows:

(a) by RST or RCM on giving to the other two years prior written notice to expire on any date after 31st December, 1979;

(b) by RCM on notice in writing if at any time RST shall cease to own the Prescribed Minimum Interest (as defined below). In the event that this Interest is not held by RST at any time before 1st July, 1972, the notice shall be one month, otherwise it shall be two years, provided that termination shall not take effect if RST restores its Minimum Prescribed Interest within three months of the date of service of the notice or the period of notice, whichever is the shorter;

(c) by RST on two years notice in writing if advice material to the conduct and development of the business of RCM is repeatedly not accepted or implemented by the "A" Directors of RCM; or

(d) by RCM on two years notice in writing if the performance by RST of its duties under the Contract shall fall below the standard hitherto exercised by the RST Group in the management of the businesses of RCM and its predecessors, so as to prejudice the efficient operation of the business of RCM or any significant part thereof, unless such a fall in standards is the result of circumstances beyond the reasonable control of RST or from obstructions by RCM.

PRESCRIBED MINIMUM INTEREST

RST and Zamanglo agreed in terms of the Master Agreement to maintain a 20 percent beneficial interest (direct or indirect) in the issued equity capital of RCM and NCCM respectively until July 1, 1972. Therefore, if RST or Zamanglo ceases to hold this interest at any time before July 1, 1972, the Master Agreements would be breached. In these circumstances, the management, sales, and marketing arrangements could be terminated by RCM or NCCM on one month's notice.

After July 1, 1972, RST and Zamanglo are at liberty to dispose . of their "prescribed minimum interest" in RCM and NCCM respectively in terms of the Master Agreements. However, in this event, RCM or NCCM may give two years' notice of termination of the management and sales contracts provided that termination shall not take effect if RST or Zamanglo restore its prescribed minimum interest within a prescribed period of time.

SALES AND MARKETING CONTRACT

Similar arrangements were made with the RST and Zamanglo groups for services to be provided under sales and marketing contracts with RCM and NCCM respectively. The details below are taken from the RST contract.

With regard to marketing functions, the RST sales and marketing contract states:

> RST shall provide and ensure the continuation of sales and marketing services for RCM of a standard that prior to 1st January 1970 were supplied or procured by the RST Group to Mufulira, Luanshya and Mwinilunga with the intention that the sales and marketing business and operations of RCM shall be maintained in a manner no less efficient and to an extent and standard no less than those given before 1st January 1970, and shall be directed towards the optimization of profit of RCM and any subsidiary companies.

The contract also includes the following provisions:

1. Exclusive agency. "RST will be the exclusive agent of RCM in every country for the purpose of finding purchasers for all ores, metals and minerals and any by-products recovered from the mining or treatment of ores, metals or minerals produced by RCM and any subsidiaries from time to time."

2. Performance. "RST's obligations may be performed by the existing sales facilities of the RST Group, but an appointment of new agents must have the approval of RCM."

3. Sales obligations. "RST shall, as RCM's agents, in accordance with the general policy of the RCM Board, use its best endeavors to secure contracts with customers at the best prices and on such terms and conditions as may be determined by RCM from time to time on the advice of RST."

Remuneration will be based on .75 percent of gross sales proceeds for all sales throughout the world of copper metal and 2.5 percent on cobalt sales. No commission will be payable on sales to the Zimco group of companies for their own consumption for purposes of fabrication.

The terms of the sales and marketing contracts with regard to commencement and termination follow those in each management and consultancy contract.

With regard to staff attachments, the RST sales and marketing contract states: "RST shall provide facilities for the attachment of employees of Mindeco or of RCM to RST's organization providing services to RCM in respect of marketing and selling. RST shall give

each such employee full and proper experience within the organization,"
at RCM's expense.

TAXATION

The Zambian Government made several tax concessions to the
RST and Zamanglo groups in connection with the takeover. The most
important of these were:

1. In order to facilitate the corporate reorganization of the
Zamanglo and RST groups pursuant to the acquisition by government
of its 51 percent interest, the Zambian Government provided for the
exemption of the Schemes of Arrangement involved in such reorganization (including the reduction of capital by RST) from all Zambian taxes
and stamp duties.

2. The Zambian Government has agreed that the overall rate
of tax payable by RCM and NCCM shall not be increased so long as
any part of the Zimco loan stock 1982 or Zimco bonds 1978, as the
case may be, is outstanding (i.e., a maximum tax rate of 73.05 percent
of gross profits).

3. The Zambian Government agreed to enact legislation to
ensure that the companies did not incur any tax that would not have
been incurred (or lose any relief to which they would have been entitled) if the takeover had not taken place.

4. The government agreed that all payments made with respect
to the bonds and loan stock would be exempt from all taxes in Zambia.

5. The government agreed that as long as any bonds and loan
stock were outstanding there could be no tax on dividends paid by
RCM or NCCM to Mindeco or other shareholders who were neither
citizens nor residents of Zambia. In addition, both RCM and NCCM
would not be subject to any discriminatory stamp duty, excise tax,
or import duty.

At the same time that the mines takeover was announced, the
Zambian Government announced certain changes in the tax laws relating to mining generally (these are discussed at length in Chapters
6 and 8). In addition to replacing royalty payments and export taxes
by a mineral tax (income tax remaining), the general provisions relating to capital allowances and taxation of prospecting expenditure
were enacted into law in the Income Tax (Amendment) Act 1970 and

the provisions relating specifically to the takeover were enacted into law in the Income Tax (Special Provisions) Acts (No. 1 and 2) 1970. The Zambian Government agreed that as long as the Zimco bonds and loan stock were outstanding none of the provisions of these acts would be altered.

EXCHANGE CONTROL

The Zambian Government agreed to exempt from exchange control the following:

1. All payments made with respect to the Zimco bonds and loan stock except to Rhodesian residents.

2. All dividends and other payments in RCM and NCCM securities to persons not resident or citizens of Zambia (non-Zambian shareholders can freely convert Zambian currency at the IMF parity rate).

3. All payments made in connection with both the management and sales contracts.

4. All "B" shares transferred to persons other than citizens and residents of Zambia.

The above exemptions are incorporated in the Mines Acquisition (Special Provisions) Act 1970.

ARTICLES OF ASSOCIATION

Dividends

RCM and NCCM will pay dividends to the holders of "A" and "B" shares in an aggregate amount equal to the consolidated net profits of RCM and NCCM respectively (and the respective subsidiaries) after deduction only of appropriations in respect of capital expenditure, expenditure for exploration and prospecting, and reserves for necessary working capital. Appropriations for capital, exploration, or prospecting expenditures require the approval of both "A" and "B" directors voting separately.

Shareholder Protection

1. Preemptive rights: Mindeco (as holder of the "A" shares) and the holders of the "B" shares have preemptive rights entitling them to subscribe to new issues of shares of the same class before such shares are offered to the public.

2. Voting rights: Certain major corporate actions by RCM or NCCM require the approval of both the "A" and "B" shareholders, voting separately. The corporate actions which require such approval are, inter alia: disposal by RCM or NCCM of a substantial part of its assets or its concessions or mining rights; the winding up, amalgamation or reconstruction of RCM or NCCM; any change in the powers of the board of RCM or NCCM or any change in the proportion of "A" and "B" directors or their voting rights; and major changes in the RCM or NCCM Articles of Association (e.g., any change in the provisions requiring separate approval of the "B" directors described below).

3. "B" director veto: The following are the main actions that require the alternative votes of a majority of both the "A" directors and the "B" directors, voting separately, "which alternative vote shall not be unreasonably withheld having regard to the interests of RCM (and NCCM) and to the interests of the shareholders":

a. The winding up of RCM or NCCM or the appointment of a liquidator for the purpose;

b. Any amalgamation or reconstruction of RCM or NCCM to which the companies are a party;

c. Any disposal of all or any substantial part of the assets of RCM or NCCM or the assignment or grant of any of their concessions, mining or other substantial rights to others;

d. Any change in the proportion of "A" directors to "B" directors, in the directors' voting rights, or in the power of the Board;

e. The engaging by RCM or NCCM in any business or activities of a nature substantially different to the mining companies taken over, or the expenditure by RCM or NCCM of any funds not in the ordinary course of its business, or the making of any financial commitments in respect of any new mining operation or facility or the expansion of an existing mining operation or facility in respect of which commitments or expansion RCM or NCCM is unable to raise such monies as may be required on commercially competitive terms or in respect of which the "B" directors are not satisfied of the commercial validity;

f. The issue of additional "A" or "B" shares or the creation or issue of any other class of share captial, or of securities convertible into share capital, or the borrowing of any funds, whether by the issue of bonds or other securities;

g. The sale of any products or the making of any purchases other than for cash, or at a price or on condition other than those in general application and use in the relevant world market, or for any currency that is not freely convertible;

h. Appropriation in respect of capital expenditure or expenditure for exploration or prospecting (discussed above);

i. Any act, dealing, arrangement, or transaction that, in the opinion of a majority of the "B" directors, is not directed toward and/or calculated to attain the optimization of production and profit of RCM or NCCM; and

j. Variation or modification of any provision of the Memorandum and Articles of Association of RCM or NCCM.

SETTLEMENT OF DISPUTES

As part of the takeover, the Zambian Government agreed to adhere to the convention establishing the International Centre for the Settlement of Investment Disputes (ICSID). In addition, the Master Agreements require the Zambian Government and RCM and NCCM to enter into formal arbitration agreements as soon as possible after the convention has been ratified.

The Zambian Government and Zimco agreed that all disputes arising under the following documents be governed by arbitration by ICSID: (1) Heads of Agreement; (2) any general agreement governing the transaction; (3) the trust deed or indenture pursuant to which the bonds and loan stock are issued; (4) the Memorandum and Articles of Association; (5) the management and sales contract; and (6) any assurances given to foreign shareholders or employees embodied in legislation enacted or agreements entered in connection with the takeover.

The Master Agreements contain an interesting provision with respect to the law that will be applied in arbitration. In particular, it is provided that all disputes be governed by "frozen Zambian law," i.e., the law of Zambia (including its rules on the conflict of laws) as in force at the date of execution of the Master Agreements, disregarding all legislation, instruments, orders, directions, and court decisions having the force of law in Zambia (other than those contemplated by the Master Agreements) adopted, made, issued, or given subsequent to the date of execution of the Master Agreements. In addition, the arbitrators may determine any dispute arising under the Master Agreements in their discretion ex aequo et bono. (It should be noted that all disputes other than those arising under the Master Agreements are determined under "frozen Zambian law" only and not by ex aequo et bono.)

OTHER GOVERNMENT UNDERTAKINGS

The Zambian Government also agreed (1) that RCM and NCCM would be permitted to conduct their operations on a commercial basis; (2) that the provisions in the Memorandum and Articles of Association of RCM and NCCM for the protection of all classes of shareholders would not be altered by any change in the law of Zambia; and that no change in the law of Zambia will alter or affect the legislation passed to give effect to the Master Agreement.

ZAMBIAN LEGISLATION

In order to facilitate the takeover, the Zambian Parliament enacted several laws that had the effect of making many of the key terms of the Master Agreements part of the statute law of Zambia. Such legislation included the following:

1. The Mines Acquisition (Special Provisions) Act, 1970. This act contains provisions, inter alia: giving the Minister responsible for Finance the power to grant all guarantees and undertakings necessary to implement the Master Agreements; exempting various documents and transactions from stamp duties and transfer and registration fees; setting forth the exemption from exchange control; and providing for the vesting of assets in the new companies. In addition, in order to give the Zambian Government the power to take immediate action in the event of unforseen circumstances arising in connection with the takeover, the act contained a clause giving the President power to make amendments to existing laws by statutory instrument

if such amendments were necessary to give effect to the Master Agreements and to do anything necessary or expedient to give full and complete effect to the Master Agreements.

2. Tax legislation. As indicated above, the provisions of the Master Agreements relating to taxation were enacted into law by the Income Tax (Special Provisions) Act 1970 and the Income Tax (Amendment) Act 1970.

3. The Mines Acquisition (Special Provisions No. 2) Act 1970. As a part of its group reorganization, Zambian Anglo-American Limited decided that it would change its domicile from Zambia to Bermuda. In order to facilitate this move, the Zambian Parliament enacted an unusual piece of legislation that enabled Zamanglo to cease to be incorporated in Zambia without winding up. Bermuda enacted complementary legislation to enable Zamanglo to continue its business in Bermuda as a going concern. The combination of the Zambian and Bermudan legislation enabled Zamanglo to transfer its domicile as a going concern without winding up.

4. Investments Disputes Convention Act 1970. As part of its agreement to join ICSID, it was necessary for the Zambian Government to provide for the recognition and enforcement of any ICSID award in Zambia. The Investment Dispute Convention Act 1970 provides, inter alia, that any ICSID award will have the same force and effect in Zambia as a judgment of the Zambian High Court.

THE MINES AND MINERALS ACT OF 1969

Although the Mines and Minerals Act of 1969 was not specifically part of the takeover arrangements, provision was made in the Master Agreements for both RST and Zamanglo to have first option on those mining rights that, under the 1969 Mines and Minerals Act reverted to the State on January 1, 1970. This legislation made provisions for the State to have an option (to a maximum of 51 percent, of any mining ventures arising from the issue of any new prospecting and exploration licence after January 1, 1970 (for further discussion, see Chapters 3 and 8).

APPENDIX

B

SOME
LEGAL
ASPECTS
OF THE
ZAMBIAN
TAKEOVER

John Niehuss

Peter Slinn

INTRODUCTION

The taking over by the State of a 51 percent interest in the Zambian copper mines illustrates many of the legal problems that arise in a negotiated government acquisition of a controlling equity interest in a foreign-owned undertaking. Where a state is acquiring a 100 percent financial interest and assuming managerial control in a single foreign company, difficult problems inevitably arise in respect of, for example, the terms of compensation. However, in the Zambian case the resolution of the legal difficulties was a task of bewildering complexity as the State was acquiring a less than 100 percent holding in undertakings that had a highly complex financial structure, on terms providing for the continuing participation by the existing management and shareholders. The purpose of this appendix is to bring out some of the more important points of legal interest arising out of the outline of the takeover terms set out in Appendix A.

Relative Bargaining Positions

The relative bargaining strengths of an acquiring government and the acquired company will naturally differ from situation to situation. Important factors in determining the strength of the Zambian Government's position in the copper takeover were (1) the extent to which the Zambian Government could run the acquired company without reliance on the technical expertise and financial resources of the RST and Zamanglo groups; (2) the importance of the acquired companies to the economy of Zambia as a whole; (3) the estimate of future copper prices and the estimated strength of Zambia's future foreign exchange reserves; (4) the ability of the Zambian negotiators and the expertise available to the Zambian Government in the financial and legal fields; (5) the fact that there had been a prior announcement (the Matero speech) on the method of valuation of assets (i.e., book value); and (6) the fact that the operating (mining) companies of the two groups were being acquired at the same time.

Key factors in determining the strength of the RST and Zamanglo positions were (1) the degree to which they had recovered their investments in the Zambian copper industry; (2) expected future cash flows from their investments in Zambia; (3) investment opportunities in the Zambian copper industry as opposed to opportunities in other parts of the world; (4) the percentage of the groups' assets in Zambia; (5) the fact that the economy of Zambia is dependent upon copper;

(6) the groups' assessment of the future investment climate in Zambia; and (7) the extent to which the groups were tied to Zambia and the strength of their desire to break such ties and be free to invest elsewhere.

Drafting of Documents

The party preparing the first drafts of the main takeover documents may gain an initial advantage insofar as it can structure the mode of acquisition in the way it wants; the other party must achieve its own objectives by suggesting changes in the tabled drafts. In the Zambian takeover, President Kenneth Kaunda asked the RST and Zamanglo groups to invite the Government to participate in their organizations, thus putting the onus on the companies to present proposals. In any event, the companies as "vendors" would have prepared drafts for Government approval in accordance with the usual practice in negotiations of this kind. In order to counter the advantage gained by the companies in preparing the first drafts and thus being able to determine the framework of the negotiations, it was essential for the Government to have expert legal advice to ensure that its own objectives were achieved.

LEGAL PROTECTION FOR THE ZAMBIAN GOVERNMENT

Since the initiative as to future action after the takeover in regulating the economy and the mining industry in particular rests with the Government, it should have had less need than the RST and Zamanglo groups to protect itself against future events. Except insofar as the government regards itself as restricted by the terms of the takeover, it is in a position to change tax laws, impose exchange control restrictions, determine trade employment policy, and generally regulate the copper industry.

Particular problems arise where, as in the present case, the acquiring government is not taking over 100 percent ownership of the undertaking concerned. An acquiring government should aim to concede only what is necessary to give the surviving private element in the company the safety, security, and incentive to remain for as long as that element's expatriate expertise and investment resources are needed. On the other hand, a government should try to preserve for itself maximum flexibility as to future action on taxation, exchange control, and trade policy, consistent with giving existing management and shareholders a "fair deal" and with creating conditions for the kind of partnership necessary for the successful running of the government-controlled company.

Expert Advice

When it comes to actual negotiations, an acquiring government may find itself at a serious disadvantage against the talent and experience that the acquired company generally is able to produce (e.g., experience in similar takeovers elsewhere and highly specialized legal counsel, merchant bankers, and accountants). In these circumstances, a government may lose much of its initial inherent advantage during the process of negotiation and actual drafting of the key takeover documents. In the Zambian takeover, the Government was fortunate to have an able chief negotiator and staff in Indeco which had had experience in 51 percent acquisitions (albeit on a relatively minor scale), a nucleus of experienced lawyers in the Attorney-General's Chambers, and the good sense to retain a team of experienced private lawyers to advise in the negotiation of the takeover. The complexity of the eventual settlement shows how essential it was for the Government to have had such expertise available. The lesson for other developing countries is clear: no considerations of expense or pride should inhibit a developing country (which may well be less fortunate than Zambia in the availability of local expertise) from obtaining the advice of independent financial and legal experts on deals of this kind.

Valuation

In any takeover, one of the most important factors is the price to be paid by the government for its equity interest; this price generally depends upon valuation of the acquired company's assets. The acquiring government has an advantage in that it can dictate the method of valuation of the undertaking to be acquired and considerably reduce the scope for argument on the valuation itself. If the precise method of valuing assets is not established prior to negotiations, this initial question affords an opportunity for prolonged disagreement and ultimate deadlock, which may lead government to coercive action and ruin the chance for an amicable settlement.

As long as government establishes a method of valuation that is recognized as fair or acceptable under internationally accepted accounting principles, the acquired company will have little ground for legitimate complaint. In the Zambian takeover, President Kaunda announced in advance that the companies would be paid "a fair value represented by book value." By thus prescribing the method of valuation, President Kaunda made the task of his negotiating team easier and precluded serious discussion on alternative methods of valuation such as capitalization of future profits, market value of the business, or physical appraisal of assets.

Management Contract

The question of management is bound to be especially sensitive in any government acquisition, particularly in those cases where the rationale of state participation is the achievement of control over the country's economy. When a management contract is granted to the acquired company, a substantial amount of guidance and control of management is left outside Government's hands. Therefore, the government must be sure that it does not give the managing company so much control over the acquired company or make the management contract so long or so lucrative as to become a political issue. Furthermore, government must be careful not to grant a management contract that has the effect of retarding the training of local personnel who will eventually run the company.

In the Zambian takeover, the Government partially protected its interests in the field of management by providing for the secondment of local personnel to the management contractors, by requiring a minimum shareholding in RCM and NCCM by the RST and Zamanglo groups, by basing part of the management fee on profits to provide a financial incentive for good management, and by providing for termination in the event of the standard of management falling below that previously achieved by the RST and Anglo-American groups.

Currency Devaluation Clause

The Zimco bonds and loan stock issued as payment for Zambia's 51 percent equity interest are payable in dollars, but there is no clause providing for adjustment in the event of devaluation of the Kwacha or the dollar. Thus, the Zambian Government might benefit if the dollar were devalued and be hurt if the Kwacha were devalued. However, it should be noted that the fact that there is no devaluation adjustment provision with respect to the Zimco bonds and loan stock is not so significant, for Zambia earns substantial amounts of hard currency from copper sales. Nevertheless, it may be prudent for an acquiring government to attempt to negotiate into the main takeover document a clause protecting the government against assuming an increased burden in the event of devaluation. Of course, negotiations will be difficult on this point for one of the main worries of any acquired company is that its compensation will be eroded by devaluation.

Control of Board of Directors

The Zambian Government as owner of 51 percent of the equity of RCM and NCCM has a majority on the boards of both companies. Thus, in the absence of other factors (e.g., the minority "B" director veto discussed below), the Zambian Government would be in a position to dominate the affairs of RCM and NCCM.

Reinvestment Guarantee on Externalization

The Zambian Government allowed RST and Zamanglo to externalize substantial sums of cash accumulated in Zambia on condition that the companies would hold a certain percentage of the amount externalized available for reinvestment. This reinvestment guarantee was not a great burden on RST or Zamanglo, for both had planned development projects that would demand all the funds that they were committed to reinvest. However, in other countries a reinvestment guarantee could be significant. While allowing the acquired company freedom of use of the externalized funds, such a guarantee would assure an acquiring government of a certain minimum amount of reinvestment.

Pre-emptive Rights

The type of minority shareholder in the acquired company is especially important to an acquiring government for it does not want a minority holder whose political or economic views would make it a difficult partner. Unless the takeover itself involved the buying out of certain shareholders the easiest way to ensure that the acquiring government has control over the major minority shareholders is to include pre-emptive right provisions in one of the takeover documents, enabling the government to acquire the shares that any minority shareholder wishes to sell. The master agreements in the Zambian takeover included a clause enabling the Zambian Government to acquire the shares of its major minority partners whenever they wished to sell. Thus, the Zambian Government has substantial control over the type of major minority shareholder in RCM and, especially, NCCM at least if the Government is prepared to acquire the shares itself to forestall "unsuitable" purchasers.

General Regulation of Acquired Companies

Any major takeover gives the acquiring government an excellent opportunity to restructure the regulations of the industry or company acquired and to negotiate changes in tax laws, royalties, and other aspects of government regulation. In the Zambian case, the acquisition of 51 percent of the mining companies was an integral part of a major change in mining policy: i.e., the introduction of a 51 percent mineral tax and the new system of mining, prospecting, and exploration rights (see Chapters 6 and 8). Thus, the Zambian Government gave itself substantial protection outside the main takeover arrangements by introducing a new regulatory pattern of the copper industry. The Zambian Government could thereby make concessions to the mining industry without the benefits going wholly to foreign shareholders.

Limitation of Concessions

As part of any takeover, an acquiring government may make concessions with respect to taxation, exchange control, and management contract terms. If it does so, it may be able to preserve for itself freedom of action in the future by limiting the duration of the concessions. In the Zambian takeover, most of the major concessions with respect to taxation, exchange control, and duration of management arrangements were limited to the life of the Zimco bonds and loan stock. Thus, as soon as the bonds and loan stock are repaid the Zambian Government will be free of most of the restrictions on its action imposed by the Master Agreement. As will be discussed below, the Zambian Government gave the "B" directors (those elected by the minority shareholders) a type of veto over certain major company policy decisions. In order to limit this power, the Master Agreement and the Articles of Association of RCM and NCCM provide that "B" director approval shall not be withheld unreasonably, having regard to the interests of the company and to the interests of the "B" shareholders as shareholders of the company. Thus, the RST and Zamanglo groups are not free to veto reasonable action by RCM or NCCM or to veto such action for reasons unrelated to their interests as shareholders in RCM and NCCM.

PROTECTION OF THE RST AND
ZAMANGLO INTERESTS

Because of the continuing advantage that the Zambian Government has in controlling the boards of directors of RCM and NCCM and in being able to effect changes in exchange control, taxation, trade policy, and other aspects of regulation of the copper industry, the question of securing legal protection for their interests was much more important to RST and Zamanglo than to the Zambian Government. RST and Zamanglo fought hard to secure their policy objectives with regard to maximum protection for their future minority interests and compensation. Therefore, the Zambian takeover affords numerous examples of the legal safeguards that can be obtained by acquired companies to protect their basic interests in the face of the natural advantage of an acquiring government. Several of the more important of these safeguards are outlined below.

Corporate Reorganization

The Zambian takeover forced RST and Zamanglo into the major reorganizations outlined in Appendix C in order to be in a position to offer the Zambian Government a 51 percent interest in their respective operating companies. The Master Agreements were not concerned with setting forth the details of the restructuring of the RST or Zamanglo groups; the corporate reorganization was left to RST and Anglo-American, whose boards had to procure the requisite consents to enable them to carry it out. In addition, the Zambian Government agreed to aid the companies in such reorganization (1) by exempting the reorganization from tax and by granting special concessions with respect to the carry-over of tax losses and the calculation of capital redemption allowances; (2) by consenting to be a party to the reorganization if necessary; (3) by undertaking to protect creditors whose obligations were assumed by RCM and NCCM; (4) by enacting special legislation to facilitate the reorganization by enabling Zamanglo to move its domicile from Zambia to Bermuda without winding up and by enabling assets to be vested in RCM and NCCM pursuant to the Scheme of Arrangement; and (5) by cooperating in obtaining stock exchange listings for securities issued in connection with the reorganization. In short, although these were forced reorganizations, the RST and Zamanglo groups were given freedom to reorganize in the way most advantageous to their interests because of the cooperation of the Zambian Government in the form of concessions with respect to exchange control, taxation, and special enabling legislation.

Payment Terms

RST and Anglo-American insisted on payment in U.S. dollar bonds and loan stock both guaranteed by the Zambian Government. Because the bonds and loan stock were issued pursuant to an indenture or trust deed common in American or British practice, the RST and Anglo-American groups ensured that the standard protective clauses incorporated in such documents were automatically incorporated into the Zambian takeover. By insisting on payment in U.S. dollars, RST and Zamanglo avoided the obvious problems that would have been created if they had been paid in Kwacha, a less acceptable international currency. By obtaining the Zambian Government guarantee of the bonds and loan stock, the companies ensured that they would have a legal right to demand payment directly from the Government in the event that the flow of dividends from RCM and NCCM to Zimco was so small that Zimco could not service its bonds and loan stock. As pointed out in Chapter 7, payment for the 51 percent interest acquired by the Zambian Government is intended to be made out of the dividends paid by RCM and NCCM to Mindeco and ultimately to Zimco. RST and Zamanglo negotiated an accelerated payment of the bonds and loan stock based on the amount of dividends paid by RCM and NCCM and thus ensured that they would share in the benefits of high copper prices, although they would not suffer if copper prices were low since payments due under the bonds and loan stock were guaranteed unconditionally by the Zambian Government.

Events of Default of the Zimco Bonds and Loan Stock

In addition to conventional events of default (e.g., nonpayment of principal or interest or transfer of assets without bondholder or stockholder consent), the Zimco bonds and loan stock contain a number of unusual events of default that would arise through breaches by the Zambian Government or RCM or NCCM of obligations relating to other aspects of the takeover: e.g., the unlawful cancellation by RCM or NCCM of the management agreements, a failure by RCM or NCCM to abide by certain provisions of their respective Memorandums and Articles of Association designed for the protection of the "B" shareholders, a failure by the Government to honor certain undertakings regarding taxation and exchange control, or an unlawful cancellation by the Zambian Government of mining leases or prospecting or exploration rights held by RCM or NCCM. These terms act as a powerful safeguard for RST and Zamanglo and a powerful restraint on the future actions of Government, RCM, and NCCM. As long as any bonds or loan stock are outstanding, there is the risk of having all of the Zimco bonds ($117,810,000 in the case of RST and $178,698, 992 in the case of Anglo-American) declared immediately due and payable if Government, RCM, NCCM, or Zimco fail to comply with certain of their obligations as enshrined in the takeover agreements.

Control Over the Financial Policy of RCM and NCCM

Both RST and Zamanglo secured added protection for themselves as bondholders and stockholders respectively and as minority share- holders in RCM and NCCM by insisting that the Managing Directors of RCM and NCCM be appointed on nomination by the "B" shareholders of each company and that the "B" directors have, in effect, a veto over certain key decisions with respect to the financial and capital programs of RCM and NCCM.

The most important matters over which the "B" directors have power of veto are: (1) the expenditure of funds not in the ordinary course of business; (2) the expenditure of funds on any new mining operation or on an exisitng mining operation where RCM or NCCM are unable to raise money for the project on commercially competitive terms or where the "B" directors are not satisfied that the project is commercially viable; (3) any other appropriations in respect of capital expenditure or expenditure for exploration or prospecting other than those referred to in 2 above; (4) any transaction that a majority of the "B" directors believe is not calculated to optimize production or profit; (5) the making of any noncash sales (e.g., barter) or sales at prices other than those prevailing in the world market or sales outside Zambia for nonconvertible currency; and (6) the issuing of additional equity capital or the borrowing of any funds.

These clauses give RST and Zamanglo substantial protection by giving them a means of preventing the Zambian Government from using its 51 percent control for social or political ends by engaging in a project that would not be economically justified in terms of standard commercial practice. Thus, the Zambian representatives can be prevented from running RCM and NCCM without regard to the interests of the minority shareholders.

Although the "B" directors' veto might well work to the general benefit of the companies in a case where it was used to prevent the implementation of some commercially damaging proposal by the "A" directors, the Zambian Government has professed the need to secure effective "control" of the mines as a major reason for the takeover. Therefore, it may be that the full achievement by the Government of its stated objectives could prove incompatible with the "B" directors' veto.

Although President Kaunda stated in his August 11, 1969, Matero speech that the Zambian Government would pay for its 51 percent equity out of future dividends from RCM and NCCM, the bondholders and stockholders will get their money if Zimco never receives a dividend from RCM or NCCM, since under the actual terms of the takeover the Government has guaranteed unconditionally payments due in respect of the bonds and loan stock. However, to ensure that the bondholders and stockholders would derive full benefit from the acceleration of repayment provisions (see above) and that the private shareholders of RCM and NCCM would receive the highest possible future dividend, RST and Zamanglo secured the inclusion of provisions in the RCM and NCCM Articles of Association requiring both companies to pay out as dividends the whole of the consolidated net profits in respect of each financial year, after deduction only of certain fixed charges and appropriations in respect of capital, exploration, and prospecting expenditure and reserves for necessary working capital as approved by the directors. This provides substantial protection for the private shareholders as the "B" directors have a veto over appropriations for capital expenditure and expenditure for exploration and prospecting.

RST also obtained protection for itself as a bondholder and as a minority shareholder by inserting in the RCM Articles of Association a standard type restriction on the amount of debt RCM can incur. Thus, RCM and its subsidiaries are limited to borrowing K350 million or twice the amount paid up on the RCM issued share capital (whichever is greater) unless additional borrowing is approved by a special resolution of the company as well as by "A" and "B" directors voting separately. A similar restriction is contained in the NCCM Articles of Association.

Management of RCM and NCCM

In addition to the safeguards for the minority interests of RST and Anglo-American embodied in the Articles of Association of RCM and NCCM, exclusive management contracts were secured with RCM and NCCM by RST and Zamanglo respectively. If RST and Zamanglo

honor their obligations under these contracts, the latter may be kept
in force until the bonds or loan stock, as the case may be, are repaid.
As was noted above, RST and Zamanglo have maximum legal protection
against unlawful cancellation of the contracts, as such action by either
RCM or NCCM would constitute an event of default in respect of the
bonds or loan stock.

Therefore, as management contractors RST and Anglo-American
have secured additional means of exercising effective influence over
the actual operations of RCM and NCCM. Thus, for example, so long
as RST is committed under the terms of the takeover to retain a
major interest, either as a bondholder or a shareholder, in the optimization of profit by RCM, RST can ensure that the RCM looks to RST
alone for the fulfillment of certain essential management functions.

Tax Concessions

RST and Zamanglo were able to negotiate several tax concessions
from the Zambian Government, for example, the undertaking that, as
long as the Zimco bonds and loan stock were outstanding, RCM and
NCCM would not be subject to taxes in excess of those provided for
by the new Mineral Tax Act and the Income Tax Act, as amended. In
making this concession, the Zambian Government severely reduced
its freedom to increase taxes on RCM and NCCM, for RST and Zamanglo
have the assurance that the present 73 percent combined rate of tax
could not be increased without breaking the master agreements.
(However, it should be noted that the present rate of 73 percent is high
when compared with other copper producing countries and that it is
not likely that the Zambian Government would want to increase the
rate in the near future. Thus the concession is not as important as
it may seem.)

The Zambian Government also agreed that, as long as any bonds
or loan stock were outstanding, all payments of interest, capital
redemption, and dividends would be exempt from taxation by the
Zambian Government; that RST and Anglo-American group reorganizations would be tax free; and that there would be no additional tax
burden (or loss of any tax benefit) for RST or Zamanglo as a result
of such reorganization. It is important to note that the tax concessions
made in the Master Agreements by the Zambian Government were
enacted into law by the Zambian Parliament and that in the Master
Agreements the Zambian Government undertook not to alter any such
laws as long as the Zimco bonds and loan stock are outstanding.

Exchange Control Concessions

The Zambian Government granted RST and Zamanglo various exemptions from exchange control. In addition, the government enacted most of these concessions into the enabling legislation passed in connection with the takeover. Thus, RST and Zamanglo succeeded in reducing the risk that their reorganizations or the subsequent debt service and dividend payments would be frustrated by arbitrary administrative action with respect to exchange control.

Externalization of Liquid Funds

RST and Zamanglo were allowed to externalize substantial sums (at least K50 million) over a two-year period. This gave the two groups the obvious advantage of freeing these funds from Zambian exchange control and using them in any way the companies wished. This was of particular advantage to the RST group for the RST funds were located outside the United States, which meant that they could be invested by Amax outside the United States free of U.S. balance of payments restrictions.

Forum for Settling Disputes and Choice of Law

Under the Master Agreements, the Zambian Government agreed to ratify the Convention on the Settlement of Investment Disputes Between States and Nationals of Other States. The Government also agreed that all disputes arising under the main takeover documents would be governed by arbitration according to the procedure established by the International Centre for the Settlement of Investment Disputes, an organization affiliated with the World Bank. In addition, it was agreed that all disputes would be determined by the law of Zambia as in force on December 24, 1969, except that disputes arising under the Master Agreements could be determined ex aequo et bono if the arbitrators so wished. Thus, RST and Zamanglo were assured that they would have an impartial forum for settling disputes and that Zambian legislation passed after December 24, 1969, would not prejudice their position in such disputes.

Special Legislation

The advantages to RST and Zamanglo of the special legislation passed to facilitate the takeover are obvious, for it not only made the mechanics of the takeover easier but also gave RST and Zamanglo double protection in that the various concessions, were given statutory effect and therefore can only be altered by further legislation. Under the Master Agreements, the Zambian Government agreed not to alter any of the laws concerned so long as the bonds and loan stock are outstanding. Thus, if such laws are altered, the government would be in breach of the Master Agreements.

APPENDIX

C

CORPORATE
STRUCTURE
OF THE
ZAMBIAN
MINING INDUSTRY

This appendix is confined to a description of the ownership of the Zambian mining industry before the takeover of the operating mining companies and a comparison of this structure with the post-takeover situation. Appendix Chart 1 shows the "family tree" existing as at December 31, 1969, while Appendix Chart 2 describes the situation on December 31, 1970. The discussion below should be read in conjunction with these charts.

PRE-TAKEOVER "FAMILY TREE" AT DECEMBER 31, 1969

The complexities of the interrelationships between Anglo-American Corporation of South Africa, Charter Consolidated, Rand Selection Corporation, and De Beers Consolidated Mines are not given in Appendix Chart 1. The direct holdings indicated ignore the indirect cross shareholdings through such companies as Anglo-American Investment Trust, Diamond Corporation, Consolidated Diamond Mines of South West Africa, De Beers Holdings, Rhochar Holdings, and African and European Investment. Suffice it to say that De Beers Consolidated Mines has an indirect holding of 41.2 percent, mainly through the Diamond Corporation, in Rand Selection Corporation, which in turn is administered within the Anglo-American Corporation group. Similarly, Anglo-American Corporation of South Africa and Rand Selection Corporation hold a 28.5 percent indirect interest in Charter Consolidated (which absorbed the British South Africa Company) through Rhochar Holdings. Both De Beers Consolidated Mines and Charter Consolidated are administered outside the Anglo-American group, but Anglo-American of South Africa serves as consulting engineers for De Beers.

Anglo-American Corporation of South Africa is the largest South African mining finance house and is head of a group that comprises a large number of companies that are administered by Anglo-American but in most cases are not subsidiaries in the statutory sense. In 1969, Zambia copper interests represented 7 percent of the total Anglo-American Corporation of South Africa investments and 15 percent of total income.

AMENDED

The Anglo-American group interest in the RST group of mines is through Charter Consolidated's holding in Selection Trust and indirectly through the interests of Zamanglo and Rhokana Corporation

259

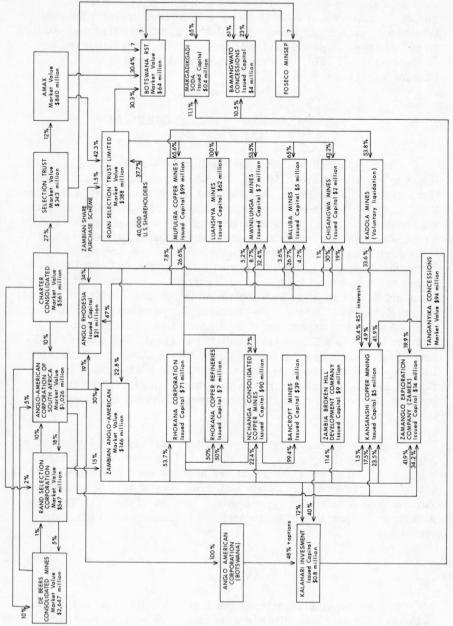

APPENDIX CHART 1

Zambian Mining Industry: The Corporate Structure at December 31, 1969

Source: Jane's World Mining Who Owns Whom (London: Sampson Low, Marston, 1970); various company annual reports.

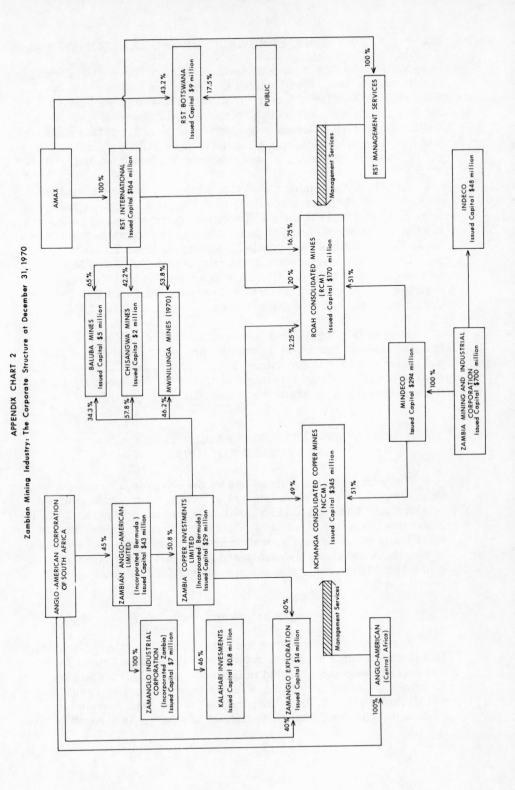

APPENDIX CHART 2

Zambian Mining Industry: The Corporate Structure at December 31, 1970

261

in several of the RST mining companies. (The origin of both Zamanglo and Rhokana's interest in Mufulira Copper Mines is described in Chapter 3.) Likewise, Charter Consolidated's interest in nearly all the RST mining and prospecting companies was inherited from the British South Africa Company holdings. One anomaly in this situation was that the Anglo-American group as a whole had a substantial interest in Chisangwa Mines, a prospecting company administered by RST.

Details of the mining companies taken over by the Government on January 1, 1970, are given in Appendix A. In addition, negotiations were concluded in 1970 for a 51 percent Government participation in Kansanshi Copper Mining Company, which is to recommence mining in 1973. Since RST has been granted a mining licence for Baluba, negotiations on Government's 51 percent interest in Baluba Mines will be concluded in 1971. Outside copper, details of Government's purchase of a 51 percent interest in Zambia Broken Hill Development Company, a lead and zinc mine, were announced in March 1971.

Most of the Anglo-American prospecting and exploration work is undertaken by Zamex, while the RST prospecting and exploration companies are Mwinilunga Mines, Baluba Mines, and Chisangwa Mines. (Kadola Mines went into voluntary liquidation in December 1969, after it had surrendered its exclusive prospecting concession.)

POST-TAKEOVER "FAMILY TREE" AT
DECEMBER 31, 1970

The arrangements entered into by the Zambian Government for its purchase of a 51 percent interest in the Zambian mining companies provided both Zamanglo and RST with an opportunity to reorganize their respective corporate structures. Appendix Chart 2 is concerned specifically with this reorganization and excludes those shareholdings in both the Anglo-American group and Amax that have remained unchanged. These basic changes are summarized below.

Anglo-American Group

Zambian Anglo-American has changed its domicile to Bermuda. Two new companies have been established: (1) Zambia Copper Investments (ZCI), also incorporated in Bermuda, to hold all the Anglo-American interests in NCCM and the various prospecting companies; and (2) Zamanglo Industrial Corporation (Zamic), incorporated in Zambia, to hold the Zamanglo industrial interests. As a result of this reorganization, Charter Consolidated interests in the RST companies have been purchased by Zamanglo. This purchase and the rational-ization of shareholding in Zamex and Kansanshi Copper Mining have ensured that ZCI is a subsidiary of Zamanglo (50.8 percent).

RST Group

The Government takeover of RST's mining interests in Zambia provoked Amax (which owned 42.3 percent of the RST shares at Decem-ber 31, 1969) to make an offer to the remaining RST shareholders for their shares. This they proposed to accomplish by an exchange of cash, RCM shares, Zimco bonds, shares of Botswana RST Limited, and an offer of Amax debentures. On completion of the deal described below, RST will become a wholly owned subsidiary of Amax. (See footnote on page 171.)

Companies Involved in the Reorganization

Notes on the various companies involved in the reorganization following the takeover are given below.

Zamanglo (Zambian Anglo-American Limited)

Zamanglo was reincorporated in Bermuda on June 26, 1970. Following the Bancroft and Mufulira schemes of arrangement (see Appendix A), Zamanglo's total holdings of securities in ZCI amounted to: 57,295,000 shares of BD$0.24 (U.S.$0.24) each in ZCI (48.54 percent of ZCI share capital); 80,850,198 units of 6 percent ZCI loan stock 1982 (45.25 percent of ZCI holding); and 18,211,858 units of 6 percent ZCI loan stock 1978 (65.98 percent of ZCI holding). The ZCI loan stock was issued against the Zimco bonds and loan stock vested in ZCI. With the changes effected in the shareholding of Zamex and Kansanshi during 1970, the Zamanglo interest in ZCI was increased to 50.8 percent.

Zamic (Zamanglo Industrial Corporation Limited)

Zamic was established in June 1970 to hold Zamanglo's industrial and farming interests in Zambia. Total investments and loans amounted to $5.22 million at June 30, 1970. The most important of these are shown in Appendix Table 5.

APPENDIX TABLE 5

Investments and Loans of Zamic, June 30, 1970

	Holding (percentage)	Book Value (million of dollars)
Chilanga Cement Limited (cement production)	8.4	0.97
Contractual Holdings Limited (holding company for several construction and engineering companies)	29.5	0.39
Duncan, Gilbey, Matheson (Zambia) Limited (potable spirit blending)	16.3	0.07
Dunlop Zambia Limited (tire and tube manufacture)	14.7	0.42
Merchant Bank (Zambia) Limited (accepting house)	20	0.14
Metal Fabricators of Zambia Limited (copper wire and cable fabricators)	9.8	0.17
Mushili Limited (farming company)	100	0.10
Zambia Breweries Limited	24.5	1.23
The Ridgeway Hotel Limited	28.8	0.26
Unitor (Zambia) Limited (welding electrode manufacturing)	18.3	0.04
Zambia Clay Industries Limited	28.6	0.27
Miscellaneous loans	- -	1.25

ZCI (Zambia Copper Investments Limited)

Ursa Enterprises Limited was incorporated in Bermuda on November 6, 1969, and changed its name to Zambia Copper Investments Limited (ZCI) on March 20, 1970. ZCI holds 60,412,100 "B" ordinary shares of K2 each in NCCM (49 percent interest) and 3,713,595 "B" ordinary shares of K4 each in RCM (12.25 percent interest). It holds all the Zimco 6 percent loan stock 1982 (US$178,698,992) and 23.4 percent of Zimco 6 percent bonds 1978 (US$27,603,200), against which the ZCI loan stocks 1982 and 1978 have been issued on a back-to-back basis. In addition, ZCI holds sundry investments that were excluded from the takeover with a total book value of $46.01 million, the most important of these are:

Zambian local registered stocks	4.37 million
Baluba Mines Limited (34.27 percent interest)	$ 1.71 million
Kalahari Investments Limited (48 percent interest)	$ 0.37 million
Zambian Government bonds	$19.61 million
Rhodesian Government bonds	$14.98 million
Malawi Government bonds	$ 0.72 million
Baluba Mines Limited (interest-free loan)	$ 0.60 million

In addition, ZCI holds liquid funds amounting to $22.39 million, most of which will be externalized.

Following the change in shareholding arising from the issue of ZCI shares for NCCM's purchase of a 51 percent interest in Kansanshi Copper Mining Company Limited and the vesting in Zamanglo of ZCI securities held by companies of the Anglo-American group in Zamex, the issued share capital of ZCI was increased to $28.8 million at December 31, 1970, making ZCI a subsidiary of Zamanglo.

RST International

Following the acquisition by Zimco of a 51 percent interest in the mining, smelting, and refining operations of RST subsidiaries in Zambia and the combining of these interests into the single

State-owned company RCM, the RST interest in RCM was 36.75 percent. Immediately following the acquisition, it was proposed that all issued shares of RST other than the 42.3 percent Amax holding be cancelled in exchange for a package. The complexities of this deal were contained in an explanatory letter to RST shareholders dated June 30, 1970. The net effect of the arrangement will be to make RST a wholly owned subsidiary of Amax. The non-Amax shareholders were offered the following in exchange for their 57.7 percent of holdings:

Cash, $6.34million

Zimco bonds 1978, $50.78million (56.3 percent of the bonds held by RST)

RCM shares, 16.75 percent

RST Botswana shares, 17.5 percent; and

Amax Debentures with Amax warrants to purchase common stock, $76.17million.

At December 31, 1970, the acquisition by Amax of the non-Amax shareholdings in RST had not been executed. Appendix Chart 2 describes the situation arising from the proposed acquisition. If the acquisition is achieved Amax will own:

1. 100 percent of RST with net asset value at January 1, 1970, of $69.5million (of which 9.1 percent will be distributed to non-Amax shareholders as cash),

2. 20 percent of RCM,

3. 43.7 percent of Zimco Bonds 1978, $90.21million,

4. 43.2 percent of RST Botswana,

5. The management and consultancy contract with RCM,

6. The Ametalco group and the sales and marketing contract,

7. The Baluba orebody and certain prospecting/exploration interests retained by RST (Chisangwa Mines and Mwinilunga Mines, 1970),

8. Miscellaneous investments outside RCM held by RST,

including Real Estates Limited (100 percent), Vainoma Estates Limited (84 percent), RST Management Services Limited (100 percent), RST Mine Services Limited (100 percent), unquoted investments with book value of $1.24million of which 50 percent were in Rhodesian companies, $12.98million loans (mainly to Zambian Government), and $6.48million frozen assets held in Rhodesia.

Zambia Mining and Industrial Corporation (Zimco)

Zimco is the Government holding company of Mindeco and Indeco. Indeco holds the State's numerous and varied industrial and trading interests, while Mindeco is concerned specifically with mining interests and holds 51 percent in NCCM and RCM.

At December 31, 1970, NCCM operated the copper mines at Rhokana, Nchanga, Bancroft, Nampundwe, and Kansanshi in addition to the Rhokana refinery. RCM operated the mines at Mufulira, Chambishi, Luanshya, Chibuluma, and Kalengwa and the Ndola Refinery. In addition to these interests, Mindeco held a 51 percent interest in four servicing companies that the two mining groups formerly controlled: Copperbelt Power Corporation, Ndola Lime, Mines Air Services, and the Copper Industry Service Bureau. One medium-scale copper mining company, Astra Leasings Limited (Mkushi Mine) also was owned 51 percent by Mindeco. Outside copper, Mindeco had a 100 percent interest in Kafubu Emeralds (International) Limited.

APPENDIX

D

**STATE
PARTICIPATION
IN NEW MINES:
ANNEXURE ATTACHED
TO
PROSPECTING LICENCES**

The following is an extract from the annexure attached to prospecting licences, defining the terms under which the State has an option to participate in subsequent mining ventures:

The Application referred to in the Licence of which this Annexure forms part is granted subject to the following terms and conditions:

(1) The Republic . . . shall have the option to acquire an interest (not exceeding 51 percent thereof) in any mining venture to be carried on upon the whole or any part of the prospecting area described in the said Licence.

(2) . . . The Holder shall notify the Minister and the option-holder referred to in paragraph (1) above of his intention to apply for a Mining Licence. Upon such notification The Republic shall, within the period prescribed in Section 46 (2) (c) of The Act, consider whether to exercise its option. An application for a Mining Licence shall not be made until such time that The Republic has exercised its option, has decided not to do so, or fails to make a decision within the prescribed period. In the event of The Republic deciding to exercise such option a Mining Licence shall not be granted to a person other than a Company incorporated under the Companies Ordinance (hereinafter called "The Company") with an issued capital comprising ordinary voting shares unless otherwise approved by The Republic.

(3) . . . the said option shall be exercisable by a notice, which shall state the percentage (not exceeding 51 percent) of the ordinary shares in The Company to be acquired, signed on behalf of The Republic and sent by registered post to the registered office of The Company PROVIDED ALWAYS that if the said option is not exercised . . . such option shall not be exercisable thereafter.

(4) The terms upon which the option referred to in paragraph (1) hereof may be exercised are as follows, namely:

(A) Unless otherwise agreed by The Republic and

The Holder the consideration for the interest
for which the option is exercised shall be cash
paid to The Holder (if shares are transferred
by The Holder) or to the Company (if shares
are issued by the Company). In the first case
the cash paid shall be a sum equal to such proportion of all expenditure (as defined in paragraph (4) (B) below) incurred by The Holder and
his predecessors in title from the date of issue
of the Prospecting Licence under The Act to the
date of exercise of the said option as may be
equal to such interest (not exceeding 51 percent
thereof) as The Republic may decide to acquire
in the Company. In the second case the cash
paid shall be ascertained by reference to the
following formula:

X equals Y times Z divided by (100 minus Z)
where X is the amount to be subscribed, and

Y is the total of the said expenditure, and

Z is the percentage interest nominated by
The Republic.

(B) (i) The expenditure hereinbefore referred to
shall mean all expenditure reasonably incurred for prospecting, exploration, development and relevant evaluation, metallurgical test-work, feasibility studies in or
in relation to The Prospecting Area as well
as a reasonable proportion of overhead and
general administrative expenses in areas
where The Holder holds or has held, or his
predecessors in title have held, mining
rights for other areas in Zambia.

(ii) The expenditure hereinbefore referred to
shall be reflected in annual accounts certi-
fied by a firm of independent accountants,
acceptable to The Republic and the accounting year relating thereto shall be agreed by
The Holder with The Republic whereupon
the said accounts shall be produced to The
Republic within three months after the end
of such agreed year.

(iii) The Republic or its duly authorized agent shall establish upon such production a record for the relevant year of such part or parts of the expenditure hereinbefore referred to and included in the accounts hereinbefore mentioned in sub-paragraph (4) (B) (ii) as The Republic may recognize as having been properly incurred for the purposes of calculation in due course of the consideration to be payable in the event of the said option being exercised.

(iv) The Holder shall be entitled to obtain from The Republic or its agent the particulars of such approval within three months after production of the said accounts in manner hereinbefore mentioned.

(C) Upon the exercise of the said option and payment of the consideration calculated as hereinbefore mentioned (unless otherwise agreed between The Holder and The Republic) The Republic may either require The Holder to make available to The Republic free of all encumbrances such number of the issued ordinary voting shares in the capital of The Company representing the percentage of voting rights in the whole of the issued share capital of The Company equal to the percentage of the interest in the mining venture for which option is exercised, or The Company to issue and allot to The Republic such number of ordinary voting shares in the capital of The Company as shall afford to The Republic the stated percentage of the resultant issued ordinary voting shares in the capital of The Company, or partly in one way and partly in the other.

(5) (i) Management, marketing and technical services necessary for the efficient operation of the mining venture shall be provided by The Company at the time of the exercise of the option in such manner as shall be acceptable to all the shareholders.

      (ii) In the event of The Company being unable
to provide any or all of the management,
marketing and technical services, required
itself, The Holder, at the time of the exercise of the said option, shall be afforded
the opportunity of providing such services
to The Company on the basis of a separate
contract provided The Holder can do this
to the satisfaction of all shareholders on
competitive terms.

(6) In the event of a dispute arising in connection with
the interpretation or the implementation of the
provisions of this Annexure the matter in dispute
will be referred to arbitration and such arbitration
will be conducted under the provisions of the Arbitration Ordinance of Zambia.

MARK BOSTOCK is the Managing Director of a Zambia-based firm of consulting economists, Maxwell Stamp (Africa) Limited. Since 1966, he has been involved in extensive and varied research work for both Government and private sector clients in Zambia and East Africa.

From 1964 to 1966, Mr. Bostock lectured in economics at the University of York, England, where he was responsible inter alia for a one-year course in economic development and administration for Zambian civil servants. Previously, he was a Research Fellow in the Department of Political Economy, University of Edinburgh, where he was involved in an economic and statistical research program in Ghana.

Mr. Bostock received an M.A. (Hons.) in economics from the University of Edinburgh.

CHARLES HARVEY has been a lecturer in economics at the University of Zambia since 1967. During this time, he has written papers on taxation, inflation, and money and banking in the Zambian economy.

From 1960-64, Mr. Harvey worked for the Bank of England, latterly for the Home Intelligence Department, mainly on the finance of the budget. From 1964-67, he was at the University of York, first as a graduate student in economics and then as Junior Research Fellow and Teaching Fellow. During this time, he was associated with an investigation into the export policies and practices of firms.

Mr. Harvey received a B.A. in mathematics and history from the University of Cambridge, subsequently converted to an M.A.

ALAN DRYSDALL is Director of the Geological Survey Department, Ministry of Mines and Mining Development, Lusaka.

ANDREW GORDON was a project analyst for Anglo-American Corporation (Central Africa) Limited until March 1971; he now works for Anglo-American Corporation (Australia) Limited.

JOHN NIEHUSS was a lawyer with the Ministry of Finance Lusaka, until December 1970; he now works for the World Bank.

PETER SLINN is doing research at the School of Oriental and African Studies, London, and is a consultant to a London law firm.